Crafts For Dummies®

What to Buy for a Basic Craft Kit

- **Craft knife**: A general all-purpose craft knife, such as an X-Acto knife, and a package of blades, such as #11. Or substitute single-edge razor blades.
- **Cutting board**: To use with a craft knife and straightedge.
- **Glue:** A small bottle of white craft glue, such as Elmer's Glue-All.
- **Glue stick:** A tube of glue, like the kind school kids use.
- **Hammer:** A small, lightweight hammer.
- **Nails:** A small box of nails, brads, and pushpins.
- **Pad, pencil, and eraser:** Always handy for jotting down notes and measurements.
- **Ruler:** A wooden 12-inch ruler with a metal edge so that it can function as a *straightedge* for cutting, or a plastic ruler.
- **Screwdrivers:** A regular screwdriver and a Phillips head screwdriver come in handy. No need to buy expensive items for craft work.
- **Scissors:** A good, serviceable 8 1/2-inch pair of scissors that can cut anything from paper to fabric.
- **Tape:** Rolls of masking tape and transparent tape.
- **Tape measure:** For measuring odd-shaped items.

What to Buy for a Basic Sewing Craft Kit

- **Needles:** A package of needles with a dozen different sizes for general sewing needs is essential for any sewing project. You may want to have a package of quilting needles in your kit, but you can also use the all-purpose needles for this type of crafting.
- **Pins:** A package of regular straight pins is essential for holding fabric pieces together temporarily. You need pins for any craft work involving fabric, even if no sewing is involved.
- **Pincushion:** Although a pincushion isn't absolutely necessary, it's handy for holding pins for easy access.
- **Scissors:** All-purpose medium-priced scissors are necessary for most crafting projects. For most of your projects, you need only a pair of 8 1/2-inch-long scissors and a 6 1/2-inch pair. If you plan to cut a lot of fabric — you're making a quilt with lots of small fabric pieces, for example — buy a heavier, more expensive pair of the larger size.
- **Thimble:** You need a thimble only when you're quilting. It protects the finger that holds the fabric from underneath, or the finger that pushes the needle in and out of the fabric.
- **Thread:** Because thread is generally an inexpensive item, I always buy the best, which is generally the most expensive. I prefer 100-percent cotton thread. Always keep two or three spools of white in your sewing kit.

Crafts For Dummies®

Cheat Sheet

Take-Along Craft Kit for Buying Supplies

When you go shopping for materials to do your crafting projects, it's helpful to have a tote bag filled with items for measuring or jotting down notes about ideas you may have gotten and want to remember for future projects.

- **Tape measure:** You always need to measure something when doing a craft project. A measuring tape made of material that won't stretch and winds up neatly into a compact roll doesn't take up much room in your craft kit.

- **Ruler:** Keep a 6-inch plastic ruler in your kit for quick, small measurements. Some times you may need to draw a straight line when you're making a quick sketch of a project to remind you of something you want to make later.

- **Pad and pencil:** Keep a sharpened pencil with a clean eraser, along with a small notepad, in your craft kit for quick notes, measurements, and reminders of material you've found in a store that you may need at a later time.

- **Tape:** A roll of tape is handy if you want to take swatches of fabric or chips of paint color samples home with you. Tape each sample to a page on your pad and jot down any information you need, such as color name, manufacturer, product information, price, width of fabric, store, and phone number for calling in an order.

- **Clear-plastic notebook binder sleeve:** When shopping in paint stores and craft and hobby shops, you often find free project sheets. Many manufacturers also provide the stores with free how-to and product information booklets. Pick these up and put them into your notebook sleeves for later use. You'll be surprised at how useful they become as a quick product reference when you get ready to craft.

- **Plain envelope:** Keep a No. 10 business-size envelope in your kit to hold swatches of fabric, paint chips, and other bits of information until you have time to tape them onto your pad and jot down the pertinent information.

- **Magnifying glass:** Sometimes product information is printed in such small type on a label that it's difficult to read. Having a small, inexpensive magnifier is extremely useful.

The IDG Books Worldwide logo is a registered trademark under exclusive license to IDG Books Worldwide, Inc., from International Data Group, Inc. The ...For Dummies logo is a trademark, and For Dummies and ...For Dummies are registered trademarks of IDG Books Worldwide, Inc. All other trademarks are the property of their respective owners.

...For Dummies®: Bestselling Book Series for Beginners

by Leslie Linsley

IDG Books Worldwide, Inc.
An International Data Group Company

Foster City, CA ◆ Chicago, IL ◆ Indianapolis, IN ◆ New York, NY

Crafts For Dummies®

Published by
IDG Books Worldwide, Inc.
An International Data Group Company
919 E. Hillsdale Blvd.
Suite 400
Foster City, CA 94404
www.idgbooks.com (IDG Books Worldwide Web site)
www.dummies.com (Dummies Press Web site)

745.5
Linsley

Library of Congress Catalog Card No.: 99-63211

ISBN: 0-7645-5140-X

Printed in the United States of America

10 9 8 7 6 5 4 3 2

1B/RU/QX/ZZ/IN

Distributed in the United States by IDG Books Worldwide, Inc.

Distributed by CDG Books Canada Inc. for Canada; by Transworld Publishers Limited in the United Kingdom; by IDG Norge Books for Norway; by IDG Sweden Books for Sweden; by IDG Books Australia Publishing Corporation Pty. Ltd. for Australia and New Zealand; by TransQuest Publishers Pte Ltd. for Singapore, Malaysia, Thailand, Indonesia, and Hong Kong; by Gotop Information Inc. for Taiwan; by ICG Muse, Inc. for Japan; by Norma Comunicaciones S.A. for Colombia; by Intersoft for South Africa; by Eyrolles for France; by International Thomson Publishing for Germany, Austria and Switzerland; by Distribuidora Cuspide for Argentina; by Livraria Cultura for Brazil; by Ediciones ZETA S.C.R. Ltda. for Peru; by WS Computer Publishing Corporation, Inc., for the Philippines; by Contemporanea de Ediciones for Venezuela; by Express Computer Distributors for the Caribbean and West Indies; by Micronesia Media Distributor, Inc. for Micronesia; by Grupo Editorial Norma S.A. for Guatemala; by Chips Computadoras S.A. de C.V. for Mexico; by Editorial Norma de Panama S.A. for Panama; by American Bookshops for Finland. Authorized Sales Agent: Anthony Rudkin Associates for the Middle East and North Africa.

For general information on IDG Books Worldwide's books in the U.S., please call our Consumer Customer Service department at 800-762-2974. For reseller information, including discounts and premium sales, please call our Reseller Customer Service department at 800-434-3422.

For information on where to purchase IDG Books Worldwide's books outside the U.S., please contact our International Sales department at 317-596-5530 or fax 317-596-5692.

For consumer information on foreign language translations, please contact our Customer Service department at 1-800-434-3422, fax 317-596-5692, or e-mail rights@idgbooks.com.

For information on licensing foreign or domestic rights, please phone +1-650-655-3109.

For sales inquiries and special prices for bulk quantities, please contact our Sales department at 650-655-3200 or write to the address above.

For information on using IDG Books Worldwide's books in the classroom or for ordering examination copies, please contact our Educational Sales department at 800-434-2086 or fax 317-596-5499.

For press review copies, author interviews, or other publicity information, please contact our Public Relations department at 650-655-3000 or fax 650-655-3299.

For authorization to photocopy items for corporate, personal, or educational use, please contact Copyright Clearance Center, 222 Rosewood Drive, Danvers, MA 01923, or fax 978-750-4470.

About the Author

Leslie Linsley is the author of more than 50 books on crafts, decorating, and home style. Her work appears regularly in national magazines, and she writes a weekly newspaper column that appears throughout the country. Leslie is often a featured guest on the Home and Garden Television Network show *Decorating With Style*. She has made guest appearances on *Today, Good Morning America, Live with Regis and Kathie Lee,* and *The Oprah Winfrey Show*. Leslie has been a consultant to many companies in the do-it-yourself market. Along with her partner and husband, Jon Aron, she has a design studio on Nantucket Island, where the couple live and own two stores. Leslie Linsley/Nantucket sells their one-of-a-kind handmade home accessories, and The Craft Place offers a complete line of craft kits and supplies for the do-it-yourselfer.

ABOUT IDG BOOKS WORLDWIDE

Welcome to the world of IDG Books Worldwide.

IDG Books Worldwide, Inc., is a subsidiary of International Data Group, the world's largest publisher of computer-related information and the leading global provider of information services on information technology. IDG was founded more than 30 years ago by Patrick J. McGovern and now employs more than 9,000 people worldwide. IDG publishes more than 290 computer publications in over 75 countries. More than 90 million people read one or more IDG publications each month.

Launched in 1990, IDG Books Worldwide is today the #1 publisher of best-selling computer books in the United States. We are proud to have received eight awards from the Computer Press Association in recognition of editorial excellence and three from Computer Currents' First Annual Readers' Choice Awards. Our best-selling *...For Dummies®* series has more than 50 million copies in print with translations in 31 languages. IDG Books Worldwide, through a joint venture with IDG's Hi-Tech Beijing, became the first U.S. publisher to publish a computer book in the People's Republic of China. In record time, IDG Books Worldwide has become the first choice for millions of readers around the world who want to learn how to better manage their businesses.

Our mission is simple: Every one of our books is designed to bring extra value and skill-building instructions to the reader. Our books are written by experts who understand and care about our readers. The knowledge base of our editorial staff comes from years of experience in publishing, education, and journalism — experience we use to produce books to carry us into the new millennium. In short, we care about books, so we attract the best people. We devote special attention to details such as audience, interior design, use of icons, and illustrations. And because we use an efficient process of authoring, editing, and desktop publishing our books electronically, we can spend more time ensuring superior content and less time on the technicalities of making books.

You can count on our commitment to deliver high-quality books at competitive prices on topics you want to read about. At IDG Books Worldwide, we continue in the IDG tradition of delivering quality for more than 30 years. You'll find no better book on a subject than one from IDG Books Worldwide.

John Kilcullen
Chairman and CEO
IDG Books Worldwide, Inc.

Steven Berkowitz
President and Publisher
IDG Books Worldwide, Inc.

Eighth Annual Computer Press Awards ≥1992

Ninth Annual Computer Press Awards ≥1993

Tenth Annual Computer Press Awards ≥1994

Eleventh Annual Computer Press Awards ≥1995

IDG is the world's leading IT media, research and exposition company. Founded in 1964, IDG had 1997 revenues of $2.05 billion and has more than 9,000 employees worldwide. IDG offers the widest range of media options that reach IT buyers in 75 countries representing 95% of worldwide IT spending. IDG's diverse product and services portfolio spans six key areas including print publishing, online publishing, expositions and conferences, market research, education and training, and global marketing services. More than 90 million people read one or more of IDG's 290 magazines and newspapers, including IDG's leading global brands — Computerworld, PC World, Network World, Macworld and the Channel World family of publications. IDG Books Worldwide is one of the fastest-growing computer book publishers in the world, with more than 700 titles in 36 languages. The "...For Dummies®" series alone has more than 50 million copies in print. IDG offers online users the largest network of technology-specific Web sites around the world through IDG.net (http://www.idg.net), which comprises more than 225 targeted Web sites in 55 countries worldwide. International Data Corporation (IDC) is the world's largest provider of information technology data, analysis and consulting, with research centers in over 41 countries and more than 400 research analysts worldwide. IDG World Expo is a leading producer of more than 168 globally branded conferences and expositions in 35 countries including E3 (Electronic Entertainment Expo), Macworld Expo, ComNet, Windows World Expo, ICE (Internet Commerce Expo), Agenda, DEMO, and Spotlight. IDG's training subsidiary, ExecuTrain, is the world's largest computer training company, with more than 230 locations worldwide and 785 training courses. IDG Marketing Services helps industry-leading IT companies build international brand recognition by developing global integrated marketing programs via IDG's print, online and exposition products worldwide. Further information about the company can be found at www.idg.com.   1/24/99

Author's Acknowledgments

Producing a successful project takes the help and talent of many people. For this support, I am most grateful to everyone at IDG Books Worldwide, Inc., especially Holly McGuire, Andrea Boucher, and Christy Beck. I would also like to thank everyone in my studio who worked on this project: Robby Savonen, Peter Pelusso Jr., Jeff Terr, Greg Worth, Susie Peterson, Ruth Linsley, and Tori McCandless. Most of all I want to thank my partner, Jon Aron, and my agent, Alan Kellock, without whose friendship and loyalty this book would not be a reality.

Publisher's Acknowledgments

We're proud of this book; please register your comments through our IDG Books Worldwide Online Registration Form located at http://my2cents.dummies.com.

Some of the people who helped bring this book to market include the following:

Acquisitions and Editorial

Project Editors: Christine Meloy Beck, Andrea C. Boucher

Acquisitions Editor: Holly McGuire

Copy Editors: Rowena Rappaport, Tina Sims, Billie A. Williams

General Reviewer: Cyndi Marsico

Editorial Coordinator: Maureen F. Kelly

Acquisitions Coordinator: Jill Alexander

Editorial Managers: Jennifer Ehrlich, Rev Mengle

Editorial Assistants: Paul E. Kuzmic, Alison Walthall

Production

Project Coordinator: Maridee Ennis

Layout and Graphics: Angela F. Hunckler, Barry Offringa, Brent Savage, Michael A. Sullivan

Special Art and Photography: Jon Aron

Proofreaders: Nancy Price, Marianne Santy, Ethel M. Winslow

Indexer: Ann Norcross

General and Administrative

IDG Books Worldwide, Inc.: John Kilcullen, CEO; Steven Berkowitz, President and Publisher

IDG Books Technology Publishing Group: Richard Swadley, Senior Vice President and Publisher; Walter Bruce III, Vice President and Associate Publisher; Steven Sayre, Associate Publisher; Joseph Wikert, Associate Publisher; Mary Bednarek, Branded Product Development Director; Mary Corder, Editorial Director

IDG Books Consumer Publishing Group: Roland Elgey, Senior Vice President and Publisher; Kathleen A. Welton, Vice President and Publisher; Kevin Thornton, Acquisitions Manager; Kristin A. Cocks, Editorial Director

IDG Books Internet Publishing Group: Brenda McLaughlin, Senior Vice President and Group Publisher; Diane Graves Steele, Vice President and Associate Publisher; Sofia Marchant, Online Marketing Manager

IDG Books Production for Dummies Press: Michael R. Britton, Vice President of Production; Debbie Stailey, Associate Director of Production; Cindy L. Phipps, Manager of Project Coordination, Production Proofreading, and Indexing; Shelley Lea, Supervisor of Graphics and Design; Debbie J. Gates, Production Systems Specialist; Robert Springer, Supervisor of Proofreading; Laura Carpenter, Production Control Manager; Tony Augsburger, Supervisor of Reprints and Bluelines

◆

The publisher would like to give special thanks to Patrick J. McGovern, without whom this book would not have been possible.

◆

Contents at a Glance

Cartoons at a Glance

By Rich Tennant

"I'd like to join a crafts club. I'm just not sure I have that much whimsey in me."

page 9

"It was Lieutenant Hooper's idea. He thought it would be nice to add some rustic charm to the unit by stenciling the tanks. This, for instance, is part of our 'Country Cupboard' attack squad."

page 101

"Okay kids, today we'll be working on sock puppets, name plates, and glue gun safety."

page 281

"Oh, that's Jack's area for his paper crafts. He's made some wonderful US Treasury Bonds, Certificates of Deposit, $20's, $50's, $100's, that sort of thing."

page 39

"Let's see, I've made an herb wreath, a fruit wreath, a flower wreath, a berry wreath, a shell wreath... Gay–what are you planning to do with those egg shells?"

page 319

"One thing I learned banging out license plates at the State Penn for six years is always use a complementary color to border your designs and establish an overall sense of depth."

page 157

"I decided to take up dried flower arranging. Most of the flowers in my house were halfway there anyway."

page 255

Fax: 978-546-7747 • E-mail: the5wave@tiac.net

Table of Contents

Introduction

● ●

Many people take up craft projects simply because crafting is fun. But another reason for getting into craft projects is because you want to *create* something. Crafts have traditionally been "of the folk," which means that they were things made by ordinary people to solve everyday problems. For example, long ago people made pottery or baskets because they needed a vessel for carrying water or to collect berries. In colonial times, women cut up the fabric from worn-out clothing to use for quilt-making in order to keep warm. These early artifacts are now cherished as American folk art, but at the time, they were just ordinary items.

That's why discovering how to make something isn't at all intimidating. You don't have to be "artistic" to make the things in this book. Most craft techniques are quite basic and easy to do, and the materials for any craft are readily available and inexpensive, so anyone can master a craft. It's just a matter of combining the technique with a pleasing design to make something you can use or give as a gift. Even if you were the kid in your home economics or shop class who always felt like you were all thumbs, you can become an expert crafter.

Although crafting is a nice way to pass leisure time, it can do so much more. Developing a variety of crafting skills opens doors to creative expression you may never have thought possible, such as selecting colors and fabrics for decorating your home to enhance your craft projects. When I make a craft gift, it is given — and received — with more feeling than something that has been purchased. Another bonus you get from making things is the opportunity to save money while creating something original that can't be bought. But one of the nicest rewards from the crafting experience is the quality it adds to your time spent at home. When you know how to do a craft, that knowledge is with you for all time, and you can work on your craft projects whenever you're in the mood.

About This Book

You may be thinking, "Which craft should I delve into first?" This book helps you decide what to make even if you don't have a clue when you begin. Take a few minutes to skim through the chapters and look at the color photographs for inspiration and project ideas before getting down to actually reading about each crafting technique in depth. Whether it's how to create a memory book or how to stencil, you can find everything you need to know right here. Even if you've never held a paintbrush in your life, this book holds your hand through the process. I assume nothing!

You may think that any dummy knows how to thread a needle, but you may be glad to discover the very best way to thread a needle in the sewing chapter. And if you drop your box of pins, you can find the best way to save your sanity with a tip on how to pick them up in less than three seconds! And these are only a couple of the many tips and great ideas you'll find throughout the book.

How to Use This Book

This book is your key to becoming a crafter. You can open it anywhere. You don't have to start at the beginning, because each craft technique stands on its own, even though some of the techniques you master for one craft may be helpful when tackling another. For example, in Chapter 11 you find out how to stencil, and in Chapter 5 you find information on making your own wrapping paper. Then in Part VI, you find directions for making holiday stenciled wrap. This crossover of skills — a feature that you find throughout this book — makes crafting so much fun.

If you're already familiar with a craft, you can look through the part of the book devoted to that craft to find many good tips for doing things quicker or easier, or even better.

You may have watched a friend or your mother doing needlepoint and thought, "I can do that." You're right — you can! And this book is just what you need to help you get started.

Most of the techniques in this book are a cinch to master, but in this book you get more than the directions; you also get tips on what kind of yarn is best and where to find materials. And this preview is just the tip of the iceberg. Crafting is exciting, and that's why this book is filled with projects you'll want to make.

How This Book Is Organized

This book is divided into seven parts and 29 chapters. Each part begins with a description of the crafts that are included in the various chapters in that part. You also find a variety of projects to make with the specific crafting techniques so that you can apply the skills you've acquired. Many of the crafting techniques are used for more than one craft and, in this case, you'll find cross references so that you can easily find the exact information you need, when you need it. I also include plenty of icons to make it easy to identify specific information such as tips, cautions, specific tools, and cost-cutting and time-saving devices.

Every part also contains a description of all the basic materials needed for the crafts in the chapters that follow. You also find the easiest and best way each one of the materials can help you with specific steps in the crafting process.

Along with all the basic information spelled out in no-nonsense terms, each craft chapter provides you with a variety of projects. I assume that you are trying a craft because you want to make something. Therefore, after you master a new skill, you'll want to apply it, so I provide plenty of projects for each craft. You can start with a very simple one and then try one that is more elaborate. After you master the basic skills, you can complete the elaborate project just as easily as the simple one — it just takes more time. For example, after you can stencil a flower on a box, you can use your newly developed stenciling skills to create a border of flowers around a room. The technique is identical, but the border project involves more steps and takes longer to complete. If you start with a simple project, you'll probably want to do more with your newfound skills.

At the end of the book is an appendix that can help you find additional resources.

Part I: Things to Know Before You Begin

You are probably eager to get started, but if you aren't sure which craft to start out with, you may want to look through Part I before rushing out to buy your first box of pins or pick out a piece of fabric. The chapters in this part start you thinking about different crafting techniques and which ones appeal to you the most. This part also gets you thinking about the projects you'd like to make, such as decorative items to personalize your home or gifts for your family and friends. However, if it's your style to buy the materials first, take the handy Cheat Sheet, found right inside the front cover of this book, with you to the store and jump right in.

Chapter 1 tells you the many benefits you can derive from crafting. It helps you choose your first craft project so that it's just right for you and tells you where to find inspiration for design. Chapter 2 discusses the basic tools that you use for any craft project and which ones are essential for a good toolbox. Chapter 3 arms you with good advice, basic directions, and simple skills for tackling any craft project.

Part II: Paper Crafts

Remember when you used colored construction paper to make holiday decorations in elementary school? Using paper to make craft projects is a little more sophisticated now, but it's just as much fun as when you were a kid. It's easy and inexpensive and can be enormously creative. This part tells you about different ways to use paper in crafting, describes the materials you need for each craft, and gives you complete directions for making a variety of projects.

Chapter 4 introduces you to popular paper craft techniques that you can use to wrap beautiful packages, preserve your memories, make gifts, and display your photographs. You get tips on where to find the supplies that you need and how best to use them. Chapter 5 is about folding, wrapping, and fashioning projects from paper. You find out how to personalize and decorate papers for extraordinary wrappings, make hatboxes, and creatively reuse paper scraps. Chapter 6 describes the world of stamp crafts. You can pick up ideas on how to create designs on paper, fabric, wood, and ceramic and how to make different things with stamps.

If you take lots of photographs but never get around to putting them in an album, Chapter 7 makes you happy that you aren't super-organized. Here you find out how to best crop your snapshots, mount them, preserve them, and mat and frame them in interesting ways. This chapter also offers a variety of projects for you and your kids to make with photographs. Chapter 8 can help you create a personal scrapbook filled with collected bits of memorabilia, including your favorite photographs. You also find information about different kinds of paper and adhesives and get great tips for finding and organizing interesting material.

Chapter 9 dispels any notions you may have that découpage is difficult. (You'll be happy to know that découpage simply means the art of applying cutouts.) Turn to this chapter for a brief history of the craft, a description of the materials you need, and complete directions for decorating boxes, plaques, and furniture.

Part III: Paint Crafts

You can choose from many different paint crafts, each of which uses different tools and materials to achieve the best results. In this part, you find everything you need to know about faux finishing, stenciling, and decorative painting.

Chapter 10 introduces you to different painting techniques and materials and gives you a basic primer on the things you should know before you begin any project. Chapter 11 is all about stenciling and includes step-by-step directions for easy projects. You also discover the best way to cut your own stencil, how to use precut designs, all about paints and glazes, and how to stencil with one or more colors. If you think that you need artistic ability to do decorative painting, Chapter 12 shows you how easy it can be. This chapter lets you in on all the professional secrets and tells you about the techniques and tools that can enable you to faux finish your walls or decorate furniture like a pro.

Part IV: Fabric Crafts and Needlecrafts

Fabric, needle, thread, yarns, and ribbons are the guts of any fabriccraft or needlecraft. But, oh, the things you can make when you put it all together! This section is chock-full of the stuff you need to stitch any project, and even includes a few crafts that you can make without stitches.

Chapter 13 describes the best tools for quick sewing projects, gives you advice about buying a sewing machine, and includes tips and tricks for measuring, cutting, and sewing simple projects. It also covers the basics of needlepoint and cross-stitch. Armed with the right materials and a primer on a few stitches, you'll be off and running in no time. Chapter 14 explains techniques for using materials to make things the no-sew way. This chapter provides lots of easy projects for gifts, decorating, and fix-ups for your home.

Chapters 15 and 16 introduce you to the basics of making patchworks and appliqué. You find out which fabrics to use, what materials you need, how easy it is to transfer and enlarge patterns, and how to make a template. I also give you some quick and easy methods for making a variety of projects.

Chapters 17 and 18 give you directions for needlepoint and counted cross-stitch projects to make in a weekend. The hardest aspect of the chapters in this part is picking the project to make first!

Part V: Nature Crafts

If you tend to be a couch potato, this section brings out your hunting and gathering instincts and gets you moving. A walk in the woods or along the seashore, or a visit to a park, garden, or garden center, yields the materials you need to do any nature craft. This section is filled with information on using nature's bounty in crafts.

Chapter 19 tells you what materials to collect, what supplies you need for collecting, and how to clean and work with the materials after you collect them.

Chapter 20 gives you the know-how to dry, press, and arrange flowers fearlessly, as well as recipes for potpourri and other projects to make with your favorite flowers. Chapter 21 tells you how to cut grasses, gather leaves, and pick pinecones for your craft projects and discusses the tools and materials that you need when working with them. If you've got a dish filled with beautiful seashells that you gathered on your last trip to the coast, Chapter 21 also offers some creative ways to preserve those mementos.

Part VI: Holiday Crafts

The months of November and December are the best times of the year for craft lovers. Many people look forward to the holiday season just because it gives them a good reason to work on crafts. The chapters in this part are designed to help you have a lot of fun at this time of year. The stores are well-stocked with craft materials such as felt, fabric, dried flowers, Styrofoam, buttons, bows, sequins, trims, decorative papers, ribbons, and all sorts of other interesting seasonal doodads.

Chapter 22 tells you what materials you need for making ornaments, gifts, and decorations. Chapter 23 covers in detail how to make a variety of ornaments for your tree, and Chapter 24 shows you how to make Christmas stockings for everyone. If presentation is your thing, you find sensational ways to create packages in Chapter 25. I also offer suggestions for hostess gifts in that chapter. Christmas cards, welcome banners, and table center-pieces are a few of the holiday decorative crafts that you can find in Chapter 26, which focuses on decorating in style.

Part VII: The Part of Tens

In Chapter 27, I offer my favorite last-minute holiday decorating ideas that don't look like they were made at the last-minute. As a testament to what crafts can do for you, in Chapter 28 I reveal ten great ways to turn your trash into treasures. Chapter 29 contains my list of the ten all-time, best-selling bazaar and fund-raising craft projects.

Conventions Used in This Book

For each project in this book, I include a list of materials needed, followed by step-by-step directions. If you need special tools to complete a project, I also list them. Sometimes the same materials, such as paper towels or newspaper, are good to have on hand for many projects. In this case, you can find the list for these handy, helpful things at the beginning of the chapter. Before starting any project in the book, follow this procedure:

1. **Start by reading through the materials list to see what you have on hand and what you need to buy. Make a list of the items that you need to purchase.**

2. **Read through the directions to see whether they include a term you don't understand.**

   If I don't define the term in that project, I usually include a cross-reference that does define the term. For example, if the directions for a patchwork quilt in Chapter 15 tell you to baste and you've never done this before —

not to worry. A cross-reference directs you to the chapter where you can find out that basting — at least in this book — doesn't have anything to do with your Thanksgiving turkey. Instead, it means to take long, loose stitches through the layers of fabric in order to hold it temporarily in place.

In my studio, I am constantly trying out new techniques and creating new designs. Because I often appear on television shows, demonstrating how to do various crafts, I try to simplify the techniques so that anyone watching the show can pick up these craft skills in a short amount of time. I use this same method for teaching crafting in this book. Therefore, whenever possible, I suggest the newest and best materials for getting the very best craft results with the greatest of ease. I always aim to design a project that is worthy of your time but that anyone can do. Therefore, all you have to do is choose the project you want to make without any concern about how difficult it may be. The projects do not progress in stages from easy to harder. They are all intended to be equally satisfying on all levels.

Icons Used in This Book

Throughout the book, I've sprinkled in *icons,* little pictures in the margins, to draw your attention. These icons help you identify the kind of information contained in the section. Read on to find out what each icon indicates.

I use this icon when you need to be especially careful, such as when you're measuring or cutting or using certain kinds of paint.

This icon marks projects that are especially suitable for you to make with your children.

If you want ways to save money on a craft project, look for this icon.

I use this icon to direct you to names of products and how to get them.

This icon points you to stuff that you really don't need to know about a project but you may find interesting anyway.

The craft vocabulary is simple, but each craft has its specific names for things. This icon highlights the words that can make you sound like a seasoned crafter.

This icon identifies ways to make it easier to do something. Experienced crafters know certain secrets that are worth sharing, and this icon guides you to that advice.

When you want to know what special gadget you need for a craft project, keep an eye out for this icon.

Where to Go from Here

Maybe you've always wanted to try stenciling. Why not turn directly to Part III and get started with paint crafts? On the other hand, if sewing is your thing and you'd love to make a patchwork quilt like the one your grandmother may have owned, turn to Chapter 15. It's as easy as that.

Most people like to get organized before starting a project, and I highly recommend this approach. Putting together a basic tool kit for all your crafting needs can be fun, and everything you need to know is in Chapter 2. Assembling this kit gets you in the mood to craft, acquaints you with craft and hobby stores, and has you racing home with more craft ideas than you thought possible. I always get inspired when I go to a hobby store. It's like being in a candy store with so much to choose from. That's what crafting is all about. You can enjoy it all — without gaining weight.

Part I

Things to Know Before You Begin

The 5th Wave   By Rich Tennant

"I'd like to join a crafts club. I'm just not sure I have that much whimsey in me."

In this part . . .

Maybe you think that crafting is a way to pass the time or keep busy. This part shows you many more reasons for crafting, and you can take advantage of any or all of them.

You can choose from many types of crafts to find the ones that appeal most to you. Hard crafts, for example, involve hard materials, such as painting on furniture; soft crafts involve projects such as needlework. Nature crafts don't require using exact measurements. But some crafts do require more accuracy, such as a patchwork quilt, which is made up of geometric pieces that you have to cut perfectly in order for them to fit together.

Before you begin crafting, you need some basic tools. Putting together your basic crafting toolbox can be a lot of fun and readies you to try out the simple skills for each craft technique.

Chapter 1

The Joy of Crafting

In This Chapter

▶ Discovering the rewards of crafting

▶ Choosing a craft

▶ Looking for craft ideas

*T*his chapter explains why millions of people do some form of crafting and how you can choose a craft that's perfect for you. It introduces you to a variety of reasons for crafting and tells you where to find inspiration for different crafts and design ideas.

The joy of crafting comes from both the experience of making the project and from reaping the rewards of your finished project. This chapter helps you create the perfect marriage of those two rewards.

Craft projects fall into two categories: Some projects you can finish in a short amount of time, and others are fun to do in short spurts over a longer period of time. If you like to see finished results instantly, the chapters of this book give you many choices in each type of crafting technique. However, as you become more skilled in a craft, you may want to work on more ambitious projects that take a little more time and give you more of the satisfaction that comes from making something with your own two hands. Those projects are in this book, too.

The Rewards of Crafting

The crafting experience has many rewards. Crafting is a relaxing way to unwind at the end of a busy day. You can craft at home, so you can work on a project while enjoying the company of your family — or even including them! The very act of crafting can give you a sense of well-being. But crafting also provides benefits you may never have thought about. Any one of the following benefits may appeal to you.

I made it myself

One of the nicest things about making something is the pride of accomplishment. Receiving compliments from friends who discover that you made the very thing that they admire in your home is a great feeling. When you give a handmade gift, it often has more meaning than one that is store-bought. Decorating with your craft projects gives your home a special quality that you get from one-of-a-kind accessories.

Self-fulfillment

According to the Hobby Industry Association, it's a fact that people who do crafting are more relaxed, have less stress in their lives, and enjoy a fuller life than those who don't.

Further statistics from the Hobby Industry Association confirm that millions of crafters spend more quality time at home with their families. In fact, they enjoy being at home more than they did before taking up a craft.

Save money

We all want our homes to look as good as possible, but sometimes we can't afford what it takes. Don't be dismayed. Decorating with the accessories that you want is easier than you can imagine. If you have some simple, basic directions for a craft project, you can make almost anything for your house. After you know the technique, you can use your imagination to create those high-priced boutique items for pennies.

Personalize your home

A few handmade items lend personality to any home. A patchwork quilt or a needlepoint pillow can instantly transform a room and make it your own. Professional decorators know that accessories are the keys to good design. After you take up a craft, you may be amazed at the decorating magic you can work. You'll have all your friends oohing and aahing over your creations.

Make money from your craft

After you become skilled in a craft, you may want to sell your work. Handmade items are often in demand. You can make things to sell at your church or school bazaar or to a local shop. There's no limit to how good you can get at your chosen craft, and the better you are, the more money you can make. Best of all, you never have to leave home to do it!

Find a new career through crafting

Teaching your craft can be tremendous fun, and every community has a need for talented people to do just that. Community school programs, craft stores, private lessons, and senior centers offer opportunities for you to teach crafts. You can make money or simply reap satisfaction from teaching others what you know.

Pass on what you know

You can teach crafts to your children and your grandchildren. By handing down your knowledge, you can start a tradition that may continue through generations and create a wonderful family legacy. Many people who make things think of their craft projects as future family heirlooms.

Picking the Craft for You

Each crafting technique in this book starts with the basics and slowly introduces more and more details about the craft. Each chapter is designed so that you can start with the easiest and most basic project and progress to more advanced activities. However, crafting is a personal choice. Select a craft based on what you think you'd enjoy doing the most and what project or design is the most appealing.

Just as with clothing, certain crafts go in and out of fashion. One year, needlepoint is all the rage. But the next year, everyone is creating memory books. My advice? Ignore all the trends. Be your own person. Choose the craft that seems to fit best with your lifestyle. Here are some tips on choosing a craft:

- ✔ If you own a sewing machine, you may want to make easy sewing projects, do appliqué, or stitch a patchwork quilt.

- ✔ If you have a feeling for design but don't think that you can draw, découpage and memory books are right up your alley.

- ✔ Many people have an affinity for nature and gardening. If you're part of this group, nature crafts are just the thing for you.

- ✔ If you like to decorate things, you'll be attracted to stenciling, faux finishing, and decorative painting.

- ✔ If you love the holidays, you have a perfect excuse to try all sorts of crafts. You can make things to decorate your home and for gift-giving. Nothing is more personal than a handmade gift.

Finding Inspiration in All the Right Places

Maybe you aren't sure which craft you'd like to try first. Or perhaps you're interested in knowing about a specific craft but not sure what project you'd like to make. Many avenues can spark your imagination and get you fired up to begin. Before delving into any one craft, take a little time to look around for ideas. This section lists some of the ways I go about finding inspiration.

Keep a notebook so that you can jot down project and design ideas as they come to you. For example, cut out an item that you like from a catalog and paste it in your notebook. Then go into a paint store and select paint samples that appeal to you for this project. Put these colors in your notebook, too. (Remember that these colors can apply to fabrics as well as paint. Using colored paper and pencils is also a great way to experiment with design ideas.) Then, as you study the project, you may come up with some basic directions for how to make it yourself.

Take a tour through a craft store

Have you ever been in a craft store? If not, you're in for a real treat. To a crafter, a well-stocked general craft store is like a candy store to a kid. You may be initially attracted to the paper craft section, and then suddenly you're drawn to a beautiful needlepoint canvas. Almost immediately, you can visualize the finished needlepoint pillow on your living room sofa. Take as much time as you need to study the different options. Then come back to this book to discover exactly which craft is right for you and which tools and supplies you need to get started.

Browse through fabric stores

You can find a wealth of inspiration in fabric stores. The colors, patterns, and textures of fabrics makes you want to discover more about crafting with fabric. Wandering through the aisles of a fabric store is like visiting a wonderful botanical garden in full bloom. Fabric stores often display finished projects so the customers can get ideas for making their own.

Take advantage of designer boutiques

Most high-priced boutiques carry handmade, one-of-a-kind accessories. Chances are that you'll find several items you'd like to make, and those items can be a wonderful source of inspiration. Look at the way they are made. Consider the technique and the design.

Most crafting techniques are not complicated or difficult to do — the attraction usually comes from the design. Good design inspires you. After you know a particular technique, you can use the technique in many different ways. For example, painted furniture is very popular and carried in many gift and home accessory stores. But you can achieve the same professional-looking results by applying a stencil design to furniture without any professional art training. You'll be surprised how easy it is.

Look through magazines

Magazines are published on every subject imaginable, including very specialized topics. However, when looking for inspiration, you can narrow your choices down to magazines on home decorating and crafts. Pore over these magazines for items you'd like to make. Look at the details in rooms that you find attractive, and study the designs that you find particularly pretty.

Dozens of publications offer special holiday issues, which are great for finding decorating or gift ideas that you can make. Don't be limited by the exact things you see. Sometimes part of a wallpaper design can be the inspiration for a design on a small gift box. One section of a patchwork quilt may give you an idea for making a patchwork pillow or sachets.

Check out cable TV shows

Many cable shows are devoted to decorating and crafts. They give you a smattering of information about do-it-yourself projects, which is just enough to inspire you to find out more. Check out the shows in your area for project ideas. TV shows can also provide good design ideas to use with various techniques.

Beware of tackling a craft project that you saw on TV without gathering more technical information! The people who demonstrate the crafts are professionals, and they have modified the steps in order to fit into the television time format. They often leave out some details — the very ones you may need for a successful outcome. Use these shows as a way to dip your toe into the water and for inspiration. Then come back to this book for complete crafting directions and all those little details for which TV time doesn't allow.

Wander around a home center

I don't know about you, but when I go to a home center, I get lost there for hours. If I could, I'd live there. Home centers have everything you need for living better and things you never knew you needed. Walk up and down the aisles with no agenda. Pick up things that interest you. Even if you don't think you have a creative bone in your body, a home center inspires you to make something.

For example, in the lumber area, you can find round wooden discs of all sizes. The perfect table top! In the garden section, you can find outdoor planters in all sizes and shapes. The perfect table base! But these pieces may need some decoration. Look through this book for the crafting technique that fits the bill. Perhaps you've been saving a bunch of paper memorabilia, such as a wedding announcement, a greeting card, a love note, a ticket stub to a favorite movie, a child's drawing, and a photograph. You can use these items to create a collage on the table that you're going to assemble from the parts you found in the home center. (Find the technique for this découpage project in Chapter 9.) And this is only one idea. Imagine how many more ideas you can come up with!

Scope out flea markets and yard sales

"One person's trash is another person's treasure." I don't know who first said it, but that sentence speaks to me. Our weekly newspaper has a column heading for "Yard Sales," and every Saturday morning traffic jams form in front of the houses listed. Everyone loves a bargain, and yard sales, swap meets, and flea markets provide a terrific way for people to help one another. The seller gets rid of excess "junk" and picks up a little cash. The buyer finds something useful for very little money. These types of sales are my favorite way to find things to use for crafting. I may come across a box of ribbons or colorful threads. Or I may discover remnants of fabric or an old piece of furniture that needs refurbishing. Recycling someone else's cast-offs is a worthwhile endeavor, especially if you use a crafting technique to turn an ugly toad into a handsome prince.

Chapter 2

Basic Tools the Crafter Can't Live Without

*P*utting together basic materials and a good tool kit to have on hand is an essential part of the crafting experience. All the projects in this book use at least some of the tools described in this chapter, so spend the time now to gather them together and you'll be forever grateful every time you want to make a project. This chapter tells you everything you need to know and makes it easy to assemble a good tool kit.

You can use a clear plastic storage box or basket to hold all your crafting tools and materials so that they are handy when you're ready to work.

Good Scissors Make All the Difference

A good pair of scissors is sharp, has clean blades, and isn't too loose or too tight. If your scissors' blades wobble, don't even think about using them for craft projects — you're asking for crooked, ragged, and ugly edges if you do. Use 'em to give your dog a haircut, if you want, but use good scissors for your crafting.

Sharp scissors are essential to any craft undertaking. I once had a pair of pinking shears that I used to cut zigzag edges for quilt squares, but they became so dull that they began to zag when they should have zigged. I had to throw the dull pinking shears away. Nothing is more frustrating than getting set up to cut out a pattern only to find that you have to struggle to cut the first piece because of dull scissors. Buying new scissors is often easier, cheaper, and more convenient than having the old pair sharpened.

Scissors come in many sizes, and you use them for many different things. Fabric shops usually carry the best selection of scissors. Start off with three different scissors sizes, and you're prepared for any creative urge that may strike you.

The following list describes many of the different types of scissors:

- **Sewing scissors** are about 6 inches long and have one pointed blade and one blunt-end blade so they don't snag fabric when trimming.

- **Lingerie shears** have long, slender, pointy blades designed to not slip on sheer fabric.

- **Pinking shears** have blades that look like alligator teeth. Pinking shears were cleverly designed to cut zigzag edges that resist raveling. They are good for finishing seams and doing decorative projects. Originally intended for cutting fabric, pinking shears make decorative edges around paper as well. In fact, craft shops often carry a variety of scissors with blades that cut scallops and other shapes for all sorts of craft projects.

- **Dressmaker's shears** have a bent-handle design that makes cutting flat-lying fabric comfortable and easy. Dressmaker's shears are the scissors of choice for cutting clothing and quilt patterns. They come in different lengths and also in a left-handed version.

- **Embroidery scissors** are small, pointed scissors used for general crafting. Embroidery scissors are essential to the crafter's tool kit. Use them for snipping pieces of thread. Use them for cutting a strand of thread to weave through your needle. Use them to snip away errors. Use them to trim fabric. Use them to trim your bangs. After you realize the practicality of embroidery scissors, you'll want to keep one pair in your craft kit and one pair handy for other household uses.

- **Cuticle scissors** are useful for extremely fine work like cutting designs for découpage, which is the art of cutting out delicate paper designs (see Chapter 9 for complete directions). The blades are short, sharp, and curved. The curve enables you to cut rounded shapes more accurately than you can with straight scissors or a craft knife.

- **Electric scissors** do the same job as regular scissors, but make cutting large quantities of fabric quicker and easier. Electric scissors come with or without a cord.

On Pins and Needles

Not all pins and needles are alike. When you go to the fabric shop to buy your crafting supplies, you need to buy a box of pins and a package of needles. Finding out about the different pins and needles in advance helps you buy the right ones for the craft projects you want to make.

Pins

Pins hold things — fabric, paper, and so on — temporarily in place until they are permanently secured. Pins are great because they enable you to look at different variations of your project before the commitment of sewing or gluing. The following list describes the four basic types of pins.

- ✔ **Straight pins** come in various sizes, with 1¹⁄₁₆ of an inch being the most common length. Use straight pins to pin fabric to fabric, secure strips of fabric or ribbon around Styrofoam balls, or for almost any craft project. (Straight pins are sometimes called *dressmaker's pins.*)

- ✔ **Color ball pins** have different colored plastic balls on the end, which make them easy to see when you want to remove them from your project. Because color ball pins aren't as sharp as straight pins, they are best for use on knit fabrics.

- ✔ **T-pins,** which are larger than straight and color ball pins, are useful for loose knit fabrics because they can't accidentally slip through the fabric and get lost.

- ✔ **Safety pins** aren't used much for crafting, but they are ideal for threading cording through a casing if you're making fabric-covered cording to trim a pillow. Just secure a safety pin to one end of the cording and weave it through the fabric tunnel. Even if you never trim a pillow, a few safety pins always come in handy for temporary closure, in case you lose a button on your shirt.

Most pins are made of steel, which is a great advantage if you accidentally spill them. If and when you spill your pins, you'll find that a small magnet becomes invaluable. Passing the magnet over the spilled pins instantly picks the pins off the floor in one easy, effortless step — one pass of the magnet over the pins, and you're back in action. If you don't have a magnet, simply tape a piece of thin, cotton fabric over the end of your vacuum hose and run it over the pins. The pins "stick" to the fabric. Hold the hose over the pin box, turn off the vacuum, and watch the pins drop into box.

Needles

Needles come in various sizes and styles. If you haven't decided which craft to do, it's best to buy a general-purpose package of needles, which contains an assortment for different uses.

No matter which needle you use, threading a needle simply takes good eyes. I find it easiest to thread a needle if I've moistened the end of the thread between my lips. Good lighting also helps. If you're using white thread, hold the needle in front of a piece of dark fabric to make the eye of the needle and the thread more visible. You may find that a needle threader comes in handy. Ask for one at your craft store.

The following list helps you take the guesswork out of needles and what they do:

- ✔ **Sharps:** Use these medium-length needles for general hand-sewing. When it comes to patchwork and appliqué work, nothing takes the place of a sharp. Sharps come in a variety of sizes and can be used on fabrics of different weights.

  Sharps are the most common needles; they're the ones usually included in travel sewing kits and in your mother's or grandmother's sewing basket. Sharps may be common and cheap, but they can be found in the most elite sewing circles.

- ✔ **Betweens:** Because they are shorter than sharps, use betweens for making tiny stitches, such as for hand-quilting projects (see Chapter 15). Betweens may also be referred to as *quilting needles*.

- ✔ **Tapestry:** Use the blunt-tipped tapestry for counted cross-stitch, needlepoint, and other techniques worked on even-weave fabric (see Part IV).

Thimbles

Some sewing mavens can't live without this miniature knight in shining armor, and others find it a nuisance. Thimbles are inexpensive devices, so if you plan to do any crafts that involve stitching, why not cover your fingers? Thimbles come in sizes from 6 (small) to 12 (large) and are available where sewing accessories are sold.

Thimbles save your hands from the wrath of the repetitious needle in certain crafts, such as quilting or cross-stitch, where you push the needle in and out of the fabric over and over again. A thimble protects the finger you press against the thread end of the needle, and another protects the finger holding the work area on the underside of the fabric. If you can get used to sewing with a thimble, your fingers will thank you.

Pincushion

Pincushions come in all kinds of shapes and designs. Probably the most familiar pincushion is the fat tomato shape with a dangling strawberry attached. The strawberry is filled with graphite, an abrasive that keeps needles and pins clean and sharp — just push the needle or pin into the strawberry periodically. A pincushion provides a convenient and easy way to store and retrieve pins and needles as you use them.

Measure Twice — Cut Once!

Use the tools in the following list to get your measurements exactly as you want them, preferably before you make a nice, clean cut. You can always re-measure, but you can't always re-cut.

- ✔ **Tape measure:** A standard tape measure extends to 60 inches. A good tape measure should be made of a material that is flexible and won't stretch — most are made of thin metal, plastic, or cloth. A tape measure is ideal for measuring anything that isn't flat. You can measure around boxes, balls, and other three-dimensional objects. A tape measure rolls into a compact circle and is handy to tuck into your purse when shopping for craft material that you may need to measure.

- ✔ **Metal-edge wood ruler or metal ruler:** The metal edge is a necessity for cutting a straight line with a craft knife. A 24-inch ruler is more versatile than a 12-inch ruler.

- ✔ **Triangles:** Plastic triangles are the straight edge's relatives. Triangles come in handy when planning quilting projects. A 45-degree triangle and a 30/60-degree triangle work for most projects.

- ✔ **Yardstick:** You must own a yardstick! The yardstick works great for marking lengths of fabric 36 inches or longer. You can also use the yardstick's width to mark quilting grid patterns.

- ✔ **Rotary cutter and cutting board:** A rotary cutter (also known as a *cutting wheel*) looks like a pizza cutter. The rotary cutter helps cut strips of fabric to use in strip-piecing quilts and other projects that require cutting through layers of fabric.

A Sticky Subject

Every good craft tool kit includes glue. You simply can't live without it. But what kind of glue should you buy? The following sections help you choose the right glue for the job.

Craft glue

You can use all-purpose craft glue for just about every kind of craft project imaginable. Craft glue is permanent, doesn't stain, and is water-soluble until it's completely dry. After the glue dries, it holds forever. Craft glue is often called *white glue* because it comes out of the squeeze bottle an opaque white. However, it becomes clear as it dries. Craft glue also goes by the names *PVA* and *polyvinyl acetate*.

School glue and tacky glue are also white, but these glues are less effective as long-term adhesives. They hold paper to paper, but the glued elements can be separated — which is a good thing if you make a mistake. School glue and tacky glue are perfect for children's projects.

Rubber cement

Rubber cement works best for gluing paper to paper. You get the best results from rubber cement, which is a contact cement, by following these steps:

1. **Coat each surface separately.**

2. **Let the surfaces dry**

3. **Mount the two surfaces together for a permanent bond.**

If neatness isn't your thing, you can clean up the excess rubber cement by rubbing your finger back and forth over the messy area or by using a rubber cement pick-up. The *rubber cement pick-up* is a square, hard eraser available in art material stores. And don't worry about asking the people behind the counter for a pick-up; they won't think you're asking for a date.

If you make a mistake with rubber cement, it's very difficult to undo without rubber cement thinner. For best results, follow the directions on the can.

Glue sticks

I can't imagine what people did before glue sticks were invented. These handy, non-toxic devices are great for gluing paper, photos, fabric, or any other light item. Glue sticks make it especially easy to create memory books and scrapbooks without any messiness.

Glue sticks operate like a tube of lip balm — you turn a dial at the bottom to expose more of the solid glue at the top. After removing the cap from the top of the tube, rub the top of the glue stick over the surface to be mounted and press down — presto!

Glue guns

Crafters must earn their "stripes" just like anyone else. One of the first steps in earning those crafter stripes is owning a glue gun. The glue gun is one of the most indispensable tools you can own. You can use the glue gun for all sorts of crafting projects and home repairs.

Don't be intimidated by the word *gun*. This device looks like a small plastic water pistol, but it becomes hot, the way an iron does, to melt a solid glue stick as you insert it into the glue gun.

When using a glue gun, first insert the solid glue stick. After the gun gets hot, squeeze the trigger. As the glue stick passes through the heated gun, it becomes hot and soft, and a little dollop of glue comes out. The hot glue forms a strong bond that secures heavy or three-dimensional elements. The glue dries almost instantly and has become the crafter's "can't do without" item on the "materials needed list" of supplies.

The hobby glue gun was created for use in crafting and comes in pretty colors and in different sizes for home and professional use. You can find glue guns in craft stores along with the appropriate-size solid glue sticks that you insert into the gun. You have to buy the packages of glue sticks for the gun separately, though. (These glue sticks are not the same as the tubes of glue described in the preceding section.)

The glue gun is a tool that should be kept away from children because, if misused, the hot glue and the gun itself can cause burns on contact.

Paint Brushes for Every Occasion

Paint brushes come in many different sizes and are made of different materials. Each has its specific use. Some projects require better quality brushes than others, depending on what the brushes are being used for. When you use the best brush recommended for a project you're sure to get the best results. The following descriptions of different brushes help you choose the ones you need.

Sponge brushes

Sponge brushes are inexpensive and are, therefore, disposable after use. Because a sponge brush doesn't have bristles, it's a great tool for applying a smooth coat of acrylic paint or water-based varnish. Sponge brushes come in ½-, 1-, 2-, and 3-inch widths.

If you take care of your sponge brush and rinse it well in warm water after each use, you can get several uses out of it before the brush falls apart. (Sponge brushes also dry quickly, especially in the sun.)

Decorative arts brushes

Rather than using expensive professional artists' brushes, select from the wide range of inexpensive reproductions. These brushes have been designed exclusively for decorative crafts.

If you are going to use only one decorative arts brush, make it the all-purpose round brush. If you want a wider variety, consider the following brushes.

- **Long liner brushes** for fine lines or calligraphy.
- **Short or long flat brushes** for backgrounds of paintings, to paint edges, and for varnishing.
- **Angular brushes** to create lines of varying widths, such as when painting a picture of a ribbon bow or other designs that require fine, curvy lines.

Stencil brushes

Stencil brushes are also called *stipplers* or *pouncers*. Stencil brushes are round, and the hairs are all cut to the same length.

To use the stencil brush, hold the brush in a vertical position and apply the paint to the surface by lightly pouncing the brush up and down. You can also use stencil brushes to do faux finishing. (I discuss faux finishing in Chapter 12.)

Clean-Up Materials That Make Life Easy

Just like cooking, crafting requires cleaning the "dishes" — with crafts, having a clean workspace and utensils is just as important as having a clean casserole dish. Keep a basket or plastic shoe box filled with rags and sponges near your workspace so that you're always prepared for spills, drips, and messy endeavors. Take a look at the following:

- **Rags and paper towels:** Use rags and paper towels to clean your workstation, tools, and crafts. A roll of paper towels is indispensable for cleaning paint off a stencil sheet and for wiping away excess glue from wood, glass, or plastic.

You can buy a bag of rags almost anywhere, but take a look at home first. Old T-shirts make great rags because they're soft and pliable. Old terrycloth dishtowels and washcloths also work well.

Soft, clean cotton rags aren't just for cleaning — they're useful for many craft projects as well, such as buffing a waxed surface or for rag rolling (see Chapter 12). Paper towels also work well for rag rolling and for applying stain to wood.

Cheesecloth is also good for cleaning up work surfaces. Cheesecloth is a cotton mesh fabric that is light and porous. It's extremely pliable and has a texture that makes it good for many faux finishing techniques. You can find cheesecloth in home centers, grocery stores, and craft supply stores.

✔ **Kitchen sponges:** Invest in a bag of kitchen sponges that come in a variety of sizes. Kitchen sponges are indispensable for all sorts of projects. For example, a tiny sponge is helpful for tasks like wiping away excess glue from a corner of a découpage cut-out. (If you don't have what you consider a tiny sponge, cut a regular-size sponge into four pieces.)

✔ **Solvents:** When possible, I always use paints and other chemicals that are water-soluble, so water is the main clean-up solvent. Water-soluble paints and chemicals make life easier, safer, and odor-free. Other useful solvents are rubber cement thinner, paint thinner (mineral spirits), and denatured alcohol (for cleaning brushes after using shellac-based primers).

✔ **Hand vacuum:** Have you ever tried to clean up embroidery floss from a carpet? Nearly impossible! But those little hand vacuums love to do just such a job. A hand vacuum makes cleaning a sewing table covered with bits of thread and tiny pieces of cut fabric a cinch. Just make sure to keep the hand vacuum in the self-charging caddy so it's always ready to operate at optimum power.

Additions for an All-Purpose Tool Kit

The items I cover in the earlier sections of this chapter are the basics, but many crafts require more specialized tools. Most of the craft projects you tackle require some specific tool or gadget to make the project easier to complete. Putting together your own tool kit ensures that you have the stuff you need on hand for your projects. (And don't forget the added bonus: Your tool kit may also come in handy for home repairs.)

Use the following items as a starting point for your tool kit.

✔ **A small screwdriver with interchangeable tips** for Phillips head and slotted head screws, or a selection of both types of screwdrivers in various sizes.

- ✔ **A small- and medium-size hammer.** When choosing the sizes for you, try out several. Pick the hammers that feel comfortable in your hand (make sure they're not too heavy).

- ✔ **A box each of small nails, brads, and push pins.** Brads are tiny nails without heads, often used on light wood when glue isn't enough but you don't need a strong nail.

- ✔ **Tweezers and/or needle-nosed pliers.** Use these for getting at those tiny little things hidden in a crevice. Tweezers and needle-nosed pliers are also used for beadwork, lifting delicate dried flowers, bending wire, and a variety of other tasks.

- ✔ **A roll of string.** You never know when it will come in handy, even if making a beaded necklace isn't your craft of choice.

- ✔ **A craft knife with a box of blades, as well as single-edge razor blades.** An X-Acto knife is a common example of a craft knife.

- ✔ **Rolls of masking tape and transparent tape.**

- ✔ **A compass.** This is the essential tool for making a perfect circle.

- ✔ **A small pad and pencil.** Use these for making notes and reminders to buy items that you need as you learn each new craft.

Chapter 3

Simple Skills for All Crafts

∙ ∙

In This Chapter

▶ Getting the right measurements

▶ Resizing your designs

▶ Making the cut

▶ Selecting colors and materials

▶ Organizing your projects

∙ ∙

*E*very craft requires basic skills and a little know-how before you begin. For example, many crafts require a design or pattern, but sometimes the design or pattern isn't presented full-size on the copy you have. You have to enlarge it. That may seem like an obstacle to your fun, but when you know how easy resizing the pattern or design is, you can zip along with no trouble.

Knowing how to cut with scissors or a craft knife isn't an art, but it helps to know how to use each type of scissors or craft knife effectively. If you've never used cuticle scissors to cut paper, for example, you may not know when to hold the scissors with the blades curving toward the work and when to cut with the blades curving away from the work. You find this type of information in this chapter so that you can put your skills into practice when making a project.

Selecting colors and materials isn't only a matter of what you like. It helps to know a little bit about colors and patterns of fabric that look best together, as well as the best kinds of material for specific projects.

In this chapter you find out how to measure, size, cut, combine colors and fabrics, and organize your projects. All the skills I show you in this chapter are useful throughout the book, and whenever you need a little help, you can come back to this chapter. If you start out knowing even these few things, you save time, money, and frustration in the long run. Then you can relax and have fun with the craft.

Measuring Right Is the Key to Success

Measuring often plays a big part in the crafting process. For example, you may need to cut pieces of fabric for a quilt or you may want to crop photographs for a memory book. Knowing how to measure correctly in the first place makes the difference between a successful project and one that's a total flop. I'm here to make sure that all your projects are successful. The following measuring devices and techniques do the trick.

Wielding rulers like a pro

Some crafts don't require precise measurements, but others do. Metal rulers are more accurate than yardsticks and wooden or plastic rulers because, by comparison, the printing on a metal ruler is sharper and more precise. When the outcome of a project is dependent on extremely accurate measurements, you want to be sure the ruler is perfectly straight on the material to be measured. When cutting fabric pieces for patchwork, for example, be sure the fabric beneath the ruler is smooth and flat. If you're stenciling a border around a room, you need to measure accurately so that you can adjust the design, if necessary, to meet at the corners.

The eye can really fool you, so don't think you can eyeball a measurement. Measuring carefully saves you a lot of time and effort. The old carpenter's rule of "measure twice, cut once" holds true for anything you need to measure.

Different projects require different kinds of rulers. Here's the lowdown on which rulers are best for certain uses:

- For drawing quilt patterns and measurements on small paper projects, 6- and 12-inch rulers are fine. Have a 12-inch ruler handy to check measurements on almost any craft project.

- Use a metal ruler when the crafting technique involves cutting with a razor blade or craft knife.

- Use 36- and 48-inch yardsticks for most fabric projects. Working with materials that are 45 inches wide requires a long ruler.

- A flexible measuring tape is most useful for measurements that don't have to be too precise and for measuring around three-dimensional objects.

- A T-square ruler combines a T-square, which enables you to line things up accurately, with a ruler to measure as you go along.

- A triangle, a protractor, and a compass are useful for measuring angles and circles, especially when designing patchwork patterns.

✔ A see-through plastic ruler with a grid is an all-purpose device with many uses. You can create graphs, check to see whether a design is squared up, and draw right (90-degree) angles.

Getting a square deal

Sometimes you may need to know the *perimeter,* which is the measurement around something, like measuring how much material you need to cover the outside of a box. Knowing the perimeter also comes in handy, for example, if you want to add a colorful binding around a square or rectangular pillow.

To figure the perimeter, add the length of all four sides. Then add an extra inch to the total to allow for some overlapping of ends.

Operating in the best circles

To find the *circumference,* the measurement around a circle, of something, you multiply the diameter by π, or 3.1416.

You may be thinking, "Why do I need to know how to figure the circumference of anything?" Here's the answer: You're having a party, and you have just made a pretty round tablecloth for your circular table. All it needs is a fringe to go around the edge. Do you eyeball it to measure the amount of fringe you need? If the tablecloth measures 114 inches across the middle (the *diameter*), what would you guess the length around it (the circumference) is? 170 inches? 250 inches? It's impossible to guess. To be absolutely sure that you buy the right amount of fringe, follow the rule for measuring to find the circumference. The fringe for your tablecloth needs to be 114 x 3.1416, or a little more than 358 inches. That's almost 30 feet! When you go to the fabric shop, buy 10 yards of fringe.

A little give goes a long way

Fabric moves if it isn't fastened down. If you're cutting small pieces of fabric from a larger piece of fabric, for example, secure the larger piece before measuring and cutting the smaller pieces in the following way:

1. **Place the large fabric piece, wrong side up, on a *cutting board* (see Chapter 2) or hard, flat surface.**

2. **Secure each corner of the fabric to the cutting board or hard surface with pushpins or masking tape, making sure that the fabric is squarely aligned and taut.**

3. **Do your measuring and mark off your small pieces with a pencil.**

4. **Using a rotary cutter and straightedge (see "Rolling away," later in this chapter), cut the fabric along the drawn lines.**

   If you're using dressmaker's scissors (see Chapter 2) to cut out the fabric pieces, remove the larger fabric from the cutting board or hard surface and cut along the measured, drawn lines.

Matching lines

You're bound to waste material when cutting and joining pieces of paper or fabric with a repeat pattern such as checks or stripes because you may have to adjust the pieces in order to match the patterns accurately. Take this fact into consideration when buying material for a project. For example, if you're making something with an appliqué pattern, draw the shape of the pieces on paper, cut out the paper shapes, and take these "templates" with you when choosing the material. Place the templates on the fabric to see how you can lay out your pattern, taking into consideration the extra fabric needed around each pattern piece for cutting and seam allowance (see Chapter 13).

Lining a box with wallpaper doesn't require the same kind of accuracy needed for buying fabric because you don't have to allow for seam allowance. If you're lining a box with wallpaper, measure the inside so that you know the sizes of the wallpaper pieces you need before choosing the patterned paper. You need a little extra for overlapping or matching the cut ends so that the pattern isn't chopped off in the middle.

Enlarging and Reducing Designs

If you find the perfect design but it's not the right size for your project, the quickest way to enlarge or reduce your design is to use a copier. You may have enlarged pictures on a copier before and know that you just set the copier to the percentage you want and press the button. But if your design is 8 inches long and you want to make it 12 inches long, how do you know what percentage to select?

At most copy centers, you can find a circular plastic gizmo called a *proportional wheel,* which is a handy thing for a crafter to own. It consists of a small plastic wheel attached to a larger plastic wheel, each marked off in inches. To figure your percentage, set the 8-inch mark on the small rule to the 12-inch mark on the large rule, as shown in Figure 3-1. The arrow points to 150 percent enlargement. Reverse the process to reduce designs.

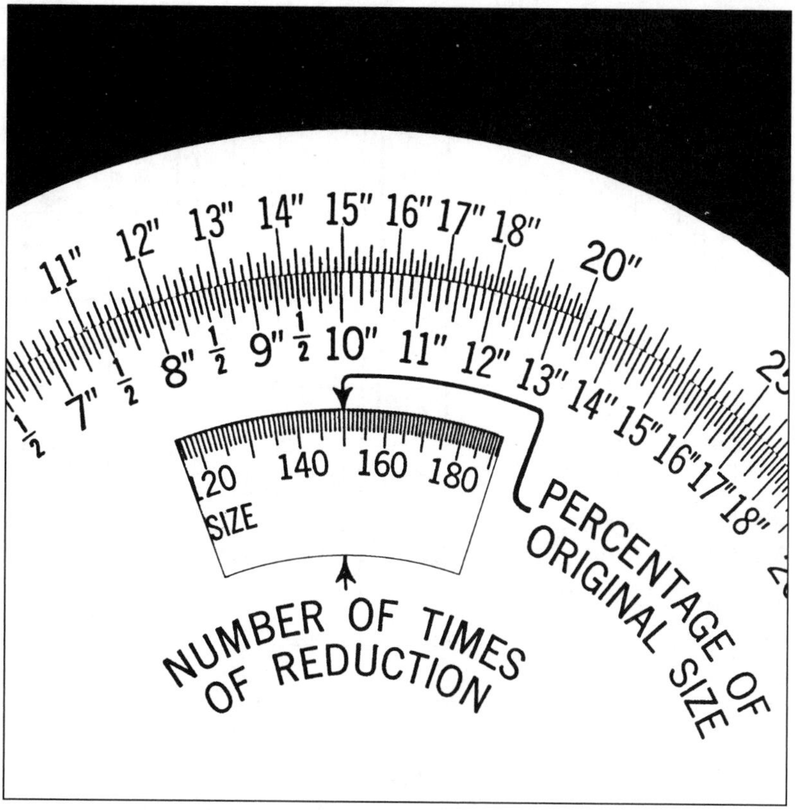

Figure 3-1:
A
proportional
wheel.

But suppose that it's Sunday and the copy center is closed. You are dying to make something, but first you have to enlarge or reduce a design. The do-it-yourself method involves transposing the drawing on one grid to a grid of a different size. Here are the steps:

1. **Trace the design in the center of a piece of graph paper.**

   Art material stores and stationers have sheets of graph paper measured off in ¼-inch, 1-inch, and other sizes. I find the 1-inch size good for most projects.

2. **Using a piece of graph paper that is large enough to fit the final size of your design, copy the original design onto the larger size in one of the following ways:**

   • Figure 3-2a shows the small Christmas stocking drawn on graph paper with ¼-inch squares. Figure 3-2b shows this design copied, square by square, onto graph paper with 1-inch squares, thereby enlarging the design four times.

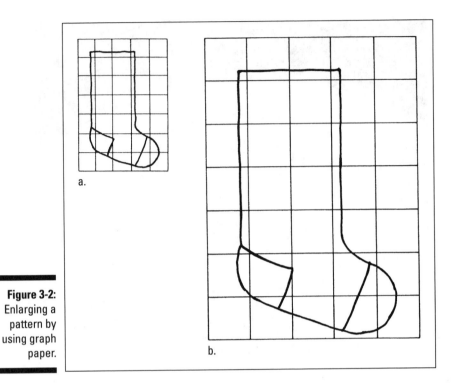

a.

b.

Figure 3-2:
Enlarging a
pattern by
using graph
paper.

- If you have only graph paper with one size squares, trace the design on it. Then on a larger piece of the same graph paper, copy the design by using one, two, three, or four squares of the large sheet to equal one square of the small sheet.

  In this way, you enlarge the design one, two, three, or four times the original size, depending on the number of squares you use.

Tape together four pieces of 8½-x-11-inch paper to make a larger piece of graph paper.

If the design is complicated, place dots on the grid lines where the design lines intersect them and then connect the dots. If you're enlarging a design for a quilt block, all you have to do is draw a grid over the block design and copy it up to the larger size. The pieces will all fit the grid because quilt blocks are planned on a grid.

Cutting Is a Cinch

You need to match up the right scissors and material for the craft you're working on. If you start with the right scissors, you can't fail. Don't even think of cutting your fabric with hair clippers or paper with fabric shears. There are scissors for everything, and when you have the right combination, cutting anything is a cinch.

Keeping your scissors clean and sharp is the most important way to ensure accurate and smooth cutting. Dull scissors create choppy cut lines.

Remember that left-handed scissors are available, too, so don't struggle with those made for righties.

Making straight cuts

Single-edge razor blades, utility knives, and craft knives provide straight, accurate cut lines. Use these against a metal ruler or straightedge for one smooth, straight cut.

When using a single-edge blade (razor, utility knife, or craft knife) to cut a straight line against a metal ruler, always place the point of the blade against the ruler and angle the blade slightly away from the cutting edge. This avoids any chance of the blade slipping over the edge of the ruler.

Choose the right cutting instrument for the job. A razor blade is fine for thin material like paper. However, if you're cutting poster board or mat board, which is thicker than regular typing or computer paper, use a craft or utility knife.

Image tip icon

A clean, sharp, blade gives you the best cutting results. Because blades are very inexpensive, this isn't a good place to economize. When in doubt, change the blade.

Rolling away

A rotary cutter looks like a pizza cutter and operates much the same way. It's excellent for making sharp cuts through many layers (cloth, leather, paper, or vinyl, thin or thick, hard or soft) at the same time. It cuts in any direction, backward or forward, straight or curved. It can be used right- or left-handed.

Remember to protect the surface on which you're cutting or use a cutting board (see Chapter 2) made especially for this purpose and sold in fabric shops. Don't even think about using the rotary cutter on top of your smooth kitchen counter or fine wood dining table without protection. One pass of the rotary cutter, and your counter or table isn't so fine anymore.

The best way to use the rotary cutter is as follows:

1. **Place several layers of same-size fabric pieces, right-side down, on the cutting surface.**

2. **Using a pencil or fabric marker and ruler on the top piece of fabric, mark off the lines to be cut.**

3. **Unlock the safety covering from the blade.**

4. **Place your straightedge or ruler on the drawn line, hold the rotary cutter firmly against the straightedge and roll the rotary cutter along the ruler edge just as you would a craft knife.**

The beauty of the rotary cutter is that the fabric doesn't pull as you roll, and the cutter can cut through several layers of fabric at one time.

Don't be timid or hesitant when using the rotary cutter. Simply press down and roll away.

Choosing Colors, Fabrics, Paints, Yarns, and Threads

Colors and textures are the heart of any crafting technique. They determine the look of your finished project. When you pick materials for a craft project, you'll enjoy working on it more if the pattern or design and the colors are pleasing to you. You wouldn't buy a dress in a color that doesn't look good on you, and for the same reason, you shouldn't choose colors you don't like for an appliqué pillow. However, many different types of fabrics, paints, yarns, and threads are available, so you'll want to match the right one for the specific craft.

Colorful decisions

Selecting colors, whether for a fabric project or paint for a painting project, is a matter of looking, learning, and, sometimes, trial and error. For example, those little colored paper samples of paint colors that are free in any paint or hardware store, called *color chips,* are intended to help you select paint colors. However, because the color is printed on paper, the chip isn't always exactly the same color as the paint. It can appear much brighter when the paint is applied.

Choosing the right color for the project is an art that you can easily acquire. It just takes practice. Start with small tubes or pint-size cans and experiment, trying out different color combinations. You will quickly become skillful at selecting colors. The same is true when matching fabric colors. Play around with fabric scraps to see which colors and prints look best together before purchasing yards of fabric. Generally, colors that don't contrast too greatly, but rather are in the same value range, are the best for fabric craft projects, unless the project calls for dark and light colors. Still, it's a good idea to choose light and darker shades of the same color.

If red is your favorite color and it looks good on you, then there's no reason why you shouldn't choose red as the color for most craft projects. However, if you're faux finishing a large piece of furniture or your bedroom walls, I strongly urge you to rethink the use of your favorite color. Introducing red in the form of a small pillow may be a better option. Replacing that pillow is much easier than repainting the entire room if you ever decide that blue is really your favorite color.

Here are some tips on choosing colors for your projects:

- ✔ **Look at the colors you wear and decorate with.** If you're unsure about what colors to use for a project or which colors go together, think about the colors you like to wear and use in your home decorating scheme. If these colors work together in your wardrobe or in your home, they'll probably look good together in a craft project.

- ✔ **Sample it first.** Paint chips are great for experimenting with color. Especially if you're making a patchwork quilt, it's easy to arrange the color pieces to see whether they look good together. Take them with you to the fabric store. Or use them to choose the colors you want for a painting project. For paints, choose a color that is one or two shades lighter than the color sample.

- ✔ **Keep it natural.** If you're unsure about the colors to use, pairing the colors of nature is a safe bet. Look around you and choose the colors you see in trees, leaves, flowers, and other products of the outdoors. Nature did it right. You can't go wrong if you follow suit.

Comparing fabrics

The fabric of choice of most crafters is 100-percent cotton. Cotton is sold in 45-inch widths and is usually quite inexpensive. You can find it in a vast array of colors, prints, and patterns. Pre-wash most fabric before measuring and cutting it for any project. Pre-washing makes the fabric softer, pre-shrinks it so that your finished project is the right size, and tests the fabric for color-fastness.

Cotton holds a crease if you want to temporarily mark a seam line by pressing the fabric into a crease with your fingers.

Polyester is easiest to work with because it is quite flexible and won't wrinkle. However, experienced stitchers, especially quilters, prefer cotton.

Polyblend means that the fabric is part cotton and part polyester. This fabric is good for tablecloths and some projects that you don't want to iron. It also resists wrinkles and stains.

Felt is suitable for projects that don't require washing, such as Christmas ornaments and decorations. Felt is easy to cut, and no seam allowance is needed because it doesn't ravel. You can buy felt in a wide range of colors and in small pieces that are 9 x 12 inches or large pieces that are 60 inches wide. The large pieces are excellent for tree skirts, banners, and table covers. When you are skillful with the rotary cutter (see "Rolling away," in this chapter), you can easily cut several layers of felt to make multiple projects.

Cross-stitch fabrics are called *even-weaves* because they are made of evenly spaced holes that form small squares or a grid. You then fill in these squares with stitches to create a design.

To begin most counted cross-stitch projects you must find the center of the fabric for placement of the first stitch. A good way to find the center of a piece of even-weave fabric is to fold the fabric in half lengthwise and again widthwise. The point at which the lines intersect is the center point.

Yarns and threads

Yarns and threads differ in texture and fiber content. Some are natural, and some are synthetic. In the directions for each type of needlework, I tell you everything you need to know about the specific yarn or thread traditionally used for that craft.

You can have a lot of fun designing with yarns and threads because the colors and shades of colors are vast. For example, after you know the basic technique for doing needlepoint, embroidery, or cross-stitch, you can create illustrations or designs from a variety of colors.

Picking paints

It's a jungle out there when it comes to paint. You can buy spray paint or paint that comes in bottles, cans, and tubes. You can choose from acrylic paint, oil- and water- based paint, glazes, glitter, and glaze.

However, you need a specific type of paint for every project, and you can find the right paint listed with each craft technique in the book. Chances are your local craft store or home center has exactly what you need. Most manufacturers have a toll-free phone number or a Web site to help you locate the nearest outlet for their products.

To use spray paint, start by reading the directions on the paint can. You should always spray-paint in a well-ventilated area, preferably outdoors where there's no wind. To sufficiently cover the surface with paint, keep moving the spray can back and forth in a slow motion. Several thin coats of paint provide a more even distribution and thus a smoother finish than one heavy coat of paint.

When applying acrylic paint, I like to use a sponge brush (see Chapter 2) because acrylic paint is rubbery and thicker than other water-based paint. Using a sponge brush enables you to avoid obvious brush strokes that are so common with a bristle brush.

Getting Organized

Crafters fall into one of two camps when it comes to organizing their projects. Some of them feel more comfortable if they organize their tools and materials and thoroughly read the directions before they begin a new project. Others like to jump in without any preparation and figure it out as they go along. But take it from me: The latter group probably spends more time and money on their projects. These folks barely get started on a craft project before they have to stop and head to a store for missing materials and tools. You'll find your crafting experience more satisfying if you buy and organize your materials in advance, find a convenient place to do your craft, and glance over the directions before you begin.

Carving out your niche

Planning an appropriate and pleasing workspace and what you need in it is the best way to begin crafting. If possible, create a work area that you don't need for other uses so that your project can go undisturbed between crafting sessions. This might be a corner of a room, a basement area, or your kitchen counter. Light your work space properly, because bright light — whether natural or artificial — is essential for good craftwork.

Some craftwork requires more space than others do. For example, if you're using a sewing machine and ironing board, you need more space than if you're making a photo craft project. If you're working with paints or other chemicals, you need a space that's well ventilated or outdoors.

Getting your act together

Store all your craft materials in a clear plastic box or bag, a basket, a tote, or other convenient container. That way, you have all your materials together so that you can easily pick up your project and work on it whenever you have the time and quickly put it all away. Cleaning up after each session is a breeze, and you don't need to worry about the cat drinking your solvent or unraveling your yarn.

If you label different containers, you won't forget what's in each one. Also, I find that when cutting different templates for patchwork or appliqué, it helps to identify each one on the back with a number or a name. The same goes for fabric pieces. Pin a note to a stack of identical cut-out pieces and write what project they are for.

Part II
Paper Crafts

The 5th Wave — By Rich Tennant

"Oh, that's Jack's area for his paper crafts. He's made some wonderful US Treasury Bonds, Certificates of Deposit, $20's, $50's, $100's, that sort of thing."

In this part . . .

Paper crafts are the easiest craft to jump into. The materials are inexpensive and the tools are few. You may already have most of what you need.

In this part you find out how to decorate paper for wrapping packages, make projects with rubber stamps, preserve and display your photographs and favorite memorabilia, create your own memory book, and do découpage (even if you aren't sure exactly what découpage is).

All kinds of wonderful papers are available for your crafts. This part tells you where to find them and how to work with them. Finishing touches make paper crafts extra special, and everything you need to know about them is right here, too.

Chapter 4

Covering the Basics of Paper Crafts

. . . .

In This Chapter

▶ Exploring different kinds of paper

▶ Reviewing the paper crafts you want to try

▶ Checking out your basic tools and materials

. . . .

Although all the craft techniques in this chapter use paper, they approach crafting with paper in different ways. No paper craft is hard to master; in fact, you have probably already done some of the techniques shown here in some form at one time or another.

Whether you are decorating paper for gift wrapping, using rubber stamp methods to make a greeting card, framing that perfect vacation photo in a novel way, putting together a memory book for your family to keep forever, or creating a découpage box for a special person, you find new methods, products, and creative ways to use familiar materials in the chapters of this part.

Sifting Through Paper Types

Newspapers, magazines, catalogs, paper bags, junk mail . . . do you sometimes feel like you're drowning in paper? Well, there's paper — and then there's *paper*. Your opinion of paper all depends on the quality of the paper and what you do with it. Better yet, your attitude about paper may become completely positive when you find out how many ways you can put it to creative uses.

Think about all the decorative papers that are easy to get: gift wrap, wallpaper and borders (including wallpaper scraps and discontinued wallpaper sample books), and colored tissues. And don't overlook ordinary but potentially useful types of paper such as construction paper, glossy pages from magazines, adhesive-backed papers, shelf-lining papers, and even plain white computer paper.

You can find more exotic papers in specialty outlets such as art supply shops and craft stores. For example, you may come across all kinds of marbleized papers available in myriad colors, beautiful rice papers from Japan, and subtly colored papers from Thailand with names like *mango, mocha, jade,* and *geranium*. Specialty stores also carry parchment papers, heavy watercolor papers, kraft papers (such as brown wrapping paper and the stuff used to make grocery store bags), cover stocks in all colors, metallic papers, and even paper that is a different color on each side.

You can find many ways to recycle paper items like greeting cards, postcards, and all those other things you've been saving, like concert ticket stubs, invitations, awards, letters, your child's drawings, and baby announcements.

Paper Crafts Anyone Can Do

The chapters of this part tell you everything you need to know about the following paper crafts. Pick which chapter to go to first, and I'm sure you'll be so inspired you'll want to go to all of them.

- ✔ **Decorative paper:** You make decorative paper for pretty wrappings. You can also buy decorative paper to cover a plain notebook or a box. Decorative paper crafts such as my berry boxes are the perfect projects to sell at a bazaar. Some decorative paper crafts are simple enough for kids to make, like their very own découpage box. It's all in Chapter 5.

- ✔ **Rubber stamping:** The simplicity of creating designs with rubber stamps has led to an enormously popular activity. You can use rubber stamps for greeting cards, announcements, invitations, memory books, and anything else you can think of. You can create designs on fabric, on wood, and even on ceramic coffee mugs. You can find all the ways to use rubber stamps and the different things you can make with them in Chapter 6.

- ✔ **Photo crafts:** Photographs are the basis for this craft. Chapter 7 shows you how to crop snapshots, mount and preserve your photographs, and use them as the main design element in a craft project. You also find out how to make a special frame for a holiday photograph.

No need to buy expensive frames once you become an expert photo crafter — and you'll save a fortune by making your own gifts!

✔ **Memory book crafts:** Creating a memory book means preserving memorabilia in a scrapbook that you design from your personal collection of keepsakes. Your memory book can include photographs, birthday cards, love letters, a child's drawings, wedding invitations, ticket stubs, announcements, newspaper articles, or scraps of pretty wrapping paper or wallpaper. Each collection represents things that have meaning, if only to you. For example, you might surprise your daughter on her wedding day with a memory book of her life from birth to the present. Memory book crafting is about putting it all together in creative ways. Chapter 8 shows you everything you need to get started.

✔ **Découpage:** This French word literally means *to cut out* and is pronounced *day-coo-pahj*. Découpage is the art of applied cutouts. Using small scissors, you simply cut out designs from materials such as wrapping paper, greeting cards, or wallpaper, arrange the elements on a flat or three-dimensional object such as a plaque or a box, and glue them in place. Many coats of varnish preserve the designs and create a smooth surface. After you get the how-to in Chapter 9, you could make a small tabletop decorated with paper souvenirs from your travels — sections from a street map of Paris, your admission ticket to the Louvre, a bill from a famous restaurant, postcards, and so on.

Gathering Your Accessories, Tools, and Materials

Each area of paper crafts has its own special accessories, tools, and materials. The following gives you a quick overview of what you need for each technique.

✔ **Decorative wraps:** If you want to decorate paper for wrapping a gift or you want to cover something with decorative papers, you almost always need a ruler, a straightedge, a craft knife or single-edge razor blade, and craft glue or rubber cement for cutting and pasting (see Chapter 2). For decorating, you may need such supplies as a stencil design (Chapter 11), paints, markers, or rubber stamps.

✔ **Stamp crafts:** To get the most out of stamp crafts (see Chapter 6), visit a well-stocked craft or stationery store, which carries literally hundreds of rubber stamp designs and almost as many ink colors. Stamp crafts are lots of fun and open up a wide range of creative possibilities from making your own stationery to creating decorative wrapping paper. Rubber stamps provide you with designs to make any plain object pretty.

✔ **Photo crafts:** Working with existing photographs is easy if you have the right tools. You need scissors and a craft knife, as well as a straightedge such as a metal ruler (see Chapter 2). Photo corners and paper borders, craft glue, a glue stick, double-faced tape, rubber cement, rubber cement thinner, rubber cement pickup (which looks like a kneaded eraser), and a *burnisher* (a flat, plastic stick that looks like a tongue depressor and is used to smooth down photos — the edge of a credit card is a good substitute) are all available in art supply stores. I introduce you to the complete art of photo crafts in Chapter 7.

✔ **Memory book crafts:** Memory book crafts employ a variety of accessories that are easy to find and a lot of fun to use. Some of these items include stickers, photo corners, stamps with decorations and sayings, cutout borders, and symbols like cloud shapes on which you can write a quote. You can also personalize a memory book with bits of lace, ribbon, a school pendant, and other trims that relate to the subject. Entire stores are devoted to memory book crafts, as well as mail-order catalogs. Check out the Appendix for information on mail-order companies and company Web sites.

✔ **Découpage:** Although découpage is an old craft, new materials are available to make it foolproof. For example, many different types of craft glue are on the market. Some dry perfectly clear (which is the kind you want), and others stay tacky so that you can undo a mistake if you glue a cutout down and then decide it doesn't look good in that spot. You can find clear water-based varnish that dries within an hour and doesn't turn yellow like oil-based varnish does. Craft stores even provide precut paper designs to eliminate tedious cutting. And you don't have to mix paint colors to get the perfect shade for your project. Now you can buy small tubes or bottles of any shade of color you can dream up. Most craft paints are water-soluble, which means no odor, no messy cleanup, and quick drying time. (See Chapter 10 for more about paint.)

Chapter 5

Wrapping It Up in Style

*T*his chapter makes you look at paper in a new light. Never again will you throw away a scrap of wallpaper, wrapping paper, or a paper bag without first thinking of its potential for use in a craft project. In this chapter you can find suggestions and ideas for decorating paper to personalize gift wraps and directions for wrapping a present perfectly.

Getting organized is fun when you have pretty containers for all your stuff. This chapter tells you everything you need to know to cover plain cardboard, plastic, and wooden boxes with decorative papers. You can even coordinate your storage boxes and desk accessories to match the décor in your room. You also discover how to create attractive home accessories by adding decorative paper trims to ordinary objects.

Making Your Own Wrapping Paper

You can easily transform a roll of inexpensive, plain white shelf paper or plain brown kraft paper into one-of-a-kind decorative wrapping paper. Simply cut a piece of paper to the size appropriate for wrapping your gift (see the section "Wrapping a Package," later in this chapter) and try one of the following ideas.

✔ The simplest way to decorate paper is by adding gold or silver stick-on stars (get them by the box from stationery stores) in a random pattern all over the paper. You can use stars that are all the same size or vary the decorative effect by using stars in different sizes.

Finish the wrapping with a wide gold or silver organdy ribbon. You can find decorative French ribbon with thin wire edges in fabric and notions stores. This ribbon is an excellent choice for making perfect bows because the ribbon holds its shape. You can also manipulate the streamer ends into graceful folds because of the wire in the edges of the ribbon.

✔ Ragging and sponging are decorative painting techniques that can be used on paper. Choose a soft pastel paint color and apply it over the paper according to the directions for doing this technique on other surfaces (see Chapter 12). Set the paper aside to dry for about 20 minutes.

Painting paper with pastel faux finishing techniques suggests a soft, cloudlike package. Finish your wrapping with 2-inch-wide grosgrain, satin, or velvet ribbon tied in a graceful bow on the top.

✔ Stenciling a simple one- or two-color design such as a snowflake, a flower, or a leaf is another decorative technique (see Chapter 11). Choose a stencil design that's appropriate for the gift or personal taste of the individual receiving the gift. You can stencil a large image that covers the top of the box, or you can repeat a small design over the entire piece of paper.

Make a card to match your stenciled wrapping paper by using the stencil design to make one imprint on a plain piece of cardboard cut to the size of a gift tag. Using a hole punch, make a hole near one corner. Tie a length of ribbon or colorful yarn around the package and use the ribbon ends to make a bow. Thread a piece of the ribbon, cording, or yarn through the hole in the card and tie it onto the bow.

✔ Making decorative swirls, polka dots, wavy lines, freehand stripes, and checks is easy to do with markers, gold and silver pens, or acrylic paint and a brush. Don't be intimidated by holding a paintbrush in your hand. The looser the designs, the more interesting your paper will be.

For your package wrapped in paper decorated with a freehand painted design, match the ribbon color to the paint color that you used to create the design. If you used a gold or silver pen, wrap the package with gold or silver cording (available in stationery or notions stores). If you decorated the package with checks or stripes, look for checked and striped ribbons to match. Most fabric stores sell a variety of decorative ribbons in a wide range of colors.

✔ Rubber stamping a design image, a name, or a saying is another way to personalize your gift wrap (see Chapter 6 for stamping techniques). Buy ink pads in different colors and use one design in alternating colors. For example, to make an easy holiday gift wrap, use a stamp that says "Merry Christmas" to create a line of "Merry Christmas" text in alternating colors of red and green across the paper. The stamp design looks like a ribbon when you wrap your package in the paper.

The color and designs of your rubber stamp paper should dictate the style of ribbon for that package. For a nautical design such as a shell, use a thick white cord (available in fabric and hardware stores) and tie it in a knot. Use a glue gun (see Chapter 2) to adhere a shell to the cord ends. If your paper is decorated for the holidays, wrap the package with red and green tartan plaid taffeta ribbon.

Wrapping a Package

Wrapping a package so that the wrapping is neat and professional-looking is as easy as 1-2-3 . Before you begin, clear off a large, clean table top or counter to use as your work area. If your package is extra large, use the floor. Begin by rolling out a strip of paper that you estimate is longer than you need to wrap your box. Next, follow the diagrams in Figure 5-1 and these simple steps for wrapping a perfect package.

For the purpose of wrapping, the long, flat sides are the *sides,* and the short sides are the *ends.*

1. **Place the box on the paper, 2 to 3 inches in from the end of the paper, and roll the box over the paper three times, making sure that all four sides of the box have touched the paper, as shown in Figure 5-1a. Add 2 inches of paper and make a pencil mark at that point.**

2. **Remove the box and, using a straightedge and pencil, draw a line across the paper at this point. Cut the paper along the marked line.**

3. **Place the box facedown in the center of the paper. Fold the paper around the box, using your fingers to crease the paper along the box edges.**

   The *face* is the top of the box that you want the recipient to see when opening the package.

4. **Fold the raw edges of each end of the paper under about an inch and smooth the paper down so that you have a sharp crease and a smooth edge.**

5. **Fold the longer side of paper over the shorter side of paper onto the back of the box and tape the paper in place, as shown in Figure 5-1b.**

6. **Fold in the ends of the paper, as shown in Figure 5-1c.**

   Each time you fold, make a finger crease along the edge of the box, which makes the wrap look neat. Fold the top flap down, then fold the sides in, and, lastly, fold the bottom flap up. Place a piece of tape on the cut edge of paper to hold it in place on the box. Repeat on the other end.

   If the top flap covers more than two-thirds of the end of the box, unfold it and trim off the excess paper so that it covers no more than two-thirds of the end.

To finish the package, add a ribbon and bow:

1. **Tape the end of the ribbon on the top of the box near one corner, as shown in Figure 5-2a.**

2. **Wrap the ribbon around the box so that the amount of the box showing at the corners is the same all around.**

3. **Pull the loose end of the ribbon tight and tape it on top of the other ribbon end that you started with.**

4. **Tape a pre-made bow (available in most stationery stores) on top of the taped ribbon ends, hiding the tape (see Figure 5-2b).**

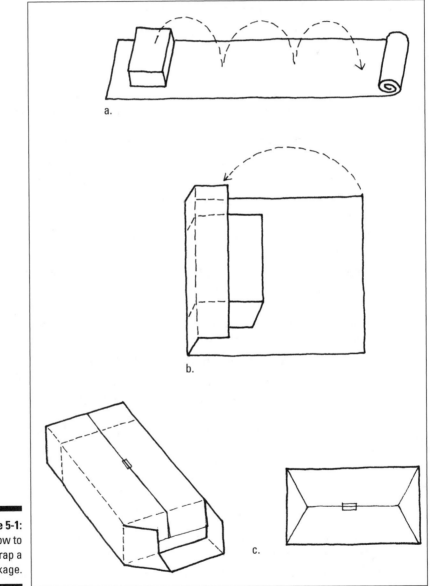

a.

b.

c.

Figure 5-1:
How to
wrap a
package.

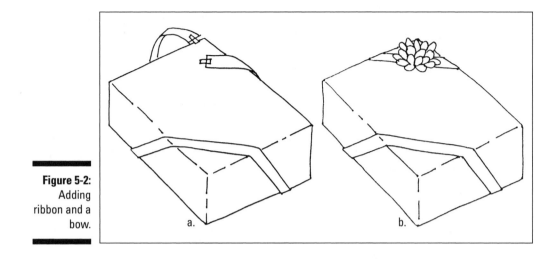

Figure 5-2:
Adding
ribbon and a
bow.

a.   b.

Making Elegant Containers of All Shapes and Sizes

Turning an ordinary object into a thing of beauty involves basic paper crafting techniques: measuring, cutting, and pasting. Using wallpaper, self-adhesive paper such as Con-Tact, and wrapping paper or other decorative printed papers, you can cover almost any object.

Paper-covered hatboxes are great for storing lingerie, thread, mementos, stationery items, and many other things. Use hatboxes to organize your things neatly on closet shelves or to accessorize a table or shelf. A decorated box can serve as a gift box or can be the gift itself. Or you can cover boxes with leftover wallpaper to coordinate accessories to match the walls.

Picking out the coverings for your boxes is a fun and creative activity. You have so many options! You can use printed papers, decorative wrapping paper, self-adhesive paper, or wallpaper to cover ordinary wooden, metal, or plastic boxes, as well as cardboard gift boxes. (Self-adhesive paper is easy to use for these projects — you can find a wide variety of designs at your local home center.)

And there are so many designs to choose from! You may decide to use florals, geometric patterns, or, for boxes for children's things, cartoon characters. You can combine two different designs — one design covering the outside and another one covering the top of the lid. After you cover the boxes, you can add trimming, such as braid, ribbon, or a wallpaper border to your boxes to give each box a finishing touch.

Covering small, square boxes

Covering small, square boxes is quite easy because you are working with straight lines. You can do wonders with plain, ordinary boxes, turning them into a work of art with just a pretty covering (see the photo in the color section of this book).

Tools and Materials:

Basic craft kit (see the Cheat Sheet at the front of this book)

A box with a separate lid

Decorative paper, preferably self-adhesive

Cutting board or protected surface

Razor blade

1. **Using a ruler, measure around all four sides of your box and add 1 inch to the total measurement.**

2. **Measure the height of the box, not including the lid.**

3. **Lay down the paper, with the wrong side up, on a cutting board or protected surface.**

4. **Using a pencil and ruler, draw one strip to the length and width of the bottom portion of your box measurements from Steps 1 and 2.**

5. **Place a straightedge across the paper at the pencil mark and cut out this strip of paper (which goes around your box) using your craft knife. Set aside the strip of paper.**

A craft knife and straightedge gives you a sharper, straighter cut line than scissors. However, in a pinch, scissors will do if you cut slowly and carefully along the drawn line. Always be sure to use scissors with a sharp, clean blade. Of course, the same goes for a craft knife blade.

6. **Measure the height of the lid of the box.**

7. **Repeat Steps 3, 4, and 5 using the lid measurements to cut this strip of paper.**

8. **With the box on the paper, draw around the base of the box and cut out the piece.**

9. **Place the lid on the paper and draw around it. Cut this piece out with an extra ⅜ inch of paper all around.**

10. **Cut the lid paper away from the corners at a slight angle, as shown in Figure 5-3, to ensure a proper fit.**

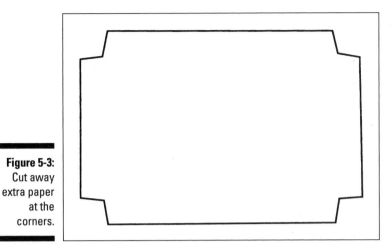

Figure 5-3:
Cut away
extra paper
at the
corners.

11. **To cover the top of the lid using self-adhesive paper, peel 1 inch of the backing paper away to reveal the sticky side. Line up the sticky paper with the corners of one edge of the top of the lid (the extra ⅜ inch of paper extends slightly to each side) and smooth it down.**

12. **Continue to pull away the backing as you smooth the self-adhesive paper down on the lid. Smooth the extra ⅜ inch of paper down onto the front edges of the lid.**

    If you're using paper that requires gluing, spread white glue evenly over the back of the paper for the lid and then apply the paper to the top of the lid in the same manner as described for the self-adhesive paper in Step 9.

13. **Repeat Step 9 to cover the bottom of the box (with no extra paper).**

14. **To cover the sides of the box, peel the backing away from one edge of the long strip of adhesive paper. Place the box on its side and align the sticky edge of the paper on one side edge of the box.**

15. **Smooth down the paper, continuing to peel away the backing as you attach the paper to all sides of the box.**

    If you are using non-adhesive paper, dot small amounts of glue on the back of the paper and spread the glue evenly over the entire piece of paper with your finger. Be sure that the paper is completely covered with a thin layer of glue. Then set the paper in position on the box.

16. **Trim away any excess paper with a clean, sharp razor blade.**

17. **If you glued the paper to the box, allow it to dry for an hour before trimming.**

Covering round or oval-shaped boxes

Round and oval-shaped boxes, like the ones shown in the color section of this book, were used to hold lingerie and sewing accessories in the Victorian era. You may find boxes in these shapes at yard sales, or perhaps you've purchased an item that came in a round or oval box. Look for pretty floral paper or one with an old-fashioned print to wrap the box for neatly organizing your things.

Tools and Materials:

Basic craft kit (see the Cheat Sheet at the front of this book)

Decorative paper, preferably self-adhesive

A round or oval box with a lid

Cutting board or protected surface

1. **To determine the circumference of the box, place the end of the tape measure on the side of the box and wrap the tape around the box until it meets the end of the tape measure (see Figure 5-4a).**

   The length of the piece of paper you need to wrap around the side of the box is the circumference of the box plus 1 inch.

2. **Lay out the self-adhesive paper on a cutting board or protected surface. Mark the length needed as per Step 1 and cut the paper, using a straightedge and craft knife or scissors.**

3. **Cut another piece of paper exactly the same size for the lining of the box.**

   You now have two lengths of paper.

4. **Measure the height of the bottom portion of the box (without the lid) and add 2 inches. Mark the height (plus the 2 inches) on the length of paper for the outside of the box and cut the extra paper off.**

5. **Now cut the length of paper for the lining without the extra 2 inches.**

6. **For the side of the box lid, cut a strip of paper the same length as the piece of paper cut to go around the side of the box. For the lining, cut another strip of paper to the same length.**

7. **Measure the height of the lid and add 1 inch. Cut one strip of paper for the outside of the lid; cut another strip of paper for the lining without the extra inch.**

8. **For the covering for the underside of the box, place the box on a piece of the paper and, using a pencil, mark around the circumference of the box and cut this piece out. Repeat for the lining of the bottom of the box.**

9. **Repeat Step 8 for the top and lining of the lid.**

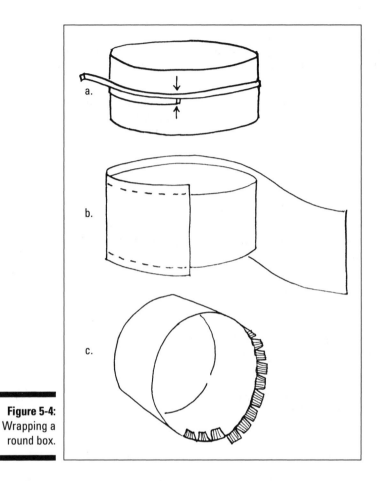

10. **Turn the box on its side and, using a ruler and pencil, draw a straight line from the bottom edge to the top edge of the box.**

11. **Take the length of paper for the outside of the box and peel away an inch of the backing paper to reveal the sticky side of the self-adhesive paper.**

12. **Center the edge of the sticky strip of paper along the pencil line on the box so that an extra inch hangs over at the top and bottom edges (see Figure 5-4b). Use your hand to smooth the paper down on the box.**

If creases occur in the paper, carefully lift the paper, pull it to smooth out the crease, and continue to smooth it around the box. If lifting the paper is difficult, smooth it down with your hand and then slice through the crease with a sharp razor blade. Use the edge of something stiff, such as a credit card, to smooth down the offending area. It's best to avoid this mess if possible, and you can if you do Steps 11 and 12 slowly and deliberately.

13. **Continue to peel away the backing paper and smooth the self-adhesive paper down around the box as you go. The ends overlap where they meet.**

14. **Make V cuts an inch apart in the paper that extends over the top edges of the box so that you can fold the paper to the inside of the box (see Figure 5-4c).**

15. **Repeat Step 14 for the lid.**

16. **To cover the top of the lid, peel away a small section of the backing on the self-adhesive paper. Position the paper on the top of the lid and smooth it down with your hand. Continue to peel away the backing as you smooth the paper down to cover the entire lid.**

17. **To line the box, follow Steps 10 through 16 by measuring the inside of the box and cutting each strip of paper without adding any extra paper to the top and bottom edges of each strip. Attach each piece inside the box and lid by pressing the paper an inch at a time around the inside of the lid, smoothing it down as you do so.**

    The lining pieces fit exactly, with no extra to fold over the edges.

18. **Attach the piece of self-adhesive paper to the bottom of the box as you did for the top of the lid in Step 16.**

Decorating boxes with finishing touches

Decorative trim such as braid, ribbon, rickrack, or a silk cord gives any box a finishing touch. You can attach trim to the edge of the lid, to the edges where the top and bottom meet, or around the bottom edge. See the photo in the color section of this book for inspiration.

1. **Measure around the area that you want to trim.**

   Using a tape measure is easiest, especially if you're trimming a round or oval box.

2. **Cut a length of trim 1 inch longer than the measurement you need.**

3. **Spread a small amount of white craft glue evenly along the back of the trim.**

4. **Position one end of the trim on the box and press it down around the area you want to cover.**

   Cut the excess trim so that the ends meet.

Paper Bag Planter

An ordinary brown lunch bag can easily be recycled and turned into an interesting vase or planter in minutes. The finished project makes a lovely centerpiece when filled with flowers or a flowering plant. The decorated bag-turned-planter is also a quick and easy vase for holding a gift bouquet of flowers. Check out the color section of this book for a photo of a paper bag planter.

Tools and Materials:

Basic craft kit (see the Cheat Sheet at the front of this book)

Newspaper

Paper bag

Iridescent acrylic paint (available in small tubes or bottles at craft stores) in the color of your choice

Paper plate

Paper towel

Drinking glass or wide-mouthed jar half the height of the paper bag

A length of natural vines, raffia, ribbon, or cord approximately 20 inches long

1. **Cover your work surface with newspaper and place the paper bag flat on top of the newspaper.**

2. **Squirt a small amount of paint (about a tablespoon) onto a paper plate.**

3. **Wad up a piece of paper towel and dip it into the paint. Dab the paint on the newspaper to remove the excess paint.**

4. **Dab the wad of toweling over one side of the bag in a random pattern for a sponged effect.**

   Allow some unpainted sections to show through so that you achieve a mottled look.

5. **Open the bag and put one hand inside the bag to create a surface to work against.**

6. **Cover the rest of the bag (the sides that you couldn't get at when the bag was folded flat) with paint by using the same dabbing method.**

7. **Set the bag down on end or over a can or glass to let the paint dry — water-based paint dries in just a few minutes.**

8. **Arrange flowers in a glass or wide-mouthed jar and insert the glass or jar into the bag.**

9. **Turn the top of the bag down two or three times to make a finished, cuffed edge.**

   If you use the bag to hold a plant, consider the size of the pot when you choose the bag; the pot should fit into the bag so that the cuff fits around the rim of the pot.

10. **Gather the bag under the cuff and wrap with a cord, ribbon, or natural vine (which is rustic but pliable) for the finishing touch. Make a bow on the front if you want (refer to the photo in the color section).**

Child's Toy Bin

A galvanized garbage can, spray paint, and a colorful paper border are the only materials you need to create a delightful container for holding toys. (See the photo in the color section.) The toy bin makes cleanup and storage easy, and it looks great in a child's room.

The colors and paper design can match the paint or wallpaper in the room. I used fire engine red for the toy bin pictured in the color section. You can paint the can lid in a contrasting color, if you want. A wide variety of delightful designs is appealing for this type of project. You can find self-adhesive paper, wallpaper rolls, and borders in any home center. Vinyl-coated wallpaper is better than regular wallpaper because it's heavier.

Tools and Materials:

Basic craft kit (see the Cheat Sheet at the front of this book)

Steel garbage can

Newspaper

Medium-grade sandpaper

1 can of colored spray paint

Decorative paper, such as a wallpaper border or self-adhesive paper

Cutting board or protected surface

1. **Cover your work area with newspapers and place the garbage can on top of the paper.**

2. **Make sure that the surface of the can is clean. If the can is rusty, sand the surface with medium-grade sandpaper and then wipe with a clean rag.**

3. **Spray paint the can and the lid, covering the surface evenly.**

   See Chapter 3 for advice on how to spray paint properly.

4. **Allow the paint to dry overnight.**

5. **Using a tape measure, measure the circumference of the garbage can and add 2 inches.**

   This sum is the length of the strip you need to go around the middle and each edge of the can.

6. **To cut strips of paper for the decorative bands, first determine how wide each strip should be.**

   A good size for the center band is approximately 6 inches wide. Use the width of the rim around the lid as your guide for cutting two matching bands to go around the lid and bottom edge.

   You can also use a border design for your decorative band in the center, in which case you don't need to measure the width of the strip. Just apply the border as is.

7. **Use your ruler to measure strips of the decorative paper that are the widths and lengths that you need. Place the paper on a cutting board, measure and mark the strips, and use scissors or a straightedge and a craft knife to cut each band of paper.**

   The back of self-adhesive paper is usually marked off with measured lines as guides for cutting.

8. **Measure the can from top (without the lid) to bottom along the seam line and mark the center of the can.**

9. **Begin with the band of paper that goes around the center of the can. If the paper is self-adhesive (which is the easiest to apply), begin by peeling away 1 inch of the backing paper and fold it under.**

10. **Line up the center of the edge of the paper with the pencil mark on the can and smooth down the inch of self-adhesive paper.**

11. **Continue to pull away the backing paper as you smooth the band around the center.**

    Most garbage cans have ridges around the outside — the cans are rarely smooth. Therefore, as you smooth the self-adhesive paper around the can, be sure to smooth it over the ridges and into the grooves.

12. **When you reach the end of the paper strip, fold back the excess paper and trim with a razor blade or cut along the folded line with scissors.**

13. **Attach the bands of paper around the bottom edge and the rim of the lid in the same way.**

    To prepare wallpaper strips for this project, measure and cut as you would the other decorative paper (see Steps 5 through 7). Place the center band facedown on a work surface covered with newspaper. Spread white glue evenly over the back of the paper, making sure that the edges are well coated. Attach the wallpaper strips as you would the self-adhesive paper, lining up the center of the strip with the center mark on the can and smoothing the paper over the ridges and in the grooves.

More design ideas

You can also try the following ideas for decorating a plain garbage can to go with your child's room theme:

✔ If you find paper with cute designs like dinosaurs or trains, you can cut out each one to apply at random over an entire garbage can, rather than creating borders.

✔ You can use decals, stars, and decorative stickers to make borders or to use as an overall design.

✔ Use a round object, such as a juice glass, as a template for drawing and cutting out colorful circles. Place the glass on colorful self-adhesive or shiny shelf paper and trace around the base of the glass. Cut out the circles and either peel off the backing or coat the backs with glue, whichever is appropriate. Apply the circles over the can and lid. You can make different-sized circles by using smaller and larger round objects as your templates.

✔ Personalize your child's toy bin with his or her name by cutting out letters from solid-colored self-adhesive paper — you can make the letters different colors or all the same. Place each letter evenly spaced on the diagonal across the front of the can.

Kids' Paper Projects

Kids love to make things that they can use — especially if they provide action fun. The following projects don't require any special skills, and you probably have the materials on hand.

Distance glider

Just as its name indicates, this easy-to-make paper airplane is designed for distance gliding. You may find that this glider is the best plane you have ever made.

All you need to make a paper airplane is a piece of 8 ½-x-11-inch plain white paper, transparent tape, and some markers or crayons. All the steps are shown in Figure 5-5.

1. **Begin by drawing a design on your paper. It can be a wavy line from the top to the bottom of your paper. Use a different color to make another wavy line right next to the first wavy line. Leave white space between each line (see Figure 5-5a). Continue drawing lines until the paper is covered with squiggly colored and white stripes.**

2. **Fold the paper in half lengthwise with the design on the inside. Fold down the two corners on one end a little short of the center, as shown in Figure 5-5b.**

3. Take the corner that you created in Step 2 and fold it back to the centerfold, extending the fold to the point (see Figure 5-5c). Turn the plane over and repeat on the other side.

4. Repeat Step 3, folding once more down to the centerfold (see Figure 5-5d).

5. Angle the wings up slightly. Tape together the underside of the plane to prevent it from opening. Use a small piece of tape on top to hold the wings together.

6. Hold the plane under the wings and give the plane a gentle push (see Figure 5-5e). Watch it glide straight and smoothly for a long distance.

The colorful design looks beautiful sailing gracefully through the air. The more you practice, the farther your plane glides.

Mini boomer

A boomerang is a piece of wood that is shaped like an airplane wing. When you throw it into the air, it comes back to you. A mini boomer is smaller and made of cardboard. It doesn't go as far as a boomerang, but it works just as well.

This project can be made from an old cereal box or a similar piece of thin cardboard. You also need a pencil, tracing paper, and scissors.

1. Trace the shape of the mini boomer from Figure 5-6.

2. Place the tracing facedown on a piece of cardboard and retrace the outline over the back of the tracing to transfer the outline to the cardboard.

3. Cut out the cardboard mini boomer. If you use plain cardboard, you can decorate it with crayons or markers.

4. Place the mini boomer on the edge of a book so that one wing hangs over the edge of the book (see Figure 5-7). Tilt the book up just a little and flick the boomer with your fingers. It shoots out into the air and returns. Practice flicking to warm up your flicking fingers.

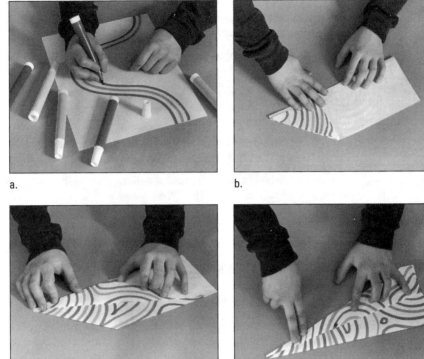

a.

b.

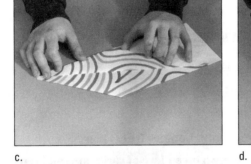

c.

d.

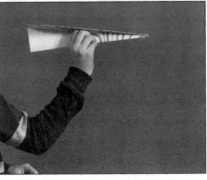

Figure 5-5:
Making a
distance
glider.

e.

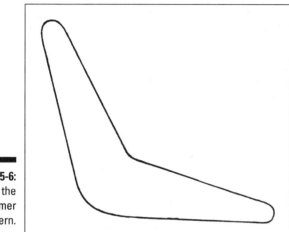

Figure 5-6:
Trace the mini boomer pattern.

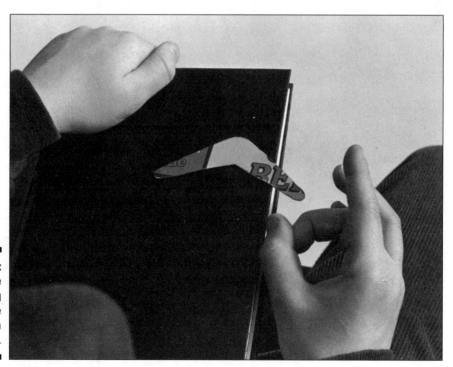

Figure 5-7:
Let one wing hang over the edge of a book.

Chapter 6

Rubber Stamping

• •

• •

*Y*ou may think that you know what a rubber stamp is. You've seen plenty of stamps on packages and envelopes. They usually read "Fragile," "Paid," "Received," "Air Mail," or "Past Due." But things have changed, and a rubber stamp revolution is going on. Rubber stamp designs and all that goes with them are the basis of a new and popular crafting activity.

Many companies have created a vast variety of rubber stamp designs that you can buy in stationery, toy, and hobby or craft stores. I'd be surprised if the number of designs currently available is less than a million. Think of the possibilities! You can decorate a leather belt, canvas shoes, a wooden table, or even your favorite coffee mug.

Rubber-stamping is for you if

✔ You like to do creative projects that involve illustrations, but you aren't in the same league as Rembrandt when it comes to drawing.

✔ You like craft techniques that can be done on a variety of materials, such as paper, fabric, ceramic, wood, and even balloons.

✔ You like crafts that are just as much fun for kids as for adults.

✔ You like to create things that have a use other than sitting on a shelf.

Getting Set to Stamp It Out

The materials for stamping are varied, depending on the project. The basic materials, however, for all projects are a stamp, an ink pad, and material to stamp on.

The rubber stamps that I talk about in this chapter have a little wooden finger grip that holds a thin piece of rubber with a raised design, called a *die,* on it. However, stamps for crafting come in many different forms. Stamps can be as small as your fingernail or as large as your hand. Some stamps have the design mounted to the front of a clear plastic box so that you can see exactly where you are placing the design when you stamp. Another type of stamp is a roller stamp, which is used to print a continuous line of a design.

Where can you find stamps? The obvious starting point is a craft supply store. Specialty paper stores, toy stores, bookstores, gift shops, and stationery stores frequently carry stamping supplies. Seeing the array and variety that you can choose from is lots of fun.

You can see a small sampling of stamp designs available in Figure 6-1.

In order to make an impression with a stamp, you have to ink the rubber design by pressing the stamp on an ink-saturated pad and then onto the surface that you want to decorate. The ink pads for stamp-crafting are made of felt or foam and come in different sizes and shapes. Ink pads are dry (you add the ink) or inked (ready to use). The ink on the pad may be one color, or the pad may hold strips of as many as 12 different ink colors. You can use ink pads for stamping over and over again. When the ink dries out, the pad can be re-inked with the same color.

If you use black ink to imprint your design, you can color in the design with colored pencils, markers, or paint.

Ink pads are available with either permanent or nonpermanent ink. When you stamp on a T-shirt, for example, you should use permanent ink. If you use water-soluble ink, it washes away the first time you wash the shirt. When you buy your supplies, be sure to read the label on the ink bottle so that you get what you want. If you're using permanent, or *solvent-based* ink, you also need solvent to clean the ink off the stamp when you're finished using the stamp or when you change ink colors.

When rubber stamping with children, use nonpermanent ink so that they can wash their hands easily. Baby wipes are great for wiping ink off fingers, stamps, and work surfaces.

Paper is the primary material used for stamping. There is no right or wrong paper — almost any paper has potential for use in a stamp craft project. Art stores have a variety of drawing and sketching pads that are suitable for stamp crafts. If you'd like to design and make your own note cards, for example, use card stock, also available in art supply stores. File folders, shelf paper, paper bags, and kraft paper (see Chapter 4) are also good for stamp projects.

Figure 6-1:
Rubber stamps are available in thousands of designs and many sizes.

Practicing Great Stamping Techniques

The first instinct you may have when faced with a rubber stamp is to immediately press the stamp on the ink pad and start stamping the design on everything in sight, which can be a lot of fun. This press-and-stamp activity just goes to show how easy the craft of stamping can be, as well as the fun that people have doing it. Despite the ease of the technique, however, you need to know some things before you start stamping that can help you create more interesting results than a random pattern on a piece of paper.

The very first thing you need to do before starting to stamp is to test the design to see how it looks and to get the hang of stamping without making a mess of things. If, for example, you press the stamp down too hard on the ink pad, you get a smudgy print instead of a nice, crisp image. Practice stamping so that you get a feeling for how much ink and how much pressure you need to produce the effect that you want.

Follow these steps to practice stamping designs on paper.

1. **Place a piece of paper on a smooth, flat surface.**

2. **Press the rubber stamp onto the ink pad so that the ink covers the raised design.**

   Check the stamp to make sure that all the raised areas are covered evenly with ink.

3. **Press the stamp down firmly with even pressure on the paper surface.**

   Don't rock the stamp back and forth; just press down. You'll get the feel of this technique very quickly.

Be sure to clean the ink off the stamp before applying another color — or before putting the stamp away — by repeatedly stamping the stamp onto scrap paper. Or wipe the ink off the stamp with a paper towel. For water-based ink, remove ink left on the stamp with a damp sponge. Use solvent, which is sold where you buy rubber stamps, for solvent-based inks. If you skip clean-up, the old ink can discolor the next color you use, and the ink colors may get mixed together on the ink pad.

Stamping for Fun and Great Results

You can find endless ways to use rubber stamps and an equally endless number of designs. So you may want to decide what project you want to do before you go to the stamp supply store. Making a letterhead for your own stationery is a good start.

Choose stamps that are versatile so that you can use them for many projects.

You can use rubber stamps to personalize all sorts of things for parties and other celebrations. Here are some ideas:

- ✔ Make your own birthday cards and invitations with a rubber stamp design. See the next section, "Personalizing a greeting card."
- ✔ Decorate the party table with a stamp design on place mats or a solid colored paper tablecloth.
- ✔ Make Christmas cards, greeting cards, and Valentine's Day cards — just some of the projects you can do with stamps. You can even decorate plain envelopes to match.
- ✔ Decorate Christmas wrapping paper and gift tags.
- ✔ Create quick and easy paper Christmas tree ornaments with your stamp designs.

Personalizing a greeting card

Nothing is more personal than a handmade birthday card. A stamp can express humor, shared experiences, a loving sentiment, or a silly thought. You can also use rubber stamps to spell out names in different typefaces and different colors. This greeting card project features stamps, decorative paper, and a border of ribbon.

Tools and Materials:

Basic craft kit (see the Cheat Sheet at the front of this book)

Light-colored decorative wrapping paper

Blank card and envelope

Scrap paper

Rubber stamp with design

Ink pad with desired color of water-based ink

Hole punch

1 yard ⅛-inch satin ribbon that matches a color in the decorative paper or the ink

1. **Using a ruler and pencil, measure and mark a piece of light-colored decorative wrapping paper ½ inch smaller all around than the front of the blank card. Cut out the piece of decorative paper.**

2. **Cover your work surface with scrap paper and place the cut piece of wrapping paper facedown on the scrap paper.**

3. **Using the glue stick, run a line of glue around the edge of the paper. Mark an X from corner to corner with the glue stick.**

4. **Position the paper so that it is centered on the front of the blank card and press it down. Run your finger around the edges of the wrapping paper to secure and smooth the paper down across the front. The ½ inch white band of card paper shows all around the decorative paper.**

   Next, punch evenly spaced holes around the card through which you weave the ribbon. Stamp the final design within the ribbon border.

5. **Use your ruler to find the center of the top edge of the card and mark it with a light pencil line. Make a hole with the hole punch about ¼ inch out on either side of this line and slightly in from the edge of the card. Repeat on the bottom edge of the card.**

6. **Make a hole at each corner of the card. Make evenly spaced holes around each side of the card.**

7. **Beginning with the two holes in the center of the bottom of the card, weave the ends of the ribbon through from the front to the back of each hole. Continue to weave the ribbon ends in and out around the card until you reach the center top two holes.**

8. **Bring the ends of the ribbon through to the front and tie in a bow. Trim the ends as needed.**

9. **Decide where you want the rubber stamp design to appear on the decorative paper.**

   If you're stamping one design only, you can stamp it in the center of the paper. But if you're making a bouquet of flowers, for example, decide beforehand where you want each flower to be and then stamp the same design several times to make the bouquet. You can use one or several ink colors, or a black outline that you can color in with different markers or pencils, as I did (see the photo in the color section).

10. **Test the design. (Refer to the section "Practicing Great Stamping Techniques," earlier in this chapter.)**

11. **Decorate the inside by stamping a message, making a decorative border with stamps, or stamping one design in a corner.**

12. **Decorate the envelope with more stamp designs.**

Now that you know how to be creative with stamp crafts, you can create greeting cards in multiples. They can all be the same, or you can make each card a one-of-a-kind creation.

Making your own stationery

Making your own stationery, envelopes, and matching note cards with your very own stamp design is easy. You can use plain white copy paper and inexpensive envelopes to decorate with borders, monograms, flowers in the corners, and even paw prints around the edges. Choose the designs that you like best or that represent you best, and you're in business. If the designs are black and white, you can use colored pencils or markers to fill in the white space with color.

Tools and Materials:

Basic craft kit (see the Cheat Sheet at the front of this book)

Scrap paper

Rubber stamp and ink pad

Plain paper

Envelopes

Colored pencils or markers (optional)

1. **Cover your work surface with scrap paper and test the rubber stamp design. (Refer to the section "Practicing Great Stamping Techniques," earlier in this chapter.)**

2. **Measure the size of the stamp design to see how wide a border it creates around the stationery and determine whether you want a continuous border with each image touching or a border with space between each image.**

   If you're creating a border of a repeat design, make sure that the design is evenly spaced and centered all the way around the paper. You don't want a wobbly border . . . unless, of course, a wavy look is what you're after.

3. **Measure in from the outside edges of the paper to the exact depth of the border that you want and mark it with a light pencil line. Mark the center of each edge of the paper to determine where you want to place the first stamp.**

4. **Press the rubber stamp on the ink pad and press down on the paper where you made a mark. Repeat on the center line of each edge. Continue to stamp around the paper in between the first imprints.**

5. **Let the ink dry and then erase the pencil lines.**

6. **Create the same border design around the edges of the envelopes if you want.**

7. **Color in the designs with colored pencils or markers if you want.**

Decorating a T-shirt with stamps

Creating your own wardrobe with stamped designs is exciting. Try it! I recommend starting with a T-shirt. But be prepared — your friends may want you to make one for each of them as well.

To practice stamping on fabric without ruining your entire wardrobe, you need to test stamping on some scrap fabric to make sure that the fabric won't bleed. The practice fabric needs to be the same material as the final project because every fabric reacts differently to ink. So if you want to stamp a T-shirt, practice on a T-shirt — not on a cotton pillowcase.

Before you start your project, make sure that you're using permanent ink because you can safely wash it without the design fading or, worse, disappearing. Wash the fabrics before printing. When dry, press the fabric so that the area you're going to stamp is free of wrinkles

Don't stamp on treated fabrics because their reaction to ink is highly unpredictable.

Tools and Materials:

Scrap paper	*Antifusant*
T-shirt	*Parchment paper (used in cooking)*
Polycoated freezer paper (available in supermarkets)	*Iron*
Rubber stamps	*Transparent tape*
Ink pad in desired colors	*Removable fabric marker (available in fabric shops)*

1. **Cover a hard work surface with scrap paper.**

2. **Lay out the T-shirt on the work surface front side up and smooth some freezer paper, shiny side up, inside the T-shirt under the area to be stamped.**

   The freezer paper prevents the ink from seeping through the fabric to the back of the shirt. You can also use cardboard or any other flat, non-porous material in place of the freezer paper.

3. **Test one of the rubber stamps (refer to the section "Practicing Great Stamping Techniques," earlier in this chapter) and then press it down on the shirt wherever you want it.**

   Most designs don't have to be placed in a precise spot — you can just be spontaneous!

4. **Before coloring in the designs, prepare the fabric with antifusant, a chemical that prevents permanent markers from running all over the fabric. First, allow your stamp designs to dry; then apply the antifusant over the entire design that you plan to color and let it dry completely.**

5. **Color in your designs with permanent markers. You need to let the color dry for 24 hours to ensure permanency.**

6. **Set the ink.**

   Permanent stamping inks and markers set into the fabric permanently when heat is applied. Read the ink manufacturer's directions for instructions on heat-sealing ink to fabric. Typically, these directions resemble the following steps:

1. **Place a sheet of parchment paper over the design with plenty of excess paper on all sides. (The freezer paper should still be in position under the design.)**

2. **Set your iron to the appropriate setting for the fabric. (If you aren't sure what iron setting to use, use the cotton setting.) When the iron is hot, iron on the parchment paper and over the design according to the ink manufacturer's directions. Remove the freezer paper and the parchment.**

3. **Rinse the T-shirt to remove the fabric marker and antifusant, according to the directions on the bottle.**

If you want to plan where the imprints will go — instead of being spontaneous — print each of your stamps on scrap paper and cut them out close to the edges, marking them A, B, C, and so on. Tape each cutout in position on the T-shirt and, with removable fabric marker, make a mark on either side of each cutout for positioning. Then remove the cutouts from the T-shirt and mark the places of each A, B, and C to match the prints. Now you can print your stamps on the shirt knowing where to place each one.

Chapter 7
Photo Crafts

. . . .

In This Chapter

▶ Preparing your photographs for display

▶ Framing your photographs in creative ways

▶ Using your photographs in craft projects

. . . .

Most of us take tons of pictures to mark special events, such as a baby's first birthday or a family get-together. We take pictures on our vacations, and we take pictures just for the fun of it. We don't like to throw photographs away, even after weeding out the best ones. Sometimes part of a photograph is good, while another isn't worth saving. This chapter shows you how to preserve the best part of a photograph and crop away the parts that don't appeal to you.

Using photographs in craft projects is a wonderful way to enjoy them yourself or to make a personalized, handmade gift. Before you begin the projects in this chapter, sort through the photographs you have thrown in a drawer or shoebox and take out the photographs you like best. And don't be discouraged if Uncle Harry is ruining the best photograph of you and your spouse. You find out later in this chapter how to do away with Uncle Harry . . . legally.

Getting Those Photos Out of the Box

If a photograph isn't just right, you can crop it to look better before framing it or mounting it into a scrapbook or photo album. Preserving photographs is easier today than ever before because the materials to do so are readily available. The following sections tell you exactly how to do it.

Cropping photos

Cropping snapshots to any size needed for a découpage project, memory book, or a collage is easy. Study your photograph to decide whether you want to use the entire picture or whether it would be more dramatic to use just part of the scene.

To use part of the photo in a craft project, follow these steps:

1. **Place a piece of tracing paper over the photograph and draw a rectangle over the area you want to use, pressing down with your pen or pencil so that you make an impression on the photograph.**

2. **Remove the tracing and, using scissors or a straightedge and craft knife or single-edge razor blade, cut along the lines around the photograph.**

   If straightness and square corners are important to you, be sure to use a T-square (see Chapter 3) or straightedge and craft knife or razor blade.

   If the area of the photograph you want to save can't be cut within a square or rectangle, use a pair of scissors and cut around the shape or image that you want to keep.

If you get the 4-x-6-inch photographs when you have your film developed, you can trim them down to fit 3½-x-5-inch frames. Cut off the excess area to help center the subject or just get rid of cluttered background. The same trick works with 5-x-7 photos to fit 4-x-6-inch frames.

Mounting photos

Mounting photographs takes a little planning because you must first determine the best method for mounting, depending on the project and the material you're using for the background. For example:

- A glue stick is effective for mounting photographs to paper or posterboard for general uses, such as scrapbooks, greeting cards, and photo albums.

- White craft glue is a good adhesive for mounting photographs to be used in a découpage project, on a wooden plaque, or on any nonporous material.

- Double-faced tape works well when mounting photographs in a scrapbook. An acid-free type of tape is available in photographic supply shops. Use it to mount photographs that you want to preserve for a long time.

- Photo corner stickers lend an old-fashioned charm to an album or scrapbook. These corners come in packages and are available in various colors, black, white, and clear.

Matting photos

Precut photo mats are designed to fit over standard-size photo prints. Standard prints are 3½ x 5 inches, 4 x 6 inches, 5 x 7 inches, and 8 x 10 inches. Larger sizes are also available. The cutout areas in the mats are slightly smaller than the prints. When you place the mat over the photograph, the mat covers the edges of the picture.

The outside measurements of the mats are designed to fit standard frames. Outside measurements of standard mats are 5 x 7 inches, 8 x 10 inches, 11 x 14 inches, and 16 x 20 inches.

Mounting a photo in a mat is a very easy process if you follow these simple directions:

1. **Place the photo facedown on a clean, smooth surface, such as a countertop or desktop.**

2. **Run a strip of 1-inch-wide clear tape across the entire top edge of the photo with half the width of the tape on the photo and the other half extending off the photo.**

3. **Turn the photo over (faceup), hold the mat over the photograph, and carefully lower the mat into position over the photograph until it makes contact.**

4. **Press down on the front of the mat where the tape is located underneath.**

5. **Turn the matted photograph over (facedown) and press the tape down firmly.**

    Fasten the tape at the top of the photograph only, not all the way around, in order to keep the photo from buckling later on due to dryness or humidity.

    The picture is now ready to be framed.

Preserving photos

No form of paper lasts indefinitely — photographic paper included. The acid in the wood that photographic paper is made from eventually discolors and erodes the paper. Preservationists have developed many ways to fight this problem in order to preserve valuable documents. Craft companies have taken advantage of the research done by museums and now produce acid-free papers, acid-free storage boxes, acid-free scrapbooks, and even pens for testing the acidity in a piece of paper.

Many photographic products bear the word *archival*. The implication is that the product will last for a very long time. But archival is a general term that can be interpreted loosely. Read the small print. Look for the term "acid free," which, by definition, means an item that has a pH of more than 7.0. (If you want to impress someone, pH stands for potential of hydrogen and is the measure of acidity or alkalinity of a solution. A pH of 7 is neutral. Anything higher than 7 is free of acid.)

If you have a photograph that is fading in an old album, consider taking it to a photographic firm that can scan your picture into a computer for permanent storage and printing.

Making Your Own Creative Frames

The subject of a photograph can often suggest the kind of frame that would enhance it the most. A great way to achieve the photo-frame connection is to collect items on your trips that you can use later to make frames for your vacation pictures. For example, on a camping trip, collect twigs from the woods to use later to frame your camping pictures. Or if you take a picture of someone holding a bouquet of buttercups, press the flowers and use them in a decorative frame for the photo. A visit to the seashore yields a variety of shells that you can use to decorate a frame with a picture of the beach.

Framing a baby picture

Fabric stores carry all sorts of interesting notions, such as unusual ribbons, buttons, snaps, sequins, beads, rickrack, and lace for trimming inexpensive frames. A baby photograph suggests a delicate frame for which you could use tiny pearl-like blue and pink beads. These beads are perfect for a baby picture frame — they reflect the daintiness of the picture.

Tools and Materials:

Basic craft kit (see the Cheat Sheet at the front of this book)

The photo you want to use

Pastel color mat in the correct size for the photograph

Pastel color posterboard (available in art supply stores)

Cutting board or protected surface

Clean cloth or dry sponge

Box of pastel beads

Tweezers (optional)

Self-adhesive picture hanging tab (available in photo shops)

1. **Attach the photograph to the mat (see "Matting photos," earlier in this chapter).**

2. **Place the matted photograph on one corner of the posterboard and, with a pencil, draw around the photo mat to make a rectangle on the posterboard.**

3. **Place the posterboard on a cutting surface and, with a straightedge and craft knife, cut along the drawn lines (see Chapter 3 for tips on how to safely use a straightedge and craft knife).**

4. **Apply a thin line of white glue around the edges of the posterboard.**

5. Place the matted photograph on top of the posterboard and press the two pieces together. Remove excess glue from the edges with a clean cloth or dry sponge.

6. On the front of the matted photograph, run a line of glue along one edge.

7. Place the first bead in the top corner on the glue. You may find it helpful to use tweezers to lift and position each bead; otherwise, you can use your fingers.

8. Continue to set the beads one after the other along the line of glue. If the white glue gets on the front of the beads, don't worry — it dries clear.

9. Repeat Steps 6 though 8 to make three rows of beads along each edge of the matted photograph.

10. Let your project dry overnight.

11. After the matted photograph is dry, attach the picture hanging tab to the center of the back approximately 1 inch from the top edge. Your baby picture is now ready to hang.

Making a twig frame

A clever frame can turn an ordinary snapshot into an eye-catching decorative accessory on your wall. For example, make a frame of twigs, pinecones, dried grasses, or other natural materials for a picture of your kids at camp or of a family picnic. The color section of this book shows a photo of this twig frame.

Tools and Materials:

Basic craft kit (see the Cheat Sheet at the front of this book)

The photo you want to use

A piece of scrap wood (pine or bristol board, available in art stores) 1 to 2 inches larger than the photograph all around

Clean, dry cloth

Glue gun and a package of glue sticks

A bunch (about a lunch bag full) of thin, small, brittle twigs

1 self-adhesive hanging tab for a bristol board backing; picture wire and 2 small screw eyes (available in hardware stores) for a wood backing

1. Apply the glue stick along the back edges of the photograph and make a large X with the glue stick from corner to corner.

2. Center the photograph on the piece of wood or bristol board and press down to mount. Use a dry cloth to smooth over the front of the photograph.

3. **Apply hot glue (see Chapter 2 for more information about glue guns) on the bristol board or wood piece that borders the photograph and then start putting twigs into the glue. Hot glue holds more firmly than craft glue and dries almost instantly, so you need to work in small areas at a time and add the twigs quickly. Continue gluing until you cover the entire border of the photograph. You may need to break up the twigs into smaller pieces to make them fit.**

   The glue dries clear, so don't worry about using too much glue — keep adding enough glue to secure the twigs. Some of the twigs may overlap onto the edges of the photograph, which creates a rustic look appropriate for the subject.

   You can use craft glue in place of hot glue for this project. But craft glue doesn't hold as well and dries more slowly than hot glue. If you're using craft glue, let the finished project dry for two days before doing Step 5.

4. **Let the frame dry overnight.**

5. **Attach a picture-hanging tab to the back of the photograph frame. If the photograph is mounted on wood, measure a third of the way down the back of the board and insert a screw eye on each side. Cut a piece of picture wire an inch longer than the width of the board. Insert the wire ends through the screw eyes and wind it back around itself to make it secure for hanging.**

A selection of memory box ideas

When you're gathering items for a memory box, use the following list for inspiration:

- Photographs
- Ticket stubs
- A performance program
- An article from a newspaper
- A birth or wedding announcement
- A special birthday, anniversary, or graduation card
- A special valentine
- A poem
- A child's drawing
- Sayings or words that have meaning to you (cut from a magazine)
- Miniature furniture
- School letters
- Your initials in three dimension, such as on baby blocks
- Old lace
- A piece of a quilt or wedding dress
- Sections of a map
- Cutouts from magazines or wrapping paper
- A pressed flower

Creating a Photo Memory Box

Partitioned boxes are sold in craft and hobby stores for the express purpose of displaying a collection of memorabilia. They used to be called shadow boxes but have come to be called memory boxes more recently. An empty memory box is shown in Figure 7-1. For an example of a finished memory box, turn to the color section of this book.

Figure 7-1: Example of a memory box.

Tools and Materials:

Basic craft kit (see the Cheat Sheet at the front of this book)

An assortment of photographs and scraps of things you've saved over the years

Glue gun and glue sticks

A display box

1. **Assemble the items you need to create your memory box.**

2. **Decide which paper items, photographs, and other flat objects you want to glue to the back wall of each section. Putting these in place first gives you the background you need to place the other objects.**

3. **Trim photographs to fit where you want to place them (see "Cropping photos," earlier in this chapter). Trim away parts of ticket stubs and**

invitations if needed; cut out favorite lines of a poem if the entire poem is too large to fit any of the spaces. Adjust each item in the display box as needed, remembering that not everything has to fit perfectly or line up exactly in soldierlike formation. This project is fun if you realize that there aren't any rules or right or wrong way to create a memory box. You can overlap paper items, gluing them this way and that. The more spontaneous you are with your selection and placement of memorabilia, the better your finished project looks.

4. You can permanently set three-dimensional items, such as a piece of ribbon, a marble, a porcelain animal, a campaign button, or a tiny teddy bear, into a section of the box with hot glue. Decide where you want to place the item. Wait until the tip of the glue gun is hot and then insert a glue stick and apply a dot of glue to the area. Don't wait. Position the item on the glue, and that's it. The glue dries quickly and holds firmly.

5. When you have the main elements affixed, stand back and look at your creation. Does it need anything more? Do you want to add any decoration to the top, sides, or front of the box? If so, don't hesitate. Just do it. Remember, spontaneity counts.

6. Display your memory box on a shelf, table, or bookcase. Or hang the memory box on a wall. For hanging information, see Step 5 in "Making a twig frame."

Making a memory box inspires you to remember things you thought you'd forgotten forever. This sort of crafting leads to more and more projects. Creating memory boxes is addictive — so beware.

Ideas for a memory box theme

Choose a theme for your memory box and try to carry it out in every way. Create a mood by the selection of colors as well as by the items and their placement. For example, if your memory box is about your trip to Florida, use sunny colors such as orange and yellow. The objects you combine with the photographs from your trip may be a coaster from the Shipwreck Bar and a postcard saying, "Welcome to Sunny Florida." Stick in an orange bubble gumball or glue in some sand and some shells that you collected on the beach.

If the memory box represents a remembrance of your school years, for example, make one corner bright and colorful by using simple objects from elementary school. The high school section might be made up of things in your high school colors. Use a section of your report card (the one with the "A" on it, of course), a picture of you at the senior prom, and the pressed corsage or boutonniere you wore.

If you are making a personal memory box, make it autobiographical. For example, cut out words from a magazine that best represent you. Add pictures of yourself that you particularly like or that were taken at the most memorable times in your life. Your memory box can be realistic or fanciful. If you always wanted to be a famous athlete or model, put your picture on someone else's body.

Chapter 8

Scrapbook Crafting

- -

In This Chapter

▶ Discovering scrapbook crafting

▶ Finding and using scrapbooking materials

▶ Preserving memories in scrapbooks

- -

Scrapbooks and photo albums are often referred to as *memory books* and *keepsake books* when purchased in craft stores. They all look alike and have one thing in common: They respond to our desire to preserve our treasured memories for ourselves and for future generations.

Scrapbook crafting takes the basic concept of a photo album and adds other elements and decorations to make it more interesting and more meaningful. Including a lock of hair from your baby's first haircut turns a simple baby album into a scrapbook. A wedding scrapbook may include wedding pictures along with a pressed flower from the bridal bouquet and a napkin from the wedding reception with the couple's names on it. Instantly, the traditional wedding album becomes a wedding scrapbook.

A scrapbook can be a simple record of events, or it can be an exciting and creative production that records memories and houses keepsakes in a more interesting way.

Keeping a scrapbook has always been popular, but never quite so formalized as today, with products available for decorating the pages of an album. Making scrapbooks with keepsake memories is a whole lot of fun! This chapter tells you about the different kinds of decorations available for scrapbook crafts and gives you ideas for creating your scrapbook. You find out where to get appropriate decorations and how to make your own decorations. You also discover how to design your own scrapbook. In this way you can create a project that brings back memories of your special times with more emotional appeal than you might get from a photo album.

Don't limit yourself to a conventional album. You can also preserve memories in a memory box (see Chapter 7), on a poster, in a picture storybook, or in a frame.

The Elements of a Scrapbook

Most scrapbooks have plain paper pages, usually black or white, while photo album pages have protective plastic coverings. Protective covers for scrapbook pages are often sold separately.

The following sections help you to put together a very personal scrapbook with a few ideas you may not have considered and some good ideas for using scrap material in creative ways.

Photographs

Photographs are the main ingredient for most scrapbooks. If you have photographs packed away in shoeboxes, stuffed into old albums, or sitting in the envelopes that came back from the photo lab, now is the time to organize them!

The process of looking through all those pictures evokes memories of the experiences that inspire you to take the pictures in the first place. Scrapbook crafting involves editing out the pictures you don't like and selecting the images that really speak to you. When you choose the pictures that you like the best, try to imagine which ones look best together. Perhaps you want to make a scrapbook of Thanksgiving get-togethers from one year to the next. Or your scrapbook crafting may chronicle your little brother at every age from 1 to 21.

When you're weeding out photographs, keep in mind that your goal is to choose the best ones and to find a common thread between them. At first, put those photographs that relate to each other (the same family members, perhaps, or taken during the same year) together in piles. Use a photo labeling pencil (look for one in craft, stationery, and photo supply stores) to identify your photographs. Put the discarded photos in a separate pile and review them again after you select the best ones. Give the old ones a second chance, just to be sure, before eliminating them altogether.

Writing on photographs with markers or ballpoint pens is not good for the photographs. If you write on the back of a photograph with a ballpoint pen, your great-grandchildren will be able to read the impressions of the pen a hundred years from now.

Albums

Craft stores that carry scrapbook supplies carry albums designed to help preserve your photographs. Look for the label "acid-free paper," which indicates archival-quality paper.

Albums come in different sizes. The larger-sized albums are the most popular for general scrapbook projects, while smaller albums are better for story-books and short subjects, such as "Graduation Day."

Albums also come in different styles of bindings:

✔ Bound albums are just like a book but they have blank pages. Use a bound album for collections that won't "bulk up" and put a strain on the binding.

✔ Expandable albums enable you to remove pages to work on them. You can easily add more pages to an expandable album when needed.

✔ Three-ring binder albums are the most versatile. These albums are usually standard size; therefore, when you need more pages, they are easy to find in most stationery stores. The pages are easy to add and remove.

✔ Some albums are designed for a specific purpose, such as a baby album, wedding album, or family history album, with theme-related decorations on the pages.

Many products are available in the way of photo and scrapbook albums, so if you have some idea of what you will be including, such as matchbook covers, pressed flowers, or a pressed corsage, you can choose the best album for your project.

Other supplies

Craft stores offer a variety of elements for decorating the pages of a scrap-book, and all the tools and materials listed for the projects in this chapter are available at craft stores that carry scrapbooking supplies. However, you probably have the basic materials needed for making a scrapbook right in your home. Mounting adhesives, such as craft glue, tape, and glue sticks, as well as photo corners, are available in acid-free versions for scrapbook crafting.

You need a pair of all-purpose cutting scissors and a craft knife. Craft stores also carry scissors with decorative edges for fancy cutting. Years ago, you could buy only pinking shears (see Chapter 2), but now you can easily find scissors that produce a scallop edge, *deckle edge* (a rough, untrimmed edge), or one of many other designs.

Photo stickers, rubber stamps (see Chapter 6), and hole punches are naturals for dressing up scrapbook pages. You can use decorative punches — ones that make small shapes such as hearts, teddy bears, stars, dinosaurs, snowflakes, and more — to decorate a page. Or you can use the type of hole punch used in an office.

Consider using any or all of these additional decorative items for your scrapbook:

- ✔ **Printed paper:** Add mood and texture to your designs with commercially-available printed papers.

- ✔ **Decorative paper that you create:** Use stenciling (see Chapter 11) and faux finishing techniques (see Chapter 12) to create your own paper.

- ✔ **Peel-and-stick ribbons:** You can find peel-and-stick ribbons in many styles and designs.

- ✔ **Embossing stencils:** These brass plates are available in a variety of designs. When you press these stencils onto the pages of a scrapbook, they make raised designs.

- ✔ **Rubber stamps:** Create designs on scrapbook pages and make borders around the pages or photographs with a variety of rubber stamps.

Scrapbook Projects

A scrapbook can be as simple or complex as you want to make it. But either way, the first thing you need to do is decide on a theme for your crafting project. This section gives you several ideas for themes for your scrapbook.

Next, you need to organize your project beforehand by gathering the materials you need. Check out the projects in this chapter to get ideas for the types of tools and materials you need for your scrapbook.

When you've gathered the materials, lay them out on your work surface so that you can plan how many pages you will use for the project. Organize the photographs by family members, events, ages, places you visited, or other categories that have meaning to you.

Examine all the elements you've collected and determine whether they all fit the theme. If the theme is *baby's first year,* for example, you probably don't want a picture of Uncle Harry on the sofa snoring. But you may want a picture of Aunt Elizabeth on the sofa knitting if, on the next page, you have a picture of baby Andrew coming home from the hospital wrapped in the very afghan that Aunt Elizabeth was knitting.

Choose a color scheme for your project. You can create a mood, such as *soft and delicate,* or *bright and cheerful,* or *romantic.* Be selective when making or choosing the enhancements that complement your theme. Don't throw everything but the kitchen sink into the project.

Going on a trip?

The following ideas may be just the ticket for your next craft project:

✔ On a trip to France, I took pictures of quaint window boxes in every little town we visited. They made a great theme for my scrapbook. I designed the pages with rubber stamp flowers and stenciled the names of each village next to the flower box. A few travel decals completed the picture.

✔ A friend came home from a trip with recipes from every restaurant she visited. She also photographed the meals in each restaurant. She combined the photos and recipes against a border of food stickers and a few restaurant business cards to make a memorable scrapbook project.

✔ Friends who traveled to England took scads of photographs of all the methods of transportation they encountered. They photographed each other or had someone photograph them getting off the airplane, in a London taxi, on a double-decker bus, on bicycles, on the train, and in the country on horses. They decorated the resulting scrapbook project with all kinds of funny sayings found on rubber stamps and stencils.

Family vacation

Try to do your family vacation scrapbook project as soon as you get your pictures back from the photo lab. That way, the experience is still fresh, and you can edit the photographs with a clear idea for selecting the images you really want to keep. The materials for this project are available at craft stores that sell scrapbook supplies.

Tools and Materials:

Basic craft kit (see the Cheat Sheet at the front of this book)

Scrapbook

Sand-colored craft paint

Sea sponge

Photographs of your family vacation at the seashore

Black or white photo corners

Pack of cutout travel stickers

Pack of cutout seashore stickers

Fine-point pen

Clean cloth for removing glue from nonadhesive decorative cutouts

1. **Using the sand-colored craft paint and the sea sponge, create an all-over background of sponged texture that has the look of sand (see Chapter 12 for how to sponge paint).**

2. **Position your photographs so that they follow the vacation chronologically.**

3. **Mount your photographs on the scrapbook paper with photo corners.**

4. **Position the cutout travel stickers between the photographs to add color and atmosphere.**

5. **Mount the seashore stickers here and there.**

6. **Write thoughts and comments about the trip to complete the design.**

Baby's first years

Parents take many photographs of their baby the first two years. Use those pictures that can't fit into the photo album in your scrapbook projects. Find a poem or a song that especially appeals to you. Perhaps it is the song that you sing to the baby before sleeping or a poem that reflects the baby's personality. Use the words of the song or poem as a running design across the pages of the scrapbook.

The best memories come in little packages

Nothing inspires the creation of a scrapbook quite like a new arrival. Have fun with colors, words, and decorations that provide hours of fun now while creating the book and later when you relive every moment, looking back.

Check out these ideas for a baby book:

✔ Preserve each of your baby's birthdays with a scrapbook project. Baby's first birthday is always a great photo opportunity. In addition to party pictures such as "baby trying to blow out a candle on a cupcake" and "baby eating with a party hat on," take pictures of baby's favorite toys, crib, or other items that remind you of the first year. Use pastel-colored baby wrapping paper for the presents and then use the same paper for the background of the scrapbook pages for the photos. Add stenciled sayings that have the word "one" in them, such as, "You're the one for me," "Numero Uno," and "One in a million."

✔ Use geometric building blocks as a scrapbook theme for a toddler. Trace around blocks to create squares, rectangles, circles, and triangles that you can cut out to use as templates. Gather your baby pictures and, using the templates, cut out the photographs in the shapes of the blocks. Cut more block shapes out of brightly colored paper. Combine the photographs and the colored paper shapes on the pages in a design that resembles a real building-block construction. Add a heading with stick-on letters, such as "Building for the Future" or "Building Memories."

Tools and Materials:

Basic craft kit (see the Cheat Sheet at the front of this book)

Scrapbook

Alphabet stencil (precut stencil in small size)

Craft paint in your choice of color

Stencil brush (small size)

Rubber stamps and inkpad (optional)

Stickers (optional)

1. **Use a small stencil alphabet and lay out the words on scrap paper first so that you know how many words fit on the page and where you want to stencil them.**

2. **Using a craft paint color of your choice and a stencil brush, stencil the words on the pages, following your scrap paper layout. (For pointers on stenciling, see Chapter 11.)**

3. **Arrange and mount the photographs of your baby among the stenciled words.**

4. **Add finishing touches with rubber stamps or stickers that fit your theme.**

'Tis the season

The first snowfall of the year is a good time to take pictures of family fun. Sledding, throwing snowballs, building snowmen, skiing, rolling in the snow, and playing with a pet in the snow are just some of the activities that I think of when snow falls. The first snow heralds the holiday season and is a good reason to do a scrapbook project.

Tools and Materials:

Basic craft kit (see the Cheat Sheet at the front of this book)

Scrapbook

Lightweight cardboard or heavy paper

Snowflake punches (large and small)

Blue craft paper

Photographs

1. **Enlarge one of the diamond shapes shown in Figure 8-1, trace it, and use the tracing to create a diamond template from the lightweight cardboard or heavy paper.**

2. **Place the diamond template on the photographs to be included in the project and draw around it. Cut out the diamond shape from each photograph.**

3. **Put eight diamonds together to form a star in the center of one page, as shown in Figure 8-1, and scatter the other diamond-shaped photos across the next page. When you like the arrangement, mount them to the page with a glue stick.**

4. **Punch snowflakes out of blue paper with different-sized snowflake punches and mount them with a glue stick all around the photographs for a festive winter theme.**

Figure 8-1:
Diamond
snowflake
template.

Stick-to-it-iveness

Children like to use stickers to decorate almost anything, including their foreheads, so using stickers for their own scrapbooks is a natural. Small children need a little guidance for a scrapbook project; older children can plan their own pages and may have them finished before you can advise them. Rubber stamp companies have a variety of licensed designs that appeal to children.

Tools and Materials:

Basic craft kit (see the Cheat Sheet at the front of this book)

Scrapbook

Photographs

Photo corners

Stickers

1. **Start with photographs of your child, cousins, friends, or family — anything that the child can relate to. Position the photos and mount them with photo corners. Older children may be able to do this step for themselves; young children may need assistance from an adult.**

2. **Calculate where to place the stickers so that they fit on the pages and mark those spots with tiny X's. Now the child can aim for the little X's when applying the stickers, thus ensuring an attractive design rather than a hodge-podge of stickers on top of each other.**

Let the seasons be your guide

Every season suggests a theme. Here are some ideas you might like to try:

- Flowers always bring back good memories. Preserve your flowers — and your memories — by pressing them into a scrapbook (see Chapter 20 for tips on pressing flowers). Try pressing flowers from your garden. Ferns press nicely, too. You can also do a project made with flowers that you pick while on a walk in a field. Preserving a corsage and other items from a school dance is another way to use pressed flowers. Another idea is to press flowers and herbs for a perfect background for photographs of women whose names are the same as a flower or herb, such as Rose, Lily, Iris, Rosemary, Violet, Fern, and Daisy.

- Halloween is the time to use a color scheme that only a football team could love: orange and black. A spooky design is good for a Halloween scrapbook project. The scrapbook section of your craft store can provide a casketful of items to use. You can find punches of a moon, a witch, a black cat, and a jack-o'-lantern. You can also find rubber stamps of spiders, bats, skeletons, and ghosts. The star of the show is sure to be those photographs of scary trick-or-treaters.

Chapter 9

Découpage

In This Chapter
▶ Describing découpage
▶ Using basic tools
▶ Crafting techniques 101
▶ Getting started with a few projects
▶ Crafting that any kid can do

*A*lthough its name may sound fancy, the craft of découpage is one of the easiest crafts to do. However, for such a user-friendly craft, the results can be amazingly impressive. In this chapter you discover where the craft of découpage originated and why it is so popular today. You find out about the basic materials you need, where to find them, and the techniques you can use to decorate boxes, furniture, plaques, and trays. You can even use découpage to recycle things that would normally end up in the garbage can. Never again will you throw away a plastic food container without first considering its potential as a beautiful découpage project. Découpage is so easy to do that even a child can master the technique.

Delving into Découpage

Découpage is a French word meaning *applied cutouts*. It involves cutting paper illustrations or designs from greeting cards, wrapping paper, calendars, wallpaper, or books and then gluing the designs to a painted object, such as a picture frame, box, tray, dresser, or wooden plaque. You can also do découpage on metal, plastic, ceramic, shells, and other materials. The designs may be whimsical, pretty, ornate, or geometric.

After you cut out a design, you glue it to the surface of the object you are working on. You then apply several coats of varnish right over the design so that you cover the entire object with varnish, protecting the design. You sand each coat of varnish smooth before applying the next coat. Years ago, crafting a découpage project could take several weeks, if not months, because the glue, paints, and lacquers took several days to dry. Because we now use improved glue, water-based paint, and varnish for crafting, you can complete a découpage project quickly and easily.

A variation of découpage is crafting on glass, which is called *reverse découpage,* because you apply glue to the front (not the back) of the cutout designs and then stick these designs under, or to the back of, the glass item. You apply the paint and varnish over the back of the cutout under the glass.

Using the Materials of Découpage

Many of the materials used for découpage are those used for other crafting techniques that involve painting. Refer to Chapter 10 for basic painting techniques and to Chapter 12 for decorative painting that you can use to create interesting painted backgrounds for your découpage projects. Here's the run-down on the materials you need for découpage:

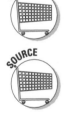

✔ **Acrylic paint:** When working with a raw wooden object, such as a plaque or a box, you have to paint or stain it. The best paint to use is acrylic paint, a water-based paint that dries quickly, covers well in one or two coats, and comes in just about any color you can dream up.

Acrylic paint is available in several different-size containers and can be found in art and craft stores. Check out these well-known brands for acrylic paints: Grumbacher and Liquitex.

✔ **Wood stain:** Minwax, as well as several other companies, makes wood stain that is easy to use and that comes in different wood colors. You can find a wide variety of stain colors in the paint department of home centers.

A little history

Découpage originated in the 17th century. Skilled furniture makers used hand-colored prints to decorate their work with elaborate designs in order to simulate the effect of hand-painted pieces. Although it originated in France, the art of découpage was imported all over the world. By the 18th century, découpage had become a popular pastime among genteel ladies who appreciated fine things and had time on their hands. The ladies were inspired by the lacquered furniture imported from China and Japan. In the 19th century, Victorian ladies made very ornate room divider screens with brightly colored, gummed-paper designs similar to decals. These screens were called *scrap albums* because the designs were created from personal memorabilia.

✔ **Latex paint:** Indoor house paint, such as latex, is also fine for découpage. Flat water-based paint covers easily and dries in minutes. If you have some latex paint left over from painting your walls, use it for your découpage project.

✔ **Brushes:** You can use a natural bristle brush or a foam brush for painting. Foam brushes are quite inexpensive (usually under a dollar), and you can clean them with hot water. A foam brush holds up for three or four coats of paint before you have to throw it away. A good natural bristle varnish brush, on the other hand, lasts a long time and is preferable for varnishing. A natural bristle brush lasts through many projects if you clean it well with hot water between uses. Each brush needs to be the appropriate size for the project in order to get the best results. For example, a foam brush needs to be at least 1 inch wide for painting a small box, and a natural bristle brush needs to be approximately ½ inch wide for varnishing.

✔ **Sandpaper:** Sanding is an essential part of the découpage process. You need to prepare almost all surfaces for découpage by sanding first, and you must also sand lightly between the coats of varnish that you apply over your paper cutouts.

The best sandpaper for decoupage is 3M Wetordry black flint paper, which you can find in hardware stores. Buy two or three sheets of #400 or #600; or, if you are crafting on an old piece of furniture with a finish already on it, you need a medium #80-100 grade sandpaper, as well. This sandpaper removes any wax that may be covering the piece. It isn't necessary to completely remove the old finish before painting — a thorough sanding job does the trick. If your piece is metal, it doesn't hurt to give it a quick once-over with fine, #400 sandpaper so that the paint adheres better.

✔ **Varnish:** A water-based, fast-drying, non-yellowing varnish is the best varnish for découpage today. Varnish comes in different finishes: satin, semigloss, and glossy — the finish is a matter of preference. (I always use a satin finish because it is neither flat nor shiny.) Varnish comes in cans from as small as a pint to as large as a gallon. For most découpage projects, a pint is plenty. Typically, a découpage project can require from 5 to 20 coats of varnish, depending on the thickness of the paper cutouts. The object is to create a build-up of thin coats of varnish until the découpage cutouts are smooth to the touch.

✔ **Designs:** The easiest sources of designs for use in découpage are greeting cards and wrapping paper. Postcards, posters, photographs, and invitations are other sources, as well as books, stickers, and calendars.

You can use some magazines for découpage, but I don't encourage using magazines for several reasons: The paper is thin and often wrinkles when it is glued to a surface, sometimes the printing ink smears when you apply varnish over the printed design, and often the printing from the back shows through when you apply the varnish over the front of the paper. If you use a magazine cutout, test the varnish on the page before applying the cutout to the object you're working on.

✔ **Scissors:** Cuticle scissors are the best for découpage-cutting. The curved, pointed shape is excellent for cutting in and out of all fine nooks and corners, such as in leaves and flower petals. Embroidery scissors are good to use when you have a large print or poster to cut apart.

✔ **Glue:** After you have cut out your designs, you need to apply them to the object with glue. Use a white craft glue, such as Elmer's Glue-All or Sobo. No other glue is as good for découpage.

✔ **Sponge:** A clean, slightly damp kitchen sponge is invaluable for pressing a cutout down firmly onto an object. You also need a damp sponge to wipe away excess glue that often seeps out from under a cutout when it's adhered.

✔ **Wax:** When the last coat of varnish is completely dry, you need to apply a coat of clear furniture paste wax to protect the finish — no matter what surface is under the varnish. Brands of furniture paste wax include Butcher's, Johnson's, and Goddard. Furniture paste wax is available in supermarkets and hardware stores.

✔ **Soft rag:** An old T-shirt cut into pieces is the perfect material for buffing the wax on your finished découpage project. However, any piece of cotton or terry cloth fabric does the job. Paper toweling is a fine substitute for a clean rag.

Getting to the Technical Know-How

Wood is the best and most traditional surface for découpage. Some of the projects that you can découpage are wall plaques, boxes of every conceivable size and shape, furniture, candlesticks, napkin rings, planters, tissue holders, picture frames, light-switch plates, salt and pepper shakers, and even a door. Most boxes, plaques, and similar containers are available in craft and hobby shops. Sometimes an unusual item can be found in an antique store or junk shop. Often you can salvage — even make beautiful — an item that is marred or chipped and isn't too appealing.

Smooth sanding

Most wooden items found in craft shops are made of white pine or birch wood. These items are fairly smooth, requiring little or no sanding. An old piece of furniture needs to be sanded before giving it a coat of paint.

Sand _with_ the grain of the wood, not across it.

To achieve a beautifully smooth finish (which is the goal of this craft), you need to sand the object several times. When sanding between coats of paint, use #400 sandpaper dry. After applying the cutouts and the varnish, lightly sand each coat of varnish with #600 sandpaper wet, a technique called _wet-sanding_. You need to sand lightly so that you don't remove the color of the cutouts. For an extra smooth finish, dip the sandpaper into a cup of warm, soapy water before you sand the last coat of varnish. Use a soft rag to wipe away all excess dirt and sand grit after any sanding with wet sandpaper.

Painless painting

When painting with a foam or natural bristle brush, always brush in one direction over the surface of the object and then lightly brush over the object in the opposite direction. Be sure to cover all areas.

If you're working on a box with hinges, you don't have to remove the hinges; simply paint around the hinges very carefully. A pointed artist's brush is handy for painting around hinges. If you get some paint on the hinges, you can remove the paint with a single-edged razor blade when it dries.

If your project needs more than one coat of paint, let the first coat of paint dry thoroughly (read the label to find out how long the paint needs to dry) before applying a second coat. If brush strokes are obvious when the paint is dry, sand lightly with fine #400 sandpaper to make the painted surface smooth.

Valuable varnishing

Many thin coats of varnish create a smoother finish than a thick coat of varnish. Brush the varnish in one direction and then drag the brush lightly across the object in the opposite direction. Each coat of varnish needs to dry thoroughly before sanding or applying another coat of varnish.

Careful cutting

When you cut out designs, the goal is to cut away as much of the excess background paper as possible. If a cutout is too large to fit onto your object, you can cut it apart and alter it to fit. You don't have to use the cutout exactly as is. Adding and subtracting leaves to or from a flower, for example, is part of the fun you can have when designing a découpage project.

Découpage Projects

Découpage has been applied to everything from large pieces of furniture to the tiniest thimble. After you master the technique, you begin to think of ideas for creating new and exciting projects using a wide variety of designs that you may find. Découpage is a great craft for making gifts, for giving a new look to worn-out objects in your home, and for personal creative enjoyment. The following projects are simple, enabling you to practice the technique.

Liven up a light-switch plate

Personalize a room with a découpage light-switch plate. You can find wooden, metal, and plastic plates in home centers, or you can make over a switch plate that you already have. Enhance a child's room by using a charming illustration from a children's book for the découpage design.

Because this project is a small item, choose an illustration that is proportionate in scale. When working on a flat, square, or rectangular item, a border design works well. I used a border of leaves and apples on my light-switch plate (see the photo in the color section) to balance the cutouts of the figures. I took these designs from a paperback Kate Greenaway book.

Tools and Materials:

Basic craft kit (see the Cheat Sheet at the front of this book)

Newspaper

Light-switch plate (wood, metal, or plastic)

Paintbrush

Paint (if the object is made of raw wood)

1 sheet each of #400 and #600 3M Wetordry sandpaper

Cuticle scissors

Paper illustration to cut out

Sponge, slightly damp

Paper towel or soft rag

Varnish brush

Water-based varnish

Furniture paste wax

1. **If the switch plate needs painting, cover your worktable with newspaper and, with the paintbrush, paint the plate and let it dry thoroughly. Apply a second coat if needed, sanding between coats. (See Chapter 10.)**

2. **Using the cuticle scissors, cut out each element of the design as close to the outline as possible so that no background paper is left.**

3. Arrange the designs on the painted light-switch plate. One by one, remove each cutout and place it facedown on the work surface. Squirt a small amount of glue in the center of the back of the cutout and spread the glue evenly to all outer edges. Position the cutout on the light-switch plate and press it down with a slightly damp sponge. Remove any excess glue from around the edges. Press the cutout down with a paper towel, soft rag, or damp sponge.

4. Continue to apply all paper cutouts in this way. Let the glue dry for an hour.

5. Using a varnish brush and working in one direction only, apply a thin coat of varnish across the entire front of the switch plate. Without adding any more varnish to the brush, drag it lightly across the plate in the other direction. Put the wet plate aside to dry.

6. Continue to apply three more coats of varnish in this way.

7. After the fourth coat of varnish is dry, wet a small piece of sandpaper by running it under tap water and lightly sand over the varnished light-switch plate. Wipe clean. Add more coats of varnish in this way if needed. To determine how many coats of varnish you need to apply, run your fingers over the finish. If the edges of the cutouts feel smooth (the design will be slightly raised), enough varnish is covering the cutouts. If not, apply another coat or two of varnish.

8. Wet-sand the final coat of varnish; wipe the plate clean.

9. Wax according to the directions on the can of furniture wax.

Dress up a dresser

Ready-to-finish furniture is usually made of inexpensive pine, which is ideal for crafting with découpage. If you are wallpapering a room, save the scraps of paper to cut out for a découpage project. In this way, you can coordinate the furniture with the design of the room. A large poster is another good source for a découpage design large enough to cover a piece of furniture.

Choose pretty wallpaper to cut out the designs to découpage the front of the drawers for a young girl's room, as I did for the découpage dresser shown in the color section. A découpage piece of furniture lends excitement to a room and gives it a one-of-a-kind quality.

Tools and Materials:

Basic craft kit (see the Cheat Sheet at the front of this book)

Newspaper

Small bureau

1 sheet #320 sandpaper

1 sheet #400 or #600 sandpaper

2-inch foam paintbrush

Latex paint in desired color

Paper design to cut out

Paper towel or soft rag

Sponge, slightly damp

Water-based varnish

Varnish brush

Furniture paste wax

1. **Cover your worktable with newspaper. Then remove the drawers and knobs of the dresser so that all surfaces are ready to sand and paint.**

2. **Lightly sand the entire piece of raw wooden furniture with the #320 sandpaper. Wipe clean.**

3. **Paint all surfaces of the dresser, drawers, and knobs separately with the foam paintbrush. Let the paint dry thoroughly. Sand lightly with the #400 sandpaper. Apply a second coat of paint if necessary.**

4. **Cut out the paper designs.**

5. **Place the dresser on its back and replace the drawers, but not the knobs.**

6. **Arrange the cutouts so that the design flows from the top drawer down across the other drawers to the bottom of the dresser. If the drawers do not close flush with the base of the cabinet, plan to apply the cutouts so that they go over the edges of the drawer fronts and continue on the cabinet between the drawers.**

Beautify a box

Craft stores carry a variety of wooden boxes for decoupage and other crafting techniques. The materials and the process for crafting on small boxes are the same as those used to découpage a piece of furniture (see "Dress up a dresser," in this chapter). However, if time and space are considerations, it takes less time and takes up less space to découpage a small box than it does a piece of furniture.

When you want the design to fit over the entire front or over the lid and base of a box, glue the cutout onto the painted surface with the boxes closed. When the glue is dry (about one hour), use a single-edge razor blade to slit across the cutout where the top and bottom of the box come together.

The inside of a box can be painted in a contrasting color or in the same color as the outside of the box. When the paint is dry, apply a coat of varnish to the inside of the box to protect the paint.

If you are working on a small night table with only one drawer, you may want to begin the design on the top and extend the design down over the front.

7. **To do the découpage, refer to Steps 3 through 9 in the section "Liven up a light-switch plate," earlier in this chapter.**

When a design flows over a piece of furniture from one drawer to another, glue the designs down with the drawers shut. After the glue dries, use a clean, sharp, single-edge razor blade to cut the design apart where the drawers open. This way, the design is perfectly aligned when the drawers are closed.

Recycled cookie tins

Cookie tins make handy containers for jewelry, scarves, and other personal items you may want to organize. Decorate them with a coat of spray paint and pretty paper cutouts. Add ribbon or lace around the rim of one for a finishing touch and a colorful knob on the top of another (see the photo in the color section).

Sheer lace comes in different widths (available in fabric shops). You can apply a narrow band of lace or ribbon around the bottom edge, middle, or entire bottom portion of the tin. The paint color shows through the sheer lace fabric and adds texture to the painted tin. You may want to apply a piece of lace over the base of the tin and then apply a band of narrow velvet or satin ribbon on top of the lace around the center or bottom edge of the tin.

Tools and Materials:

Basic craft kit (see the Cheat Sheet at the front of this book)

Metal tins (any size or shape)

Newspaper

Can of spray paint (any color)

Paper illustrations to cut out

Sponge, slightly damp

Paper towel

Water-based varnish

Varnish brush

Furniture paste wax

Tape measure

Lace, ribbon, decorative braid, or rickrack for trimming in a length to fit around the tin

Decorative knob (sold in hardware stores)

1. **Cover your work surface with newspaper. Follow the directions on the paint can to spray paint the lid and base of the tin separately. Most spray paint needs to dry overnight. If the paint color is light, you may need two coats of paint.**

2. **When the paint is completely dry, do the découpage crafting (refer to Steps 3 through 9 in the section "Liven up a light-switch plate," earlier in this chapter).**

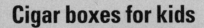

Cigar boxes for kids

Decorate a cigar box with paint and animal cutouts. The designs can be stickers or cutouts from an old book. Kids can make their own designs on colorful construction paper or by drawing and coloring a design on plain, white bond paper. The photo in the color section shows one suggested design. The blades of grass were made by cutting strips of green construction paper.

Use acrylic paint or poster paint and a foam paintbrush to cover all sides of the box. Let the paint dry. Cut out the designs and glue them where they look best on the painted box. Let the glue dry. Varnish over the designs to make them permanent. Let the varnish dry. Apply three more coats of varnish, allowing each coat to dry before applying the next coat.

3. Measure the circumference of the base of the tin and cut the trimming (ribbon, lace, and so on) to this measurement.

4. Place the decorative trim facedown on the newspaper and squirt a small amount of glue on the back of the trim. Spread the glue evenly over the back with your finger.

5. Position one end of the trim on the tin and, using a paper towel, press it down all around until the ends meet.

6. Glue a painted knob to the center of the lid of the tin and set it aside to dry overnight.

Part III
Paint Crafts

"It was Lieutenant Hooper's idea. He thought it would be nice to add some rustic charm to the unit by stenciling the tanks. This, for instance, is part of our 'Country Cupboard' attack squad."

In this part . . .

*P*aint crafts is a general term that covers a broad range of techniques and skills used to achieve different painted effects. Faux finishing, fantasy finishing, stenciling, and freehand painting all fall under the category of paint crafts. As you work your way through this part, certain words will begin to roll off your tongue as easily as your own name. With a little practice, you'll be stenciling, ragging, sponging, dragging, glazing, speckling, crackling, spattering, marbleizing, veining, graining, and even flogging like an expert. The only problem you may have is deciding which technique to use. The decision can be downright distressing — oops, that's another term. However, it doesn't matter which technique you choose, because every one of these painting techniques turns something plain into something pretty — or at least something more interesting.

The projects presented in the chapters of this part are small and not complicated. These projects let you practice the basic skills and techniques so that you can then do any project, including walls and floors.

Chapter 10

Getting Started with Paint Crafts

● ●

In This Chapter

▶ Finding out about paint crafts

▶ Brushing up on tools and materials

▶ Getting ready to paint the town red . . . or any other color

● ●

Most paint crafts, such as stenciling and decorative painting (which includes faux finishes and freehand designs), start with easy, basic steps. Getting good at a paint craft technique is just a matter of feeling comfortable with the materials. You find out what these steps are and get introduced to these materials in this chapter.

Some of the effects you can achieve (such as faux marble) make a painted surface look like something it isn't. You may become a first-class faker! Other methods, such as sponging and ragging, utilize a glaze that's applied over a background paint color to give depth, texture, sheen, and an overall richness to a flat, painted wall. Decorative paint crafts employ stenciling and illustration to add designs to painted furniture and accessories. And if you think that you can't draw a straight line, you'll be happy to know that squiggly lines make terrific decorative patterns.

Exploring the Different Paint Crafts

The next two chapters deal entirely with stenciling and decorative painting, but I introduce you to these two topics in the following sections. I show you how to use these techniques to create an interesting design that's perfect for your environment. For example, I live on an island and wanted to create a nautical design in my bathroom that has a water view. It was a cinch to do with a sailboat and seashell stencil design around the window frame. This section shows you how easy it is to do this sort of thing in your home — even if your theme isn't nautical.

Stenciling

Stenciling is the process of applying paint to a surface through a previously cut-out pattern. Although the process is as simple as that, you can use it to produce beautiful and dramatic results. Stenciling is one of the most popular paint techniques because it's so easy to master and the results are so rewarding. Furthermore, the design potential is limitless, and you can stencil a design on almost any material.

Nineteenth-century houses were frequently decorated with stenciled walls and floors. Early stencilers used stencil brushes, stencils (usually cut out of thin metal), and paint. Today we use almost the same materials; however, most stencils are now made of plastic, rather than metal.

Faux finishing

Faux (a French word meaning *false*) finishes simulate the look of something else: real leather, marble, wood, tortoise shell, stone, or another interesting, irregular texture on a surface, most often walls and furniture. When artfully applied to furniture, for example, it can be difficult to tell whether the finished piece is made of real marble or of inexpensive pine.

To achieve these faux finish textures, you use ordinary materials like brushes, rags, paper towels, or plastic wrap to apply two or more paint colors or glazes to a surface. Other faux finishing techniques include spatter painting, sponging, ragging, and combing.

Faux finishing is popular because it can give a room personality, whether you apply it to home accessories, furniture, walls, or floors. You begin by painting the surface with a base coat. After this, you apply a translucent glaze overcoat. While the glaze is still wet, you create a texture on the glaze with a sponge, a cloth, a rag, a special comb, a roller, or brushes of various sizes. You manipulate the glaze (which stays wet long enough to do the job) to form patterns or different color effects that range from subtle to bold. Whether you are doing a large wall or a small chest, you have a great deal of control over this very forgiving technique.

Assembling Your Basic Materials

Special tools and materials enable you to do paint crafts effectively. The popularity of stenciling and decorative painting has increased the availability of tools and materials, and many manufacturers provide free instructional booklets. When you go to a home center to buy the materials to comb your walls, for example, the salesperson knows what you're talking about and doesn't send you to the haircare department. Most craft stores have all the materials you need for small- and medium-sized projects. For large projects, like decorating walls and floors, home centers sell the paint in larger quantities, as well as large brushes for this purpose.

Choosing brushes

Painting the background color is the first step in decorative painting. You don't have to master any fancy techniques, and ordinary paintbrushes do the trick. You use large brushes for large projects, and small brushes for small projects. Diagonal-cut brushes are handy for corners and tight spots. It's as easy as that.

Special brushes help you achieve the best decorative painting results on top of the background paint texture. Art stores usually carry a wide variety of brushes for professional artists, and you can also use these brushes for other craft techniques.

Buying the recommended brush for the technique is important. Although you can substitute another type of brush, the results may be less than perfect. Why waste your time?

Stencil brushes

Stencil brushes come in different sizes and grades, and one size does not fit all. For example, a stencil brush that's 2 inches in diameter is designed for large areas, and it doesn't work well for a small, delicate design. Make sure that you have the right brush for what you're doing. If you are doing only one project, you need to buy only the brush or brushes that you need for that project. You can always add brushes as you do more projects.

Top-of-the-line stencil brushes are made of hog bristles. You probably don't think that a hog has such desirable hair, but it sort of makes up for his unfortunate looks and personality. Black or gray bristles are top-of-the-line; white bristles are stiffer and less desirable. Hog-hair stencil brushes are costly, and most craft stores probably don't carry them. If you buy your supplies in a craft store, simply choose the best brush available in the size that's appropriate for your stencil design. Price usually indicates the quality of the brush.

I do a lot of stenciling in my studio and have stencil brushes of all sizes and qualities. The better brushes that I purchased years ago are still in excellent condition. The poorer-quality brushes work fine for only a few projects.

The secret to keeping stencil brushes happy is to be downright obsessive about cleaning each brush every single time you use it. Warm water (not hot), a little soap (not a lot), and loving care do the trick.

Decorative design brushes

Traditionally, artists' brushes are made of red sable. These brushes are unsurpassed in all areas, and just like sable coats, they are costly. Today's technology has produced synthetic brushes that come in all styles, weights, and fiber types. These brushes are reasonably priced and particularly good for painting decorative designs with acrylic paints.

Brush manufacturers designate the sizes of brushes in different ways. Some use numbers, some use inches, and some use the metric system. I use the eyeball method: I look at the rack of brushes and pick the one that looks like the right size for the job.

Faux finishing brushes and tools

You can create faux finishes or fantasy finishes with ordinary paintbrushes and materials. Specialized brushes and tools are available to help achieve specific effects like wood graining and marbleizing. If you have a set of basic brushes, you can supplement them with a special brush or tool made just for that project. For example, if you want to create the look of real wood on a painted surface, you can't do it without a graining tool. Such a tool really is available, and it works like magic.

Although many of the following tools may seem unfamiliar to you, they are readily available in craft stores, paint stores, and many home centers.

✔ A *dragging brush* or *flogger* has long flexible bristles. You use it to drag straight stripes through glaze. Use a *wallpaper brush,* which is much wider, on large projects.

✔ A *graining brush* is made up of irregularly spaced bristles. When you drag the brush down through the glaze, it leaves a pattern similar to the grain found on a piece of wood.

You can easily make a graining brush by removing sections of bristles in a cheap paintbrush to create spaces between the bristles.

✔ A *softening brush* has medium-length, soft bristles. It softens brush strokes and gently blends colors together.

✔ A *stippling brush* looks like an oversized toothbrush with stiff bristles. It creates gradations of shade or color in painting. One color is stippled over another color that shows through in places.

✔ A rubber *graining tool* creates different wood grain patterns, including grain with knots in it. This tool has a dowel handle with a rounded rubber block on one end. A wood grain pattern is cut into the rubber block. When you drag the tool down or across a wet painted surface, it creates a pattern that simulates the look of real wood.

✔ A *three-sided comb* is a triangular-shaped tool with rubber notches on each side. Each comb produces a different effect: fine, medium, or coarse patterns. These edges create straight or wavy, evenly spaced or irregularly spaced lines in the wet paint or glaze.

✔ *Metal combs* are designed for fine combing and last longer than a rubber comb. Metal combs are excellent for doing many combing and graining projects.

Combing/graining tools are easy to make. Cut a piece of stiff cardboard, approximately 4 x 8 inches. From the 8-inch side, create a serrated edge by cutting little triangle shapes, like teeth in a jack-o'-lantern, along the entire length. They don't have to be perfect. Use this tool for creating stripes in a glazed surface. Another way to make a combing tool is to cut a plastic coffee can lid in half and serrate the straight edge. These tools generally hold up through only one project, but that may be all you need, and you'll save some money on materials.

✔ *Sea sponges* are used for (guess what) sponging! Unlike your kitchen sponge, sea sponges are natural and irregularly shaped. The irregularity enables you to create a variety of textures.

If you're in a bind and you can't find real sea sponges, you can adapt a kitchen sponge: Pull the sponge apart (be brutal) so that you end up with irregular pieces of sponge with chunks pulled out of it.

✔ *Goose and turkey feathers* are unbeatable for creating veins in a faux marbled surface. You can also use small, pointed *artists' brushes* to create this effect, but many crafters find that feathers afford more control for creating realistic-looking marble. (Now you know what to do with those wayward pillow feathers.)

✔ You use an *art eraser* to make white or negative veins in a glazed surface. This square, hard eraser is available in art supply stores.

✔ Even your old *toothbrush* can become a valuable tool, and not just for cleaning the grout between bathroom tiles. A toothbrush is the favored tool of spatterers. By rubbing your thumb over the paint-covered brush, paint spatters onto the surface.

Use this technique only on small projects, to avoid wearing out your thumb, your toothbrush, and your patience. For larger spatter projects, use the traditional method of dipping a 1-inch brush into paint and hitting the brush against a stick in order to spatter the paint onto a surface.

✔ Thin latex *gloves* enable you to work effectively while protecting your hands from the inevitable mess of paint, stain, varnish, or other messy liquids. If you're planning to do lots of crafting, you can buy an economy-size box of gloves. You remove the gloves through a pop-up top opening just like in a box of tissues. Look for the gloves in home centers.

Using rags to get richer finishes

You can create patterns and textures with a variety of materials. The first rule of creating painted textures is *use whatever works*. For example, rag rolling uses common rags. Crunched up or rolled into a cylinder shape, a rag can be used to create all kinds of textures and patterns. *Cheesecloth,* which is a soft, gauzy material, is often used in combination with coarser rags. By using rags to apply a glaze finish, you can literally go from rags to riches.

For a slightly different effect, you can use scrunched-up newspapers, plastic wrap, or paper towels to apply paint. The best thing about all these materials is that you can toss them out after you finish the job.

Steel wool is an excellent material for dragging through glaze to create fine textures. For most projects, use medium-coarse steel wool.

Wear protective rubber gloves and goggles when working with steel wool.

Craft stores carry special gloves for creating unusual faux finishes. The gloves look like oven mitts and are made with a dry-mop-like fabric on the palms. You apply paint to the palm side and create different paint textures by pressing your hand onto a painted surface. Paint rollers with textured patterns are available for the same purpose.

Picking paints and glazes

Faux finishing is a process of two or more steps that involves painting a surface with a base coat of opaque paint and then covering the painted surface with a colored, translucent glaze. You manipulate the glaze in various ways to create textures, and when it dries, the glazed surface has a rich, deep quality that you can't achieve with paint alone.

Before the advent of water-based paints, many potential crafters shied away from paint projects such as faux finishes. Such projects were messy to clean up, and you had to use solvents like turpentine to clean a brush covered with oil paint. All that is behind us now. Craft paints are now water-based, and they are available in any color you can dream up. Best of all, they come packaged in neat little squeeze bottles. In fact, all the supplies you need for paint crafts have been updated to make the projects easy to do, and cleaning up is now a cinch. All these factors put the emphasis on fun rather than frustration, and here's the best news of all: Anyone can create fabulous results, even you. After you do a few projects, you may discover that you really have a talent for it.

Before telling you to use water-based paints and glazes, I'll give you the last (well, almost the last) word about traditional oil-based finishes. An oil glaze dries slowly so that you can work with it for a long time. This slow drying process enables you to work on it over and over until you like the effect. Water-based paints and glazes are not that forgiving, because the water in them starts drying as soon as it hits the air. However, water-based products are so user-friendly that it's hard to justify choosing the oil-based products. The solution is to work in smaller areas at a time so that the drying time doesn't become a problem.

Buying the right paint for the right job is an important rule in paint crafts. For most stencil projects, a small amount of acrylic paint is enough. Craft stores carry premixed acrylic paints in small plastic containers. You may have as many as 200 colors to choose from, including basic colors, country colors, folk colors, metallic colors, and various glazes and washes.

Art materials stores have acrylic colors in 2-ounce tubes for mixing your own colors or using right out of the tube. Tube acrylics have a good consistency for stenciling.

Craft stores have faux finishing paints and glazes in small plastic containers and half-pint and pint cans. These paints and glazes are also available in quart and gallon sizes in home centers; they come in decorator colors that are appealing for use on walls. Complete faux finishing kits, which contain everything you need to do one small project like marbleizing a night table, are also available.

Paint manufacturers and craft product manufacturers have lines of paints, glazes, mediums, and varnishes designed and packaged for decorative finishing projects. They are labeled "all-purpose latex paint" or "clean up with water." Even though they are all most likely water-based products, check before you buy. Here's some advice about buying paints:

- For large projects, such as sponge painting a bathroom, get your materials from a home center, which packages paint in quarts and gallons. Glazes are in containers larger than those found in craft stores.

- For a medium-size project, such as a child's dresser, buy the base colors in cans from a craft store. They usually carry half-pint and pint sizes.

- For a small project, such as a keepsake box, look for the 2-ounce plastic bottles in your craft store. Paints, glazes, mediums, fabric paints, and many other useful liquids are packaged in these containers in craft stores.

✔ For a small or medium-sized project that requires a lot of materials, such as faux marble or faux tortoiseshell painting, I recommend purchasing a complete kit. The kit contains everything you need to do the project. Be sure that the project you're planning isn't too large for the quantities of materials in the kit. Kits can be economical because you don't have to buy large amounts of each item. You also save time by not having to look for everything you need. The marbleizing kits even include a feather.

Picking just the right combination of colors for your project can be a lot of fun but also daunting. Because you have so many colors to choose from, manufacturers have tried to simplify the process by developing special colors for faux finishing. The base paint colors and the glaze colors are designed to go together. This doesn't mean that you *have* to use the mocha paint with the burnt sienna glaze. But this system makes your decision easier by grouping the colors in a carefully selected range to show you what colors you can use together to achieve pleasing results.

Mixing your own glaze

Glaze is a combination of water-based paint, acrylic medium, and water. *Acrylic medium* is a milky white liquid that, when mixed with paint, makes a translucent mixture. Acrylic medium is available in art material stores, craft stores, and home centers that carry decorative finishing materials.

Here's a recipe that offers a very basic generalized formula for mixing your own glaze. Pour 1 ounce of paint into a bowl and then add acrylic medium a little a time, up to 1 ounce. Mix the paint and the medium together. Add water, two or three drops at a time, and mix thoroughly. (If you need a larger quantity of glaze, you can start with larger amounts, but keep the same proportions.) Mix the paint and the glaze together and then, as you add water to thin the mixture, try out the glaze to make sure that it is not too watery. You don't want the glaze to be too thin and watery, nor do you want it to be too thick to apply easily.

When applying glaze over a large painted area like a wall, do it in small sections (2 x 4 feet). This way, the glaze doesn't have time to dry while you're working on it.

Making Your Basic Preparations

Yard sales and flea markets have become treasure troves for finding potential makeovers. These sources, along with your relatives, can often provide items that have seen better days. With a little patience and skill, you can easily turn an old castoff into a gem. The following sections help you do just that.

Off with the old, on with the new

If you're planning to redo an old piece of furniture, the first job is preparing the piece to receive the paint. This task may involve removing an old finish, filling holes, sanding, and sealing the surface with a primer. If there are knots in the wood or rust on the metal, you don't want them to bleed through your new paint finish. If the wood surface has holes or niches, fill them with wood filler and then sand after the filler dries. The prep work may seem bothersome, but the end result looks better when you take the time to do the preparations. If your project has a clean, smooth surface before you paint, it will have a nice smooth finish when you are done.

If the surface is already painted but smooth, it simply needs a light sanding in order to accept the new coat of paint. If the surface is painted but uneven, you may have to use a *palm sander* (a small sander that fits in the palm of your hand) to smooth the surface. If the surface is caked with layers of chipping paint, it's not worth the effort required to get it to the point of acceptability, unless it's a sensational piece. By *sensational,* I mean good lines, interesting shape, practical size, and potentially useful. If all these attributes apply, by all means put forth the effort to remove the old finish.

Sanding your way to a smooth finish

Every yard sale find or cast-off from a relative doesn't have to be stripped of the old finish. The first time I learned this, it was music to my ears. Most of the time, cleaning and sanding are all that you need to do. Sand before you apply primer. Sand after you apply primer. Sand between coats of primer and paint. First you sand to rough up a shiny surface, and then you sand to smooth down a rough surface. Save this job for a time when you have a lot of energy to burn or frustration to release. Sanding a piece of furniture may be just the outlet you need.

Sanding isn't a hard job, but you do need to treat your hands kindly by wearing rubber gloves.

Sandpaper comes in sheets that you can cut to your desired size. It comes in different numbered grades — the higher the number, the finer the grit. See Table 10-1 for information on the grades of sandpaper and the uses for each grade.

If you are in the middle of a project that needs sanding and you don't have the recommended grade sandpaper for the next step, always use a finer rather than coarser grade of paper than the one suggested.

Table 10-1	Grades and Uses of Sandpaper	
Grade Number	*Grit*	*Uses*
50-60	Coarse	Remove rough paint from an old piece
80-100	Medium	Sand raw wood to be painted
120-150	Fine	Smooth primed surfaces
160-240	Very Fine	Smooth stained surface
280-320	Extra Fine	Remove imperfections from painted surfaces between coats of paint
360-400	Super Fine	Smooth imperfections from a varnished surface between coats
Over 400	Ultra Fine	Smooth last coat of paint or varnish

If you are not sure about which sandpaper to use, try using the grade of paper you think is right in a small area before sanding the entire surface.

A primer on primers

A *primer* is a sealer that is made up of properties that even out and seal a surface to be painted. Sealers create a barrier between the original surface and the paint that is applied over it, preventing water or paint solvents from penetrating the surface. Sealers are especially important for painting raw wood. If you don't prime an unfinished piece of furniture before painting it, the paint may appear shiny in some spots and dull in other places. Without a primer, the knots in knotty pine or the rust on metal bleeds through a coat of paint, creating discolored areas.

A primer/sealer such as BIN prepares the surface of most wood or metal objects. BIN is available in small and large cans as well as a spray, and it dries very quickly. Because BIN is rough on brushes, I recommend using a disposable foam brush to apply it; you can just throw away the foam brush when you're done.

If you get any BIN on your hands, clean up with denatured alcohol.

If you're repainting a previously painted surface that needs sanding down to the bare wood in a few spots, apply dabs of primer only over those spots. You don't need to prime the entire surface.

The unvarnished truth about finishes

An unfinished chair that has been primed, sanded, painted, and stenciled is a finished project that will last for a long time. A coat of varnish protects a painted surface and gives the piece a satin, semigloss, or high-gloss sheen, depending on the finish you choose. Varnish is a clear, protective coating that can be used over stain or paint, and the color shows through the varnish.

Many types of finishes are available: polyurethane, water-based varnish, lacquer, and alkyd-based varnish. Polyurethane is an oil-based resin that must be cleaned with turpentine, paint thinner, or mineral spirits. Lacquer and alkyd-based varnishes were often used by early furniture-makers and are rarely recommended for craft projects.

Whenever possible, I always recommend water-based materials. Therefore, I usually recommend a water-based varnish for the final finish. Water-based varnish dries quickly, is easy to clean up with warm water, and is tough enough to protect most projects that get normal use. Although it looks milky white in the can, water-based varnish dries to a clear finish.

The best protection for an outdoor project is high-gloss polyurethane.

A good varnish brush is made of natural bristles and, when cleaned between uses, will last a long time. A foam brush is good for one or two applications.

If you apply polyurethane with a foam brush, you must dispose of the brush after you use it. The foam may disintegrate in the cleaner.

Here's how to apply varnish:

1. **Hold the brush at a 45-degree angle and gently apply the varnish over the surface in parallel strokes in one direction only.**

   Lift the brush at the end of each stroke to avoid dripping. You don't have to overlap strokes.

2. **After you cover a surface with varnish, make it smoother by gently dragging the brush, without more varnish, over the surface again in the opposite direction, across the first strokes.**

3. **Look for and smooth away any drip marks.**

   If drips are left to dry, they will be difficult to remove without careful sanding.

To detect drips in a varnished surface, look at the wet surface in good light and from different angles. Because varnish is a clear substance, seeing the drips before they're dry is difficult.

Staining isn't straining

You don't have to use paint as the base coat for a project — you can stain it instead. Stain penetrates the wood and colors it in a wood tone; paint is a coating that goes on the surface of the wood to color it.

There's no strain to using stain. Applying a wood stain to an unfinished piece of furniture is an easy project. The stained background can then receive a stenciled or painted design. Because wood stains come in a variety of colors, you can choose a stain to match any wood in your home.

I recommend using a gel stain for craft projects. Even though I generally promote using water-based materials, when it comes to stains (which come with a water base as well as an oil base), an oil-based gel stain is easier to apply evenly. You apply a gel stain by rubbing it onto the surface of the wood with a soft rag or cheesecloth.

Don't forget to wear rubber gloves when applying any kind of stain.

Factoring In Time Considerations

You will save time and avoid frustration if you organize your materials before starting a paint craft project. After you pour the paint into a container, you don't want to be running all over looking for a brush. Read the tools and materials list for each project and make sure that you have everything you need before starting.

When calculating the time you need to complete a paint craft project, remember to include drying time between coats. I like to start a paint project in the morning so that I can prime and apply a base coat that will dry by the afternoon, when I can continue the project. Alternatively, I do the prep work in the late afternoon and let it dry overnight so that I can do the crafting the next morning.

Never let paint dry on a brush. If you take the time to clean your brush before it dries, it won't have a bad hair day the next time you want to use it.

Chapter 11

Stenciling

. . . .

In This Chapter

▶ Gathering your materials

▶ Cutting your own stencils and doing other preliminary work

▶ Getting down to the stenciling — at last

▶ Stenciling one- and two-color projects

▶ Making five easy projects

▶ Transforming a ready-to-finish dresser with stenciling

. . . .

*T*he craft of stenciling is the application of color to a surface through cutout designs. A *stencil* is the cutout pattern or template for the design. You can use the cutout many times to create a repeat pattern, such as for a decorative border around a room.

The best thing about stenciling is that it enables anyone to apply a painted design perfectly on any surface. You don't need any special talent. The tools and materials are basic and inexpensive, and the design potential is limitless. After you master the basic technique for stenciling, you can use it to make gifts, to decorate unfinished furniture, or to add interest to plain walls in any room of your home.

In this chapter, you find all that you need to know about the basic materials, where to find them, and how to use them. You discover how easy it is to cut your own stencils so that you can design home accessories and furniture to match fabric designs, wallpaper, or even china patterns. This chapter takes you through each step of five easy stenciling projects to get you started, and one furniture stenciling project to introduce you to working on a larger object. From this point, you'll be able to stencil anything as small as a mouse or as large as a house. You can even stencil your mouse pad!

Stenciling's humble beginnings

Stenciling was first introduced in this country in colonial times when traveling European artisans went from town to town throughout New England offering their services. Often in exchange for meals and lodging, the stencilers added patterns and decorative borders to otherwise drab walls.

Stencil designs provided an inexpensive alternative to wallpaper. Early stencilers painted swags and tassels to imitate gathered drapery, columns, and elegant urns, as well as flowers, pinecones, leaves, and fruit. The pineapple was a very popular design, representing hospitality. Today the pineapple is still the most widely used stencil design for furniture, fabric, and walls.

Perhaps the most familiar uses for stenciling are the fruit and flower motifs found on Boston rockers and Hitchcock chairs. Another popular stenciled item copied from Early American days is the canvas or oilcloth floor covering. These floor coverings were often stenciled with elaborate scenes and borders, the effect intended to be that of an expensive carpet or floor painting.

Gathering Your Stenciling Materials

All the materials you need for stenciling are readily available and inexpensive. You can find stencil supplies in art and craft stores or home centers with a craft department. Basic supplies are a stencil brush, paint, and a precut stencil design. If you are making your own stencil, you need stencil paper and a craft knife as well.

Stencil paper

Precut stencils come in a variety of designs and sizes for almost any sort of project you might like to do. The projects that I present in this chapter use original designs that I provide. When you've cut out these stencil patterns, you can use these stencils on a variety of projects of different sizes.

To cut your own stencil design, you need *stencil paper*. This special wax-coated paper is slightly stiff and prevents the design from slipping while you work with it on a surface. Stencil paper is not your ordinary supermarket wax paper that comes on a roll. This wax paper is available in sheets and is about the thickness of a manila file folder. It is transparent, which makes it easy to work with.

You can also use acetate or vinyl for cutting a stencil. These materials last longer than stencil paper, are inexpensive, can be cleaned with a damp sponge, and stick to a surface as well. You can buy acetate or vinyl in rolls by the yard or use the sleeves from photo albums. These materials are also transparent.

Manila folders and Mylar are other materials for cutting a stencil. Manila folders are fine for a one-time use on a small object, but these materials get wet and frayed after having paint tapped over them many times. Mylar is as good as acetate but may be harder to find. Furthermore, both of these materials are not transparent, which makes cutting out the design more difficult.

I prefer the wax stencil paper because it is easy to cut, lasts long enough to finish any project, and is relatively inexpensive. However, if you can't find it in your area, the Mylar and acetate are fine substitutes.

If you are copying a design or need to enlarge a design, you need tracing paper and grid paper (see Chapter 3 for enlarging a design). However, you can enlarge almost any design on a photocopier, opening the world of design to you. If you think a design would look great on a table but it's no bigger than a thumbnail, you can enlarge it to a more suitable size.

Cutting tools

You need a craft knife to cut your own stencil. The craft knife should have a narrow handle that is easy to hold like a pencil. An X-Acto craft knife with a #11 blade is best.

The best way to ensure perfectly cut stencils is to use a sharp blade, so buy an extra package of blades when you buy the knife. That way, you can replace the blade as soon as it begins to dull.

Brushes

Stencil brushes come in various sizes. For most projects, you need two or three brushes in a small and a medium size — a different brush for each color in your stencil design.

The better the brush, the better the results. Brush quality is an area where saving money is not always practical, but the best brushes are not always the most expensive. Ask your art store dealer for advice about which brushes are the best quality for the money.

Buy only natural-bristle stencil brushes. Regular paintbrushes are an absolute no-no for stenciling. You need the real thing.

Paint

Acrylic paint is the most practical type of paint for stenciling. You can buy acrylic paint in small tubes and in every color imaginable. Water-based acrylic paint washes off hands and brushes but is permanent on most surfaces. Acrylic paint is especially ideal for fabric stenciling because you can launder a stenciled piece of fabric and the stencil will not wash away.

When choosing the paint colors, also buy a tube of white paint. If a color is too strong or too bright, you can add some white paint to make it lighter and softer in shade.

For a stencil design on furniture or walls, you can use acrylic or latex paint. If you choose latex paint, get satin finish or semigloss rather than high-gloss, because a high-gloss finish isn't usually desirable on furniture or walls.

You need only a small amount of paint for most stencil projects. A pint of latex paint is plenty for almost any furniture or wall project. For most craft projects, like stenciling boxes, picture frames, and plaques, you use acrylic paint that comes in 1- and 2-ounce containers.

Other essential items

If you put together the basic craft tool box (see the Cheat Sheet at the front of this book), you probably have most of the tools that you need for successful stenciling. However, you also need the items in the following list:

- ✔ A small saucer is ideal for mixing paint colors. Because you are using water-based paint, cleaning the dishes is easy (just use warm water). You can also use paper plates — use one for each different paint color. When you finish your project, you can throw away the paint-covered plates.

- ✔ Masking tape holds your stencil in place over the surface. Buy the ¾- to 1-inch-width roll of tape.

- ✔ A straightedge is especially important when creating borders. You also need a fine marker to trace the design.

- ✔ Remember to protect the table on which you cut your stencil. The cutting surface should be heavy cardboard or a wooden board.

- ✔ You need a small sponge or dry cloth to wipe away any slight errors.

- ✔ An artist's brush with a small, narrow point is indispensable for touching up, adding a dot of color in the center of a flower, or adding details such as veins on leaves.

- ✔ An artist's palette knife (from an art supply store) is useful for mixing acrylic paint colors but not necessary.

Preparing to Stencil

If you have never stenciled before, you're in for a pleasant surprise. Stenciling is such an easy craft that as soon as you start your first project, you're on your way to professional status as a stenciler.

By following some general tips and how-to's, you'll be stenciling like a pro in no time. These tips can be most helpful, especially when working on your own designs or on several projects at once. The following sections tell you the best ways to do the various steps in stenciling. Refer back to them as needed.

Cutting a stencil

If you cut your own stencil (instead of using a precut stencil), you start with a design that you have drawn or traced from a source such as a book, wallpaper, wrapping paper, or perhaps fabric. The projects in this chapter use stencil designs provided in this book.

1. **Using a pencil and tracing paper, trace the design you've chosen.**

2. **Tape your stencil paper to the front of your traced design. If you use a manila folder to cut a stencil, tape the traced design to the folder and plan to cut through the tracing paper design.**

   You should be able to see the design through your stencil paper, vinyl, or acetate material. Do not tape your stencil material to the cutting surface. You want to be able to move the paper around as you cut the stencil.

3. **Holding the craft knife as if it were a pencil, apply enough pressure to cut along the marked lines, pulling the blade toward you.**

   Use long, smooth strokes and turn the stencil with your free hand as you cut. Avoid short, choppy cuts.

   Cut the small areas first to keep the stencil from weakening.

4. **When two lines meet at a corner, cut just slightly past where they intersect.**

   This technique gives you sharp angles. If you make an error or cut too far into a line, you can apply tape on both sides of the stencil paper.

Building bridges and laying ties

Sometimes a design is so fragile that it could fall apart by the time you finish cutting it. Or if you are cutting stencils of letters of the alphabet, the solid area of a P or an O, for example, may fall out. In order to hold the elements together, you can leave narrow strips of the stencil paper uncut. These strips are called *bridges* or *ties* (see Figure 11-1).

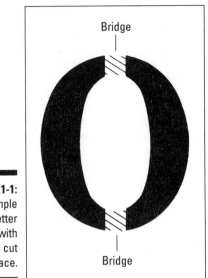

Figure 11-1:
An example
of the letter
"O" with
bridges cut
in place.

To create a round stencil such as the letter O, you must keep the center piece intact. To do this, cut the O in segments separated by ½-inch bridges that are not cut. These bridges hold the stencil together and create part of the design.

Using two-color stencils

If two or more colors touch, having a stencil for each color is a good idea. For example, if you have a red flower with a green stem and leaves, first cut a flower stencil without the stem and leaves. Then cut a stem-and-leaf stencil without the flower. When you stencil with two colors, make sure that you align each stencil properly in relation to the other stencil on your object. You can ensure correct placement of your stencils by using register marks (see the next section).

Matching up register marks

Register marks help you match up each element of the stencil design. For example, when cutting a stencil for a second color, cut out part of the elements from the stencil for the first color. Those parts that are repeated on each stencil are called *register marks,* and they help you get the parts of the design in the exact position you want them.

For example, suppose that you have a floral stencil design in two colors, red for the petals and green for the stem and leaves. In that case, you cut out part of the design of the red stencil — such as two petals of the flower — in the green stencil as well. Figure 11-2 shows the flower stencil on the left and the stem-and-leaves stencil, with two of the flower petals also cut, on the right. After you stencil the first color (the petals of the flower), position the second stencil (the stem and leaves) in place on the object. Because you have cut out elements from the red stencil onto the green stencil, you can use the petals to guide your placement of the green stencil.

This technique ensures perfect placement of each element of the design. Your stencil will be in register each time you repeat the design. Without the register marks, you can't tell exactly where to place the design on the second stencil.

If the colors touch, remember to cover that part of the flower when stenciling the stem and leaves. Simply mask it out by taping a piece of paper over the "register" area of the stencil.

Figure 11-2:
Cut out two petals of the flower in the stem-and-leaf stencil to serve as register marks.

Creating a stencil border

A repeat design is often used as decoration to create borders around the top of walls and around wainscoting, windows, and floors. Borders can be narrow or wide, geometric or floral. Or you may prefer a continuous band interrupted regularly by another design, or individual, repeated spot designs that create a border effect. You can also achieve a border effect with a series of individual shapes, such as ducks or teddy bears, evenly spaced around the walls of a child's room.

When stenciling a border design, the stencil needs register marks (see the preceding section) so that you can match up the continuing design. To establish register marks, cut part of the design to the right and left of the central cutout, as shown in Figure 11-3. As you continue to stencil, place the design on your surface to the right or left of the previous application so that the register mark is over the matching stencil you have just completed. When repeating the second stencil, don't stencil the cutout register marks on either side of it. This way, you keep a continuous design in perfect balance and evenly spaced throughout the project.

Figure 11-3:
Border
stencil
design with
registration
cut-outs on
right and
left.

If you're stenciling a border design, use a strip of masking tape to create a straight line, above which you stencil the design. After you finish, remove the tape to reveal your perfectly straight border — or at least as straight as your masking tape!

Save and reuse that stencil copy!

After you have cut a stencil design, make a copy for future use. Tape the cutout stencil design to plain white paper and, using a pencil, draw around the inside of each cutout area. You can then tape this design copy to your surface with masking tape to get an idea of how the stencil will look.

Mixing paints

If you can't find the exact color paint you want, mixing any shade of color is easy, but it takes a bit of trial and error. A palette knife is useful for blending acrylic paint on a flat dish or small saucer. However, you can use any flat utensil, such as a butter knife, a Popsicle-type stick, or a putty knife, for mixing. If you're mixing several different colors, use a separate paper plate for each color.

To mix a pastel color, for example, squirt about 1 tablespoon of white acrylic paint onto the plate. To this, add the tiniest spot of color. Blend the paints until no streaks of white or color are visible. Add more of the color, a tiny bit at a time, blending well after each addition, until you get the color you want. Then mix enough paint to finish the project. If you run out of paint in the middle of a project, remixing and matching the originally mixed color is difficult, especially after the paint is dry.

When stenciling a large item, place a wet paper towel over the dish of paint to keep it from drying out.

Putting brush to paint

The biggest mistake you can make when stenciling is putting too much paint on your brush. If the brush is too overloaded with paint, the paint seeps under the stencil, causing the edges of your design to be fuzzy rather than crisp and sharp. The center of the stencil will be heavy with color, which is not desirable.

Follow these steps for a successful stenciling project:

1. **Position the stencil on the object to be stenciled and tape the sheet at each corner so that it doesn't slip.**

2. **Dip the brush into the paint, holding your brush in an upright position so that the paint coats the end bristles evenly. Tap the brush up and down on newspaper several times to remove all excess paint.**

   The paint should go on almost dry. A dry brush achieves a clean, sharp design. I can't emphasize this advice enough. Using an almost-dry brush is the most important key to a successful stencil, yet it's the hardest technique for a beginner to understand. The paint on your brush should feel dry to the touch.

3. **Hold the brush perpendicular to the surface you're stenciling and tap the paint onto the area to be stenciled, as shown in Figure 11-4.**

   This repeated tapping motion is called *stippling*. If you use this hard pounce, the paint from the nearly-dry brush covers the area inside the stencil, and you avoid smearing and bleeding under the stencil. If you need to add more paint to the stencil, repeat Steps 2 and 3.

4. **Let the paint dry on an area and then apply another coat if needed.**

5. **After you have completed one stencil design, carefully lift the stencil sheet to check the design.**

   When stenciling a repeat design, such as a border around a room or a row of the same flowers across a dresser, wait after stenciling one design onto the surface to let this design dry thoroughly before moving the stencil sheet to the next area to be stenciled. If paint gets on the underside of your stencils, be sure to clean the stencil before putting it back in place for another round so that the paint doesn't smear the surface on which you're stenciling.

6. **If you're using a two-color stencil, apply one color to all appropriate areas before moving on to the next color.**

   Apply the light color first, followed by the darker color.

   Save a little paint of each color for possible touch-ups.

7. **For each succeeding color, place the appropriate stencil on the surface to be stenciled with register marks in place. Use a new or clean brush for each color and continue to stencil.**

   When you peel the stencil sheet away for the last time, you will be amazed. The design will be crisply executed, inspiring you to do more.

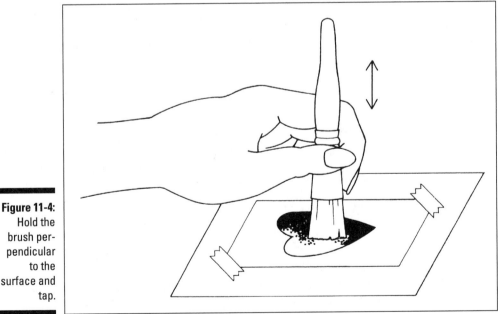

Figure 11-4:
Hold the brush perpendicular to the surface and tap.

Always clean your brush in warm water (or thinner) and be sure that it is thoroughly dry before using it again. I often put my brushes on a radiator or in the sun to dry. A hair dryer also speeds up the drying time. Never let paint dry on the brush.

Correcting mistakes

Use a damp sponge to wipe away any mistakes immediately, while the paint is wet. Small errors like rough edges are not a problem. With stenciling, the eye adjusts to the overall design, not the little details that you see when working on a small area.

Stenciling fabric

Because you can stencil almost any fabric, the possibilities are extensive. For example, you can stencil curtains to match a wall or furniture pattern. You can stencil fabric to make pillows or upholstery, a tablecloth, napkins, wall hangings, and clothing.

Acrylic paint is the easiest to work with for the best results on fabric. You can also use specially-made fabric paint.

Unlike stenciling on a painted surface, you can't correct your mistakes when stenciling on fabric.

Follow these steps to successfully paint on fabric:

1. **Before stenciling, wash the fabric, dry it to slightly damp, and then iron it.**

   Prewashing the fabric removes any *sizing* (a printing chemical), and if the fabric is going to shrink, it will do so before you stencil it.

2. **Pad your work surface with several layers of newspaper or a blotter and then tape the fabric to the surface so that it is taut.**

   If there are two layers of fabric on top of the newspaper, be sure to place more newspaper or a blotter in between the layers of fabric to prevent paint from seeping through the top layer and being absorbed by the bottom layer.

3. **Use the same stippling motion that you use on a hard surface (see the steps in "Putting brush to paint").**

   Remember to tap off all excess paint from your brush. If the brush is too wet with paint, the design becomes heavy and blurred. Using an almost-dry brush ensures your success and keeps the fabric soft and pliable, rather than stiff, where the designs appear.

As you approach the edge of the stencil, tap inward, away from the edge, so that your color is evenly placed.

4. **Apply the colors in sequence (light colors before dark) for each design as instructed for the project.**

   Before you move the fabric to stencil another area, place clean blotter paper or newspapers under the fabric so that excess paint doesn't come through from the underside.

As on hard surfaces, acrylic paint dries on fabric almost immediately and is colorfast. After you apply acrylic paint to the fabric, you can wash the fabric without fear that the color will fade or run. Fabric paints, however, must be *set* to make them colorfast. You can set fabric paint with a warm, dry iron. Place a dry cloth over the design and iron over it for three to five minutes.

Stenciling Snowflake Wrapping Paper

A one-color stencil design is the easiest to cut and apply. You can use the snowflake design that I provide in Figure 11-5 to create your own wrapping paper. Check out the color section of this book for examples.

You begin by creating an overall design on a roll of ordinary shelf paper or *kraft paper,* the kind of paper you use for mailing packages. Or you can choose pretty wrapping paper with a small, overall background pattern on which to apply the snowflake design. You don't have to use white paint just because snowflakes are white. You can use red or green paint on white paper for a holiday wrapping. For help with basic stenciling techniques, refer to the sections "Preparing to Stencil" and "Putting brush to paint," earlier in this chapter.

Tools and Materials:

Basic craft kit (see the Cheat Sheet at the front of this book)

Newspaper

Tracing paper and pencil

Stencil paper

Snowflake stencil design (in Figure 11-5)

Plain shelf paper or kraft paper

Small stencil brush

White acrylic paint

Small dish or paper plate

1. **Cover your worktable with newspaper.**

2. **Prepare your work surface for cutting the stencil (see "Other essential items," earlier in this chapter).**

3. **Trace the snowflake design. Use the tracing to cut out each element of the stencil, according to the directions in "Cutting a stencil," earlier in this chapter.**

Figure 11-5:
The snowflake design is a one-color stencil.

4. **Spread the wrapping paper out flat on a hard surface and tape each corner down.**

5. **Position the stencil in one top corner to begin stenciling the design in a random pattern over the paper.**

6. **Squirt a small amount of white paint onto a dish or plate, dip the brush into the paint, and then tap the brush to remove the excess paint, as described in the section "Putting brush to paint," earlier in this chapter.**

7. **Apply the paint to the stencil design as described in "Putting brush to paint."**

8. **Let the paint dry and then move the stencil to the next area and continue to stencil the designs all over the paper background.**

Stenciling a Snowflake Box

You can also stencil the snowflake design on a small box, which is an easy way to create a special gift. Craft stores carry all sorts of boxes in different shapes and sizes. Boxes for crafting are made of wood, paper, and tin, which are all fine materials for a stencil project. See the photo of a blue box with a white snowflake stencil in the color section of this book.

Tools and Materials:

Basic craft kit (see the Cheat Sheet at the front of this book)

Newspaper

Acrylic paint in a background color for the box, such as blue

Acrylic paint in a contrasting color for the stencil design, such as white

Sponge paintbrush

Small dish or paper plate

Tracing paper and pencil

Stencil paper

Snowflake stencil design (in Figure 11-5)

Small stencil brush

1. **Cover your worktable with newspaper.**

2. **Paint all exterior sides of the box with blue acrylic paint and sponge brush. Let the paint dry thoroughly.**

3. **Prepare your work surface for cutting the stencil (see "Other essential items," earlier in this chapter).**

4. **Trace the snowflake design. Use the tracing to cut out each element of the stencil, according to the directions in the section "Cutting a stencil," earlier in this chapter.**

5. **Tape the cutout stencil firmly in position on one area of the box.**

6. **Refer back to Steps 4 through 7 of the preceding project to complete the box.**

   When stenciling the design on the box, you can make the design interesting with the placement of the snowflakes. For example, you might stencil a snowflake in such a way on the box so that it goes from the top to the front, or the top to the side, instead of stenciling one design on the top and another on each side and front.

7. **When the box is completely stenciled and the paint is dry, you can finish the inside of the box with a coat of paint (blue or white) Or you can line the box with pretty wrapping paper, wallpaper, or self-adhesive paper (find the how-to in Chapter 5).**

Stenciling a Leaf-and-Berry Box

A two-color stencil requires cutting two separate stencils, one for each color of the design. After you cut the stencils, you can use them to make a variety of projects. The green and red leaf-and-berry design, shown in Figure 11-6, makes a nice decoration on a box, shown in the color section of this book. For help with basic stenciling techniques, refer to the section "Preparing to Stencil," earlier in this chapter.

Figure 11-6:
The leaf-
and-berry
design is a
two-color
stencil.

Tools and Materials:

Basic craft kit (see the Cheat Sheet at the front of this book)

Wooden box, approximately 5 x 6 inches

White and green acrylic paint for painting the box

Leaf-and-berry stencil design (from Figure 11-6)

Newspaper

Tracing paper and pencil

Fine-point marker

Stencil paper

Hole punch

Stencil brushes

Dish or plate for the paint

1. **Paint the top of the box white and paint the sides of the box green. Let the paint dry thoroughly.**

2. **Trace or make a photocopy of the design. Tape the design to your cutting surface and tape the stencil paper over the design.**

3. **Use the craft knife to cut out all stems and leaves, but not the berries.**

4. **Tape another piece of stencil paper over the first one. Create register marks by tracing over two leaves on opposite sides of the design. Mark an X on the stencil paper over every berry design. Remove the second piece of stencil paper.**

5. **Using the hole punch, punch out every X to make the berry holes.**

   The design is small enough for the hole punch to reach all the berries if you trim the stencil paper around the entire design.

6. **Tape the leaf/stem stencil in position on top of the box. Stencil all leaves and stems with the green paint. Let the paint dry thoroughly.**

   Clean the brush with warm water and let the brush dry, or use another brush for the second color stencil.

7. **Position the berry stencil over the leaf design so that the register marks match up (see "Matching up register marks," earlier in this chapter) and tape it down. Stencil the berries with red paint. Let the paint dry thoroughly.**

8. **Finish the box by painting the interior or lining it with pretty wrapping paper or wallpaper that coordinates with the design and color of the stencil (see Chapter 5 for hints on lining a box with paper).**

   You can also use the leaf-and-berry stencil to decorate a plain white greeting card — buy blank cards with matching envelopes in stationery stores. Or stencil a piece of plain paper for framing, as you might do with a painting, and buy a mat and frame to fit your finished stencil design. Both of these projects are shown in the color section of this book.

Five Easy Pieces

Personalizing any gift or home accessory with a stencil design or saying is an easy project. Add a decorative touch to a tiled trivet, an old-fashioned salt box, wooden boxes, or a breadboard to hang on the kitchen wall. I use typical country symbols for these projects (see the photo in the color section of this book), but you can find precut designs in a variety of styles and subjects to suit your home decorating style and taste.

For help with basic stenciling techniques for any of the projects in this section, refer to the section "Preparing to Stencil," earlier in this chapter.

Stenciling tiles

In this very easy stencil project, you can decorate inexpensive ceramic tiles, such as those found in tile shops and used in bathrooms or as a backsplash in the kitchen. If you buy a plain tile trivet (sold in gift shops, kitchen stores, and home centers), you can stencil the tiles to create your own expensive-looking trivet with delicate floral stencils. See a photograph of my finished trivet in the color section. The trivet I made has four 4-inch tiles set in a wood frame; however, you can find one-tile trivets as well.

This project is a delightful and practical gift that takes only minutes to stencil. The acrylic paint adheres to tile as well as to most other surfaces. Decorate each tile with a pattern of five repeats of the flower, cut as one stencil to position on one tile (see Figure 11-7). Stencil each flower in one color; the flowers are far enough apart so that you don't need to mask out or cut separate stencils. Personalize the color scheme for your own home or the home of the recipient.

The instructions for the project call for soft gray, pastel pink, and pale green paints. If you can't find soft gray, add a drop of black paint to a tablespoon of white paint and combine with a palette knife or other utensil (see the section "Mixing paints") until the color is consistent. You can soften any color in this way. If you can't find a pastel pink paint, for example, mix red with white, and mix green with white if you can't find pale green.

You also can use the floral stencil as a repeat pattern to create a border on a piece of furniture, as an overall pattern on the top of a small night table, or across the front of dresser drawers. Or use the stencil design to decorate a plain lampshade.

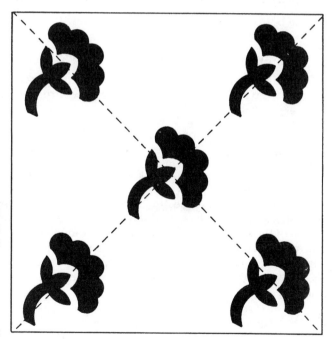

Figure 11-7:
Use this floral stencil to decorate white ceramic tiles.

Tools and Materials:

Basic craft kit (see the Cheat Sheet at the front of this book)

4-inch glazed or unglazed tile or trivet

Tracing paper

Stencil paper

Stencil brushes (one for each paint color or, if using one brush, wash thoroughly between paint colors)

Pale green, pastel pink, and soft gray acrylic paints

Paper plates or shallow dishes (one for each paint color)

1. Trace the complete design (all five elements) shown in Figure 11-7. The dotted lines in the figure are for positioning the stencil on one 4-inch tile.

2. Tape the stencil paper on top of the tracing and place both on a cutting surface. Cut out the stencils.

3. Position the stencil on one tile and tape it down at each corner.

4. The top left and bottom right corner designs are green. Stencil these first, using a small amount of pale green paint on your brush.

5. Stencil the bottom left and top right corner stencils with pale pink paint.

6. Stipple the gray paint onto the center flower stencil.

7. If you're stenciling more than one tile, remove the stencil and position it on the next tile. Continue until all the tiles are complete.

All-purpose boxes

You can use the stencil designs shown in Figures 11-8 and 11-9 to decorate a variety of objects. When used on 5- and 8-inch boxes, the designs fill the area nicely (see the photo in the color section of this book) and demonstrate how you can position a stencil design so that it flows from the top to the front of an object. Both of the stencil designs for this project involve two colors that touch. These projects give you a chance to practice cutting and stenciling separate elements to make up one image. After you master a simple stencil project, you can apply the same principles to a piece of furniture with a more elaborate design.

Stenciled boxes are good bazaar sellers and are easy and fun to make. You can paint the inside of the boxes or line each one with pretty paper or fabric.

Figure 11-8:
Tomato
stencil
design for
all-purpose
boxes.

Figure 11-9:
Berry
stencil
design for
all-purpose
boxes.

Tools and Materials:

Basic craft kit (see the Cheat Sheet at the front of this book)

Wood, tin, or paper box

Yellow, red, and green acrylic paint (if you're using the tomato design)

Lavender, green, and purple acrylic paint (if you're using the berry design)

Gift wrap, self-adhesive paper, or wallpaper (use to line the boxes)

Saucers or paper plates (one for each paint color)

Hole punch (for berry stencil)

Newspaper

Tracing paper and pencil

Stencil paper

1-inch paint brush

3 stencil brushes (one for each paint color)

1. **If you're using the tomato design, paint the box yellow inside and out. If you plan to line the box, paint only the inside rim. If you're using the berry design, paint the box lavender in the same way. Set aside to dry.**

2. **Trace each stencil design. Tape the tracing to a piece of stencil paper and place it on a cutting surface.**

   Because each design is a two-color stencil, you need to cut two stencils for each design — one for the green leaves and another for the berries or tomato. Use the hole punch to cut out the berries from the stencil paper.

3. **Make two separate tracings of each design to use as a placement guide.**

4. **Begin by using the uncut tracing of each stem-and-leaf design to position your stencil.**

   To do this, place the tracing on top of the box so that half of the design is on the top of the box and half of the design is on the front of the box (see the photo in the color section for positioning.) Crease the paper on the top edge so that it stays in position temporarily.

5. **Place the stem-and-leaf stencil for each design over the tracing in position on the box and carefully remove the tracing paper from underneath.**

6. **Tape the stencil to the box.**

7. **Squirt a small amount of green paint onto a flat dish or saucer. Stipple the paint onto the cutout area. Let the paint dry.**

8. **Replace the tracing in position as a guide for registering the second stencil. Place the second stencil over the tracing, carefully remove the tracing paper, and tape down the stencil.**

9. **Using the red paint, complete the tomato stencil design or, using the purple paint, complete the berry design. Let the paint dry.**

10. **Measure all the interior sides and the bottom of the box. Cut out the paper pieces (you can use gift wrap, self-adhesive paper, or wallpaper).**

11. **Using white craft glue, first affix the paper to the sides. (If you're using self-adhesive paper, you don't need glue.) If any excess paper extends beyond the top rim, you can trim this excess paper with a craft knife after the glue is dry.**

12. **Set the bottom piece in last.**

Kitchen plaque

Express yourself with a stenciled breadboard (shown in the color section of this book) that can serve as an attractive decorative accent for your kitchen.

This project calls for stencil letters, which come precut in many styles and sizes and are available in most art stores and home centers. Sheets of stencil letters are often sold for making signs. You can find breadboards in hardware stores and home centers, or you can use a wooden plaque, available in a variety of sizes at craft stores.

The size of the letters and the number of words in a saying determine the design. If you use graph paper to plan the layout, you can figure out the best way to stencil a saying on any size object. For this project, you stencil "Home is where the heart is" on the plaque, along with hearts. The heart stencil pattern is shown in Figure 11-10, and the layout for the plaque is shown in Figure 11-11. You enlarge the pattern 240 percent to fit the breadboard. The easiest way to enlarge the pattern is with a copy machine. If that option isn't open to you, find out how to enlarge a pattern manually in Chapter 3.

Figure 11-10:
This heart pattern is shown actual size.

Figure 11-11: Enlarge this pattern 240 percent for the layout.

Tools and Materials:

Basic craft kit (see the Cheat Sheet at the front of this book)

Breadboard or wooden plaque

Tracing paper and pencil

Precut stencil letters

Stencil paper

1-inch paintbrush

Stencil brushes

Yellow, red, deep blue, and green acrylic paints

4 saucers or paper plates (one for each paint color)

1. Using the 1-inch brush, paint the front surface of the breadboard with yellow acrylic paint. Let the paint dry; give the breadboard a second coat of paint if needed.

2. Paint the rim all around with green paint. Let the green paint dry. Apply a second coat if needed.

3. Make a rough sketch of your design by drawing the outline of the breadboard on tracing paper. Then draw the words through the stencil letters in position on the tracing paper to make up each line of the saying.

4. **Draw a light pencil line down the center of the board. Beginning with the line for the upside-down heart (refer to Figure 11-11), draw light horizontal pencil lines evenly spaced for each line of the saying.**

   Or you can place six strips of masking tape, evenly spaced, above which you can stencil each word.

5. **Count the number of letters in each word, divide by two, and space them accordingly to the right and left of the penciled center line.**

   Because letters can vary in width, spacing the letters perfectly can be difficult. However, you probably can adjust the spacing fairly accurately by eyeballing it, ending up with what looks like a perfect design.

6. **Begin with the letter O. Hold the stencil to the left of the vertical line, resting on the second horizontal line (refer to Figure 11-11).**

7. **Stencil the letter with deep blue paint. Let the paint dry.**

8. **Place the letter M to the right of the vertical line, opposite the O, and stencil as you did the O.**

9. **Continue to stencil the rest of the saying. Every other line of type is green, alternating with deep blue.**

   Stencil letters may require touch-ups. Save the paint until the project is finished. Place a wet paper towel over the dish to keep the paint from drying out.

10. **Trace the heart design in Figure 11-10.**

11. **Tape the stencil paper over the tracing on a cutting surface and cut out the heart with a craft knife.**

    A rounded design, such as the heart shape, is hard to make perfectly smooth. However, when you stencil the heart, it looks perfect even if it isn't.

12. **Refer to Figure 11-11 and, using red paint, stencil a heart on each side of the center line as shown. Stencil two more hearts to the left and right of the first two stenciled hearts, as shown in the figure.**

13. **Turn the heart stencil upside down and stencil one heart in the center of the top line on the board, as shown in Figure 11-11.**

Salt box

In colonial times, people kept their salt in a small box hanging in the kitchen. The stenciled decoration on this project (see the photo in the color section) reflects the colonial practice of decorating small pieces. The familiar school-house design, shown in Figure 11-12, is often used for quilt appliques and is quite fitting for this wooden object, which is a readily available reproduction of the original. You can use this accessory — a nice country accent in a kitchen — to hold sea salt, matchbooks, garlic, and other dry spices.

Figure 11-12:
School-
house
design for
salt box
stencil.

Craft stores and hobby mail-order supply catalogs carry salt boxes made of raw wood, ready for paint.

Tools and Materials:

Basic craft kit (see the Cheat Sheet at the front of this book)

Small wooden box

Newspaper

Tracing paper and pencil

Stencil paper

1-inch paintbrush

Pink, blue, and yellow acrylic paints (or colors of your choice)

Stencil brushes

Saucers or paper plates (one for each paint color)

1. Using the 1-inch paintbrush, paint the box pink. Let the paint dry and then apply a second coat if needed.

2. Trace the schoolhouse design in Figure 11-12.

3. Tape the stencil paper over each tracing on a work surface and cut out the schoolhouse shapes, but not the window squares. Make register marks on the stencil so that you can position the windows.

4. Remove the stencil sheets and tracings. Using the register marks as a guide, cut a second stencil of the windows, in position, as they appear on the schoolhouse.

5. Center the schoolhouse stencil on the top of the box and tape it in position.

6. Stipple blue paint onto the background until you fill in the area. Remove the stencil.

7. Center the schoolhouse stencil on the front of the box, aligned under the stencil on the top of the box. Apply paint as you did for the stencil on the top.

8. Center the schoolhouse stencil on the side of the box and apply the paint. Repeat this step on the opposite side of the box. Let the paint dry.

9. Place the window stencil in position on the stenciled schoolhouse on the top of the box. Be sure that it's centered correctly.

10. Apply a small amount of yellow paint to each of the three cutout areas for the windows.

11. Repeat Step 9 on the front and sides of the box.

Painted Dresser

In this project, you apply a faux finish to a ready-to-finish dresser with a sponging technique (see Chapter 12) and stencil the drawers with precut stencils (see the photo in the color section). The graceful bow and ribbons, combined with the rose garland that I use, create a feminine design. You can choose from many different stencil designs for a project like this. Select the designs that appeal to you and that fit with your interior decor. The background paint color I use is soft pink, the bows are blue, and the roses are stenciled with dusty rose.

Tools and Materials:

Basic craft kit (see the Cheat Sheet at the front of this book)

1 ready-to-finish dresser

1 quart pale pink latex or enamel paint (or the color of your choice)

2-inch-wide paintbrush

1 pint pale gray water-based glaze

Natural sponge

Light blue, dark blue, green, and pale rose acrylic paints

Stencil brushes

Precut stencil designs (I used ribbon/bow and flower garland from Plaid Enterprises for this project)

Water-based varnish (optional for protective finish)

1. Paint the entire dresser with pink latex or enamel paint. Let the paint dry and apply a second coat.

2. Mix one part glaze with three parts paint to create a sponge-texture background (see Chapter 12 for application directions). Let the glaze dry.

   If you don't want a sponged background, the painted dresser is ready to accept the stencil design.

3. Position the bow stencil in the center of the first drawer front and tape down each corner of the stencil.

4. Apply the light blue paint onto the cutout stencil area. Repeat with the dark blue for the second bow color.

5. Repeat Steps 3 and 4 on all drawer fronts. Let the paint dry.

6. Position the vine stencil on one side of the bow and, using the green paint, stencil the design onto the dresser. Repeat on the other side of the bow.

7. Repeat Step 6 on all drawer fronts.

8. When all the vine stencils are dry, position and tape down the stencil for the roses. Apply the pale rose paint. Repeat on all drawer fronts.

9. (Optional) To protect the painted surface of the dresser, brush on a coat of clear, water-based varnish in a satin or semigloss finish. (See Chapter 9 for more information on applying varnish.)

Chapter 12

Faux Finishing

• •

In This Chapter

▶ Mastering various decorative paint finishes

▶ Decorating furniture like a pro

• •

*T*he technique of applying decorative finishes to furniture has a long history both in this country and Europe. It's an excellent way to give an ordinary piece of furniture a touch of class. Crafters have developed techniques for faking many finishes such as marble, tortoiseshell, and bamboo.

Decorative painting can mean various faux finishes or may indicate a faux finish with a stencil or freehand design painted on top of it. Many pieces of folk furniture and accessories, for example, are valued for the painted designs created by the person who built the chair or table. These craftspeople were not necessarily artists, but this fact did not prevent them from adding a simple painted design to their handiwork. Favorite designs are simple flowers or vines, repetitive borders of brush strokes, and even random squiggles of different colors.

Freehand decorative designs can be applied on top of a faux finish background for added interest and a bit of whimsy. For example, a little flower motif may be just the thing to add interest to the back slats of a sponge-painted chair. It's easy to paint a two-color checkerboard pattern on top of a table, draw a winding ivy vine around a mirror frame, or add a random pattern of colorful polka dots over a child's bureau.

Faux Finishing

If you have never tried faux finishing before, you have an advantage: Tradition or convention does not restrict you from experimenting. The basis of decorative painting is the freedom to try out different ways to achieve a look that you think is pretty. The description of how to do each technique is a guide rather than a rule. When you know the basic techniques, developing your own way of doing things is easy.

The most important element of decorative painting is color selection, which is a highly personal decision. If you like the color, then the color is perfect for the project.

When adding a decorative design to a piece, choose colors that reflect the wallpaper or other items in the room for a coordinated look.

Faux finishing projects require the following basic equipment:

- ✔ Disposable paper or plastic plates to hold the paint or glaze
- ✔ Thin latex gloves
- ✔ Newspaper to protect your work surface
- ✔ Paper towels
- ✔ A sink or pail of water to clean sponges and brushes

You need all these basic items on hand when you tackle any of the projects in this chapter.

Sponging, stippling, and spattering

Although the three techniques that I describe in this section — sponging, stippling, and spattering — may sound rather ordinary, they can produce elegant results. All three techniques empower you with the ability to achieve a soft, multicolored surface of great depth.

Sponging on and off

Sponging with sea sponges (see Chapter 10) is the easiest, quickest, and most fun of all the faux finishing techniques. For example, an easy sponging combination is a base coat of one color with two colors of glaze sponged over it.

Note: Although the colors in this example are different, they belong in the same family. No one color should overpower the others. Glazes are subtle, so the effect is soft.

Follow these steps for successful sponging on:

1. **Apply a base coat of a pale color such as beige or ecru with a regular paintbrush. If you're painting a wall, apply the base coat with a roller.**

2. **Dampen and squeeze dry a sea sponge.**

3. **To apply the first glaze color, dip the sponge in the glaze (medium green, for example) and sponge it off on a newspaper to remove the excess glaze.**

   Check out Chapter 10 for more information on glazes — and a recipe for making glaze.

4. **Sponge the surface in a random pattern.**

   To avoid an even pattern, continually turn the sponge in different directions as you sponge the surface. (Don't turn the sponge when it is on the surface or you will smear the glaze). Sponge the entire surface, allowing the background color to show through here and there.

5. **Allow the glaze to dry (it dries quickly) before sponging on the next color.**

6. **Gently sponge the second glaze (blue-green works well in this example) over the entire surface, leaving open areas here and there.**

   You need a clean sponge for each color. Either use a separate sponge or rinse the sponge thoroughly in warm water between paint colors.

7. **Stand back and study what you have done. You will immediately think, "I need a little more color here and here."**

8. **Continue to sponge on color until the surface looks good to you.**

9. **When the second color is dry, go back and sponge more with the first color glaze — if you want to. That's the fun of sponging.**

10. **Continue to add more of whichever color you think is needed until you think you're done.**

An alternative to sponging on is sponging off. This technique is a little trickier.

1. **Apply the base coat of a pale color such as ecru, following the technique in the first step of the preceding set of steps.**

2. **Use a paintbrush to apply the glaze (medium green, for example) to the surface.**

3. **Dampen a clean sea sponge and wring it out so that the sponge is almost dry.**

4. **Sponge off the glaze using the same technique as in Step 4 of the preceding steps.**

   The sponge becomes covered with glaze while sponging it off. Wash and wring out the sponge often during the process.

5. **Continue to sponge off the glaze until you achieve an overall subtly textured pattern.**

Stippling

Stippling is another name for *pouncing,* which is a fancy way to describe tapping the ends of brush bristles up and down over a glazed surface to create a textured or mottled finish. Stippling gives depth and texture to a glazed surface. The stippling brush, which looks like a giant toothbrush, is designed to produce this effect. Stippling is a tedious technique to do on large areas, so I recommend that you use it only on small, smooth surfaces without blemishes. Here's how stippling is done:

1. **Paint a base coat of a light color.**

2. **When the base coat is dry, paint the surface with a darker-color glaze.**

3. **While the glaze is still wet, use the stippling brush to make gentle up-and-down pouncing motions over the wet, glazed surface.**

   The goal is to produce a blended texture of colors. The more stippling, the lighter and more subtle the result becomes.

To clean the stippling brush, simply rinse it in warm water.

Spattering

Spattering is the technique of applying tiny flecks of contrasting paint colors to achieve an overall field of color. Spattering different colors over one another achieves an effect similar to what you see in a *pointillist* painting, which is made up of little dots of paint. The farther away from the painting you get, the more the dots seem blended together.

I recommend a small-size project for spatter painting for two reasons:

✔ Completing a large spatter project takes a long time.

✔ Spattering is messy, so you need to protect a large area around the project (with newspaper or a drop cloth) to prevent paint flecks from getting on everything. If possible, do it outdoors.

If you want to try spattering, follow these steps:

1. **Paint a base coat of your choice and let it dry.**

2. **Spatter the paint by using the tool appropriate for the job.**

   For a small project, such as the seat of a chair, you can rub your thumb (toward you) over a toothbrush to spatter the paint (away from you and onto the chair seat). For larger projects, such as a floor, use a 1-inch stiff bristle brush for the spatter painting and a brush handle against which to smack the spatter brush. Each time you hit the stick, flecks of paint fly onto the painted surface. The distance between the brush and the surface and the texture of the paint determine the size and shape of the flecks.

Ragging, dragging, and combing

Creating patterned, lined, and striped textured surfaces by ragging, dragging, and combing is easy. The textures can be hard-edged and strong, or imperfect and subtle, depending on the colors you choose and the way you employ the technique. Choose your style. Imperfect sounds good to me.

Suggested spattering color combinations

Different combinations of paint colors result in different results. Here are some suggested ways to combine paint colors for different looks.

Complementary colors: Paint a bright blue base color and spatter over it with green paint. The colors blend in a vibrant way. Do the same with green and yellow; yellow and orange; orange and red; red and purple; or purple and blue.

Contrasting colors: A traditional spattering color scheme is a Chinese red base coat spattered with black. A country style combination is a white base coat spattered with medium blue. A rich look is obtained with a deep green base coat spattered with bright red.

Soft colors: Spattering similar shades of color over one another will achieve a subtle-looking surface. For example, try a base coat of light tan spattered with burnt sienna flecks, or a base coat of pale gray spattered with a grayish pink color.

Multiple colors: If you have a small amount of different paint colors, use them all to create a color spatter pattern. Alternate light and dark paint colors and let the specks fly. This is a terrific stress-reducing technique.

Ragging on and off

Scrunch up a rag, dip it in glaze, press it onto a painted background, and you're ragging. The best faux finishers create amazing surfaces with this humble technique. Ragging, a good technique for medium- and large-size projects, is usually done on walls. Just follow these steps:

1. **Paint the surface with a base coat and let it dry.**

2. **Dip your rag in glaze, wring out the rag, and press it onto the surface.**

   This is a trial-and-error technique. You have to press the rag on with different amounts of pressure to see which results you like best.

3. **Continually turn your rag to avoid creating an obvious pattern. Allow some of the base coat to show through to get the best effect.**

4. **From time to time, check your work from a distance to see whether the pattern is blended together.**

5. **If you want a richer finish, wait until the first coat of glaze is dry and then rag on a second glaze color.**

The opposite technique is ragging off.

1. **Apply a base coat and let it dry.**

2. **Paint an area with glaze and press the rag into the surface to remove some of the glaze.**

3. **Rinse and wring the rag out often and turn it repeatedly, using the same motions as for ragging on (see the preceding set of steps).**

   To get a lighter result, keep ragging the glaze off.

Ragging off creates a more subtle effect than ragging on.

Dragging

Dragging is just what it sounds like. When you drag a stiff-bristled brush through wet glaze, you create a pattern of coarse or fine parallel lines. Dragging is quick to do and a good technique for medium and large projects. However, dragging a wall can be difficult because keeping the lines straight can be challenging. A medium-sized project such as a tabletop or molding around a door or a cabinet is a good first project.

When using the dragging technique on walls, I recommend that two people work as a team — one can apply the glaze, and the other can drag it.

If you want to try dragging, follow these steps:

1. **Apply a medium-color base coat of paint and let the paint dry.**

2. **Use a paintbrush to apply a darker color glaze over the base coat.**

3. **Using a clean dragging brush, drag the brush down the glaze in one smooth motion in order to keep the lines straight.**

4. **Wipe the brush clean.**

5. **Continue to repeat the dragging motion over the entire surface, wiping the brush clean after each stroke.**

Dragging steel wool creates a grained effect similar to dragging with a brush. Steel wool creates a very fine pattern, whereas the dragging brush creates a bolder pattern. Use a coarse steel wool, available in hardware and paint stores.

Be sure to wear protective gloves when dragging.

Combing

Combing is a fast technique that is perfect for creating all kinds of fanciful finishes. The comb is a small tool used to create distinct patterns like simulated wood graining. You can use triangular combing tools, metal combs, cardboard or plastic combs that you make yourself (see Chapter 10), or an ordinary hair comb.

When you drag a comb down or across a wet, glaze-coated surface, you get a definite strip of lines. If you drag another strip right next to the first strip, the strips probably won't match or be identical, unless you are a world-class comber. That is why most crafters use combing to create variegated patterns.

Combing effects are intended to look rustic and handcrafted, like the designs found on many pieces of Early American furniture. Combing is the perfect technique for those who don't strive for perfection.

Use combing on small- and medium-sized projects such as boxes, side tables, dresser tops, and mirror and picture frames.

The following steps get you combing — a craft project, not your hair.

1. **Using a paintbrush, apply a base coat of paint on the surface of a project such as a wooden box. Let dry.**

2. **Apply a coat of glaze. While the glaze is wet, drag the comb in one direction (horizontal or vertical) through the glaze to create a pattern.**

3. **Allow the glaze to dry thoroughly.**

If you want a more interesting finish than one created by dragging the comb through the glaze in one direction, try the following suggestions to make interesting patterns in the glaze with the combing tool.

✔ **Crisscross pattern:** Drag the comb through the wet glaze in one direction to cover the entire surface. Then drag the comb in the opposite direction across the entire surface. If you don't like the effect, you can't go back and fix it, but you can wipe the entire crisscross away with a damp paper towel or cloth, reglaze the surface, and start again.

✔ **Curved patterns:** Use the comb to make S curves in the wet glaze, creating an effect that looks like waves. Or you can make fan-shaped curves by combing over the glaze in a half-circle motion.

✔ **Basket-weave patterns:** A square tabletop is perfect for applying a basket weave combed pattern. Divide the tabletop into four squares by marking light lines with a pencil. Apply the wet glaze and comb the first square vertically. Comb the next square horizontally. Continue alternating in this manner with the remaining squares. Stand back and admire your work.

Traditional combing is usually done with light and dark shades of similar colors, such as the colors of wood. Contemporary combing uses a broader color palette. You can achieve an exciting effect by using a bright yellow base coat with a dark red basket-weave pattern.

Color washing

Color washing is a free-form technique used for distressing a surface. The results have a rustic quality reminiscent of the walls in an old farmhouse or in the interior of an adobe house. This technique is a great way to liven up a wall surface and hide defects as well. Color washing calls for thin, almost transparent glazes that dry with the delicate tones of a watercolor painting. Here's how you do it:

1. **Apply a base coat of paint and let it dry completely.**

2. **Thin the glaze with water until it has a watery consistency.**

3. **Apply the first glaze in X patterns at random, with a broad brush. You can make these X's in a haphazard way. Neatness isn't necessary because the next color blends with this first glaze.**

   For example, if the project is a tabletop, you can paint broad X's here and there on the surface. Or you can put the glaze on in circles or cloud-like puffs. The idea is to make the glaze not look too uniform or mechanical.

4. **Feather the edges of the glaze with a softening brush.**

   A softening brush has long, soft hairs and is designed for blending colors. You can find softening brushes in hardware, paint, and craft stores.

5. **When the first glaze is slightly dry, apply the second glaze (following Step 3) over the areas not covered by the first glaze.**

6. **Smooth the edges of the second glaze with the softening brush, merging the two glazes where they overlap.**

7. **Use the first glaze again (as in Step 3) and work back over the surface, or apply a third glaze (as in Step 3) and blend in for a richer finish.**

You can use different color glazes together to create different results. Here are some ideas.

- **Bright and sunny:** Use a base coat of pale green glaze with buttercup yellow and deep gold.

- **Rich and leathery:** Start with a base coat of deep ochre, followed by burnt sienna and then burnt umber or dark brown. The mixture of these three tones (working from light to dark) creates a deep leathery look that is perfect for a den.

- **Cool and crisp:** For a lively, fresh look, paint a surface with a base coat of white with a dash of green. Color wash with a glaze of medium cobalt blue and then a glaze of darker Prussian blue.

Faux graining

Early American chairs were often made from more than one type of wood and couldn't be stained to look like a chair made from fine wood. So the furniture maker used a graining technique to make the finish into "oak" or "cherry." The graining technique was not always convincing, but despite that fact, or maybe because of it, rustic grained chairs are valued collectibles today.

If you look at professional graining, you can't tell whether the wood is real or not. That type of graining is 90 percent talent and 10 percent technique. *Fantasy graining,* a term I am more comfortable with, is 50 percent technique and 50 percent fun. Graining is an extremely enjoyable activity and amazingly foolproof.

The tools for graining are the same or similar to tools for combing: plastic, rubber, or metal combs and handmade combs with varying teeth sizes. The triangular three-sided rubber comb may suffice for most types of graining. The rubber graining tool is a must if you want to show knots in the wood. Use a rubber graining tool by dragging it down the surface in a rocking motion. The result is a strip of grained wood with a knot in the middle.

If you are trying to fake the look of something real, like wood, it helps to have the real thing in front of you while you work. If you look at a piece of pine, cherry, oak, or other wood, you notice that there is very little difference between the dark and light parts of the wood. Therefore, try to match the background color and the color used to create the pattern of wood grain as closely as possible.

1. **Paint the base coat on a surface and let it dry completely.**

2. **Paint the glaze over the base coat.**

3. **Pull your comb or other tool down the surface, thus creating lines similar to the real wood.**

Try different colors to create truly fantastic finishes. For dramatic effects on small projects, use purple glaze over an orange base, or pastel green paint over pink glaze, or black glaze over a blue base. The wildest color combinations become quite pretty when combined with a graining technique.

Faux marble

Using paint to reproduce the look of real marble is a challenge, even for an accomplished artist. However, many amateurs have been trying their hands at faux finishing, and these personal interpretations have become popular, even with interior designers. So even if you think that you are all thumbs, try the faux marbling technique. It's a lot of fun.

By looking at real marble or photographs of marble, you can see that marble can appear white, green, reddish black, or other colors. If you study a marble surface, you notice that it has depth, and it looks as if there are layers of color and texture.

Items that often are made of marble, such as small tabletops, bowls, boxes, and other accessories, make good projects for marbleizing.

Follow these general steps for marbleizing:

1. **Using a paintbrush or foam brush, paint the surface of an object to be marbleized with a base coat of latex paint and let it dry.**

2. **Pour about 2 teaspoons of paint onto a paper plate. Add 2 teaspoons of clear acrylic medium and mix together to make the glaze. Add a couple drops of water if the mixture needs thinning.**

3. **Study your picture of marble. Notice both the color and pattern of the veins.**

4. **Dip the point of an artist's brush or turkey feather (see Chapter 10) into the glaze and then drag it lightly across the painted surface. Manipulate the point of the brush as you drag to simulate the thin and thick parts of veins.**

Veins are characteristic of marble and vary a great deal. They can be dark or light, and solid, translucent, or transparent.

Decorative Furniture Projects

Ready-to-finish furniture is perfect for a decorative finish. You don't have to remove old paint from the surface before you begin. If you don't mind the extra work involved in cleaning up an old piece, yard sales, auctions, and flea markets offer more unusual furniture. Or look through the classified ads for a piece of old furniture that you can transform into something new and better than the original.

Faux marble side table

The faux marble side table shown in the color section has a faux marble top and grained legs. The base color is light blue. The top of the table is 16 inches square, which is a good size for a first marbleizing project.

Be sure to have some pictures of marble surfaces handy so that you can refer to them when painting on the marble veins.

Real marble often has a glossy surface. Marble that has been in use has a low-luster sheen. Finish your project by giving the entire table a protective coating of water-based satin or semigloss varnish.

Faux marble craft kits are available in craft supply stores. These kits come in four different marble colors. A faux marble craft kit contains everything you need to complete a project like a side table — including the turkey feather.

Tools and Materials:

Small table

4 ounces pale blue paint for base coat

2 ounces medium blue paint for sponging

2 ounces clear acrylic medium

Sea sponge

Smoothing brush

2 ounces pale gray paint for veining

Artist's brush and/or turkey feather

2-inch foam brush

Protective gloves and goggles

Steel wool (coarse grade)

Water-based varnish

Varnish brush

1. **Paint the entire table with a base coat of light blue and let it dry.**

2. **Pour about 2 teaspoons of medium blue paint into a paper plate. Add 2 teaspoons of clear acrylic medium and mix together to make the glaze. Add a couple drops of water if the mixture needs thinning.**

3. **Dampen and wring out the sea sponge. Dab the sponge in the glaze mix and press it on paper towels to remove excess glaze.**

4. **Sponge the surface of the tabletop by moving your sponge in different directions to make a random pattern.**

   As you sponge, use the dry smoothing brush to soften and feather the edges of the sponged areas. Allow some base coat to show through the sponged areas.

5. **Pour 2 teaspoons of pale gray paint into a plate. Mix in 2 teaspoons of acrylic medium. Add a teaspoon (more or less) of water to thin the mixture.**

6. **Study your picture of marble. Notice both the color and pattern of the veins.**

7. **Dip the point of the artist's brush or turkey feather into the gray glaze and then drag it lightly across the glazed surface.**

   Manipulate the point as you drag to simulate the thin and thick parts of veins. Veins are characteristic of marble and vary a great deal. They can be dark or light, and solid, translucent, or transparent.

8. **In a paper plate, mix 2 tablespoons of medium blue paint with 2 tablespoons of clear acrylic glaze.**

9. **Turn the table on its side and place it on newspaper.**

10. **Using the 2-inch foam brush and the paint/glaze mixture, coat the legs and the side of the table that's facing up.**

11. **Put on protective gloves and goggles. Using a dry ball of steel wool, drag it down the length of the side of the table and continue down the table legs to create fine lines in the wet glaze.**

    To create even finer lines, drag the steel wool down the surface again.

12. **Repeat this process on all four sides of the table.**

Sponge-painted country table ensemble

See the photo of my country table ensemble in the color section of this book.

Tools and Materials:

Basic craft kit (see the Cheat Sheet at the front of this book)

Ready-to-finish country table

Fine and extra-fine sandpaper

2-inch paintbrush

White water-based paint

Medium French-blue water-based paint

Clear glaze

Sea sponge

1 large white basket (spray paint it if you need to)

Two lampshades (any color; I used black)

Stencil of a ribbon and bow design in a size to fit comfortably on the front of the table you're working on

Stencil brush

Varnish brush

Semigloss water-based varnish

1. **Prime and seal the country table (see Chapter 10). Let it dry and then sand lightly with fine sandpaper.**

2. **Using a 2-inch paintbrush, coat the table with white paint.**

3. **To make the sponging glaze, mix equal parts of blue paint and clear glaze.**

4. **Dampen the sponge and wring it out. Dip the damp sponge into the blue glaze mixture. Sponge off excess glaze onto newspaper.**

    Sponge over the entire surface of the table, leaving some of the background showing here and there.

5. **Following the directions in Step 4, sponge over the white basket and the two lampshades with the blue glaze.**

6. **If, after sponging the items with the blue glaze, you want to lighten the effect, simply sponge over the blue with a mixture of white paint and clear glaze.**

7. **Prepare to stencil the bow on the front of the drawer by locating the center point.**

To do this, measure across the front and use a pencil to draw a light vertical line to mark the center. Next, measure from top to bottom and mark the center on the vertical line. Place the center of the stencil design at this point. Tape the stencil in place.

8. **To stencil the design, refer to the section on two-color stenciling in Chapter 11.**

9. **After you complete the sponge painting and stenciling, use the varnish brush to apply a coat of water-based varnish to all surfaces.**

10. **Let the varnish dry thoroughly and smooth out the surface with the extra-fine sandpaper.**

Whimsical jelly cabinet

This jelly cabinet, shown in the color section of this book, combines different techniques — all of which are easy to do. You can apply the fanciful painted teacup design to the front panels or drawers of any cabinet. For this project, you sponge paint a yellow background with gray glaze and paint the door molding dark blue with black trim. The door panels are painted light blue. You draw the teacups on paper, decorate them with freehand painted designs, cut them out, and glue them to the front panels. As a finishing touch, glue paper doily shelf trim on the painted cabinet under each row of teacups.

Tools and Materials:

Basic craft kit (see the Cheat Sheet at the front of this book)

Jelly cabinet or cabinet with a door

Screwdriver

Primer /sealer

2-inch paintbrush

Fine and extra-fine sandpaper

Light blue water-based semigloss paint

Dark blue water-based semigloss paint

Medium-size artist's brush

Black water-based semigloss paint

Yellow water-based semigloss paint

Light gray water-based glaze

Sea sponge

Teacup pattern (in Figure 12-1)

Paper doily trim

A variety of acrylic paint colors or fine-point permanent markers for teacup decoration

Varnish brush

Water-based varnish

1. **Carefully place the jelly cabinet on its back on the floor. Use the screwdriver to remove the doorknob, the door catch, the hinges, and the door itself. Set them aside.**

2. **Using the 2-inch wide paintbrush, prime and seal the door and the rest of the cabinet according to the directions in Chapter 10. Clean the brush in water.**

3. **Using the 2-inch paintbrush, paint the door panels light blue. Clean the brush in water and then paint the door frame dark blue. Let the paint dry completely.**

4. **Using the artist's brush, apply black paint to the grooves around the door panels (if your cabinet has grooves).**

   This job is easier than it may seem at first glance. If the paint gets on the other painted surfaces, don't panic. Wait until the paint dries and retouch the messy areas.

5. **Using black paint, coat the doorknob, wooden door catch, hinges, and all screw heads.**

6. **Using the yellow paint, coat the main part of the cabinet. Let the paint dry completely.**

7. **Using the gray glaze, sponge over the entire surface of the main part of the cabinet (see the section "Sponging on and off," earlier in this chapter).**

8. **Plan the placement of the teacups by measuring and dividing the area on the door into three parts for the three "shelves" of teacups. (Refer to the color photograph.)**

   Allow room for the doily trim. Draw light pencil lines across the door panels where you will apply the top of the doily trim.

9. **Make the necessary number of photocopies of the teacup, shown in Figure 12-1. (If necessary, reduce or enlarge the drawing by using the method in Chapter 3.)**

10. **Cut six pieces of doily trim slightly wider than the width of the door panels.**

11. **With white craft glue, mount each doily strip in position where you have drawn lines on the door panels. When the glue is completely dry, trim off the excess paper with a craft knife.**

12. **Create fanciful designs on the teacups with acrylic paint or permanent markers.**

   The charm of the design lies in the fact that there are so many teacups and they can all be different from one another. Check out the color photo of this project to get some ideas.

   To determine whether a marker is permanent, make a mark on paper. Wet your finger and rub the mark. If it smears, it is not permanent.

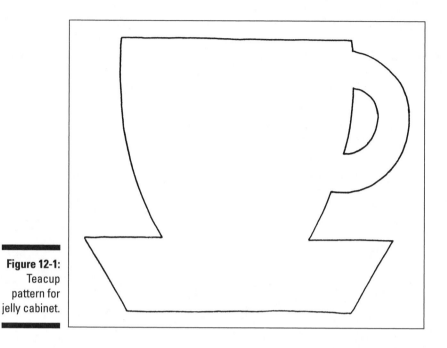

13. **Cut out each painted teacup and glue each one in position above the strips of doily edging.**

14. **Using the varnish brush, apply the water-based varnish to the entire surface, coating the paint, paper, and doilies.**

15. **Let the varnish dry completely and apply a second coat.**

16. **Replace the cabinet door, hinges, doorknob, and door catch. If necessary, repaint the screw heads with black paint after they are in place.**

Part IV
Fabric Crafts and Needlecrafts

The 5th Wave   By Rich Tennant

"One thing I learned banging out license plates at the State Penn for six years is always use a complementary color to border your designs and establish an overall sense of depth."

In this part . . .

Fabric and needles are the meat and potatoes of crafting. With just a few scraps of fabric and a needle, you can make a patchwork quilt to keep yourself warm, exciting appliqué pillows for your sofa, needlepoint gifts for your friends, and counted cross-stitch pictures for a child's room.

In this part, you even find out how to make something with fabric alone — forget the needle. Curtains without stitching? Pillows you don't have to sew? Yes. And they take only minutes to make. But why stop there, when you can find out all the tips and tricks for stitching like an expert.

Chapter 13

Fabric Crafts 101

· ·

In This Chapter

▶ Checking out the different types of fabric crafts

▶ Filling your sewing basket with the right tools

▶ Stitching basics for the beginner

▶ Using tried-and-true tips from crafters past

▶ Poking your needle into needlepoint and counted cross-stitch

· ·

*I*f you think that *fabric crafts* is synonymous with *sewing,* you're in for a delightful surprise! Fabric crafts include no-sew crafts that use sewing materials, patchwork, appliqué, needlepoint, and counted cross-stitch. The chapters in this part tell you everything you need to know about making something wonderful with fabric — even without one stitch.

You won't be on pins and needles for long, because the ABCs of sewing are easy to master. When you know how to measure, cut, pin, and stitch, you can sew like a pro, and you can find directions for those skills in Chapter 3, and find a few more introduced in this chapter.

You probably already have in your home everything you need to start a fabric craft project, and if not, all the tools and materials are readily available at craft stores, fabric shops, and even the fabric department of your local discount department store. A fabric shop or department is an exciting place to begin a fabric craft. Facing all those colors and patterns is like visiting a garden in full bloom and deciding which flowers to pick for a bouquet. The fabric supplies are all there for the choosing, and you're only a few stitches away from a finished project.

This chapter introduces you to the following fabric crafts, each of which is featured in a chapter later in this part:

✔ **No-sew** projects work great for those times when you need a fresh look or a quick solution to a decorating problem. Perhaps company's coming and you don't have time to stitch up new pillows to disguise your shabby sofa. Don't despair. Whipping up attractive fabric pillows with clever folds, tucks, and ties — and not one stitch — is quick and easy.

✔ **Patchwork** is the process of stitching together, either by hand or on a sewing machine, small pieces of colored fabric in a predetermined pattern to make a whole cloth, such as the top of a quilt or pillow. The same patchwork pattern can look completely different, depending on the choice of fabric colors and prints you use. You may use solid red and white fabric, for example, to make a bold, contemporary patchwork pillow or quilt. The same project, made with two lively calico prints, produces a country-style look. In fact, designing patchwork projects on paper with colored pencils, before setting foot into a fabric shop, provides great fun.

✔ **Appliqué,** a French word meaning, "to put on," entails applying cut-out fabric pieces on top of a fabric background. You usually design the fabric pieces that create the appliqués to portray something realistic, such as flower petals, a basket, or leaves. You can apply appliqué with hand sewing or a sewing machine.

Appliqué probably originated when someone put a patch over a hole in his or her garment to extend its life. Today, the world considers appliqué work decorative instead of utilitarian. But thinking of appliqué as merely a patch, in its lowliest form, makes trying your hand at this craft less intimidating.

✔ **Needlecrafts** include needlepoint and cross-stitch. Both these needlecrafts require a needle; wool, cotton, or acrylic threads; a background fabric (upon which you do the stitching to create a pattern or design) known as *canvas* or *even-weave;* a thimble (which is optional); and scissors. In this chapter, you find out how to perform basic needlecrafts — needlepoint and counted cross-stitch. This chapter tells you about the different needlecraft materials, how you can best work with those materials, and how to execute a few basic stitches. With these basics you can make beautiful pillows, seat covers, illustrated pictures, eyeglass cases, and countless other projects for your home or as gifts. This chapter shows you why needlecrafts have always been a most enjoyable pastime for many generations of crafters.

The Well-Equipped Sewing Basket

Sewing projects begin with a well-equipped sewing basket. You can use a hatbox, plastic sweater box, shoebox, a cookie tin, or any type of container to hold your supplies neatly and within easy access. The following list outlines the supplies you need for fabric crafts:

✔ **Scissors:** Dressmaker's shears and snipping scissors are crucial components in fabric crafts. To cut fabric accurately, you need a pair of 8- or 10-inch bent-handled dressmaker's shears. The blades open wide and take in fabric the whole length of the blade to help you avoid choppy cuts. You use 4-inch snipping scissors to cut thread and for other small jobs. (See Chapter 2 for more about scissors.)

✔ **Measuring tape and rulers:** A 60-inch flexible measuring tape includes numbers on both sides, rolls up, and is easy to store. A tape measure is used for awkward measurements such as round things and for measuring something when you need only a rough idea of the measurement. Use an 18-inch plastic ruler for short measurements and a yardstick for longer measurements.

✔ **Pins:** Use pins to hold your craft's fabric together temporarily. A box of all-purpose pins satisfies your pin needs for almost any sewing project. If you want to make a quilt, special quilting pins are available but not essential. However, quilt-making requires a lot of pinning, and these special pins are a great shortcut that make your job quicker and easier. (See Chapter 2 for more about pins.)

✔ **Needles:** A package of basic needles includes several different size needles and will get you through most sewing projects. However, quilting requires special needles (see Chapter 2).

✔ **Pincushion:** When you work on a sewing project, taking pins out and putting pins into the fabric is inevitable. A pincushion conveniently holds your pins for easy access. Pincushions also help keep pins and needles sharp (see Chapter 2 for more details).

✔ **Thimble:** A thimble is a cap that protects the finger you use most to push needles through fabric. A thimble keeps the end of your finger from getting sore. In fact, hand-quilting without a thimble is quite difficult. (See Chapter 2 for more about thimbles.)

The following items don't fit in your sewing basket but are also basic to fabric crafts:

✔ **Iron:** The iron is an essential sewing tool. After stitching two pieces of fabric together, you must press the seams. Usually, seams are pressed open, but occasionally, when stitching small patchwork pieces (1-inch, for example) together, it's easier to press the seams to one side. The standard rule when stitching any two pieces of fabric together is: stitch, press, stitch, press. Making beautiful fabric projects without an iron is impossible.

✔ **Sewing machine:** Sewing involves hand-stitching and/or using a sewing machine, but more advanced sewing crafts often require the use of a sewing machine. Even the simplest sewing machine can sew forward, backward, and zigzag. After you learn how to use this marvelous machine, you only need to turn a dial or two and presto — you're sewing. Sewing machines enable you to create everything from embroidery to making buttonholes.

Although many different types of sewing machines exist, certain fundamentals apply to all sewing machines. Most machines use a number 14 needle to sew most fabrics. Likewise, machines use number 50 mercerized cotton or synthetic thread, and the machine is usually set for 12 stitches per inch.

Tips for buying a sewing machine

Selecting a sewing machine is similar, in many ways, to buying a car. You consider the sewing machine's features, durability and dependability, and expect it to last a number of years with minimum care and repair. A sewing machine's number and type of features affects its price. Consider the features that you select for your machine as an investment in the development of your sewing skills. Certain sewing machine features are basic necessities, while others are special extras that may come in handy. Always "test drive" a sewing machine before buying it, much the way you would when buying a car. And don't think you have to become an overnight expert on sewing machines. The salesperson can tell you what you need to know, based on the information you give him or her about what types of sewing projects you intend to do.

The following is a checklist of basic features:

✔ The machine starts and stops smoothly and doesn't jam (get stuck and come to a jerky stop) when you sew off the fabric's edge.

✔ The bobbin (the spool that holds the thread that stitches the fabric's underside) doesn't vibrate while sewing and feeds the thread evenly.

✔ The bobbin winds simply and easily inserts into the bobbin case.

✔ The machine is easy to thread. The salesperson should show you how to thread the machine when you're checking out different machines that you are considering.

✔ The needle inserts into the machine easily.

✔ The attachments are varied and easy to change. The attachments may include a zipper foot (for stitching zippers into clothing or other projects) or an attachment for creating ruffles, for example. Each attachment makes the price of the machine go up, so it's up to you to decide whether or not the attachments are necessary for your sewing needs. The projects in this book use only the basic sewing machine without anything more than straight stitching — the equivalent of a car without any "add-ons."

✔ The machine contains needle plate markings to guide seam widths. The part of the sewing machine under the needle area, where you place the fabric, usually has different lines or grooves marked for ¼-inch, ½-inch, and 1-inch seam allowances. The fabric is placed along the line indicating where the stitches will appear in order to achieve the seam allowance required for that particular project. All the projects in this book require a ¼-inch seam allowance, which is standard.

✔ The machine performs accurate (straight and smooth) reverse stitching.

✔ The machine enables you to control stitch lengths and widths. Most machines have a dial for setting the stitch length and width (such as for a zigzag stitch) as per directions for the project on which you are working.

✔ The machine has adjustable tension and pressure knobs.

✔ The machine has a light that illuminates the needle area without shadows

✔ The foot pedal operates easily and comfortably. You decide for yourself when you try the machine. It's just like putting your foot on a car's accelerator and brake pedals.

✔ The machine is easy to clean.

✔ The machine includes an instruction book that you can understand!

When buying a sewing machine, look for a product that performs all the functions you need now, as well as functions that you think you may use in the future. Prices for sewing machines range from $150 to $3,500, and a basic machine costs approximately $500. If you don't think you'll need to program ten different embroidery stitches, don't spend the extra money. Selecting a known brand, buying from a reputable dealer who offers good service, and asking the opinion of friends who are accomplished sewers are three good ways to ensure the quality of your purchase.

Taking Your First Stitch

Sewing craft projects, such as patchwork and appliqué, involves basic stitching, but sewing craft accessories is much easier than making clothes that have to fit. After you master threading a needle (whether by hand or a sewing machine needle), the rest of the process is easy. This chapter describes everything you need to know to make all the sewing projects in the following chapters.

The *running stitch,* shown in Figure 13-1, is a good one to begin hand-sewing with. Follow these steps:

1. **Cut a length of thread as long as your arm, poke one end of the thread through the eye of the needle, and knot one end of the thread.**

2. **Bring the needle up through the fabric from the underside and pull it through as far as you can until the knot reaches the underside of the fabric.**

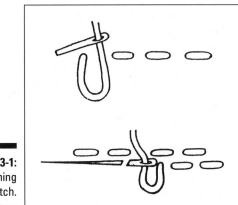

Figure 13-1:
The running
stitch.

3. **Insert the needle back down through the front of the fabric, approximately ⅛ inch from where the needle emerged.**

4. **Bring the needle back up to the front of the fabric, ⅛ inch in front of the last stitch.**

5. **Continue to weave the needle in and out of the fabric in ⅛-inch, evenly spaced stitches.**

6. **Finish sewing on the fabric's underside with a fastening stitch, or leave a 4-inch loose thread and use it to make a knot close to the underside of the fabric.**

   To make a fastening stitch, finish a row of stitches with the needle on the underside of the fabric and bring the needle under the thread of the last stitch two or three times to secure. Pull the thread through firmly, but don't pucker the fabric.

7. **Cut the thread end.**

Congratulations on your first sewing masterpiece!

Tips and Tricks of the Trade

As you repeatedly perform tasks, you develop ways to get the job done quicker, easier, and altogether better. You may also discover new products along the way that help you with your task. These tips, tricks, and shortcuts that you discover pass from one person to the next and sometimes from one generation to the next. The craft of sewing is so seasoned that it definitely contains some tips and tricks of the trade. The following tips help you with the sewing projects in this part.

On your mark

Use a special quilt pen to mark lines on your fabric when you quilt (see Chapter 15). These inexpensive pens (sold in fabric shops) are made especially for making marking lines to follow when hand-stitching, as for quilting, on fabric. The pen lines eventually fade, or you can wash them away. You can use a plant mister after you finish quilting to eliminate the pen's marks.

Always mark patterns on the underside of the fabric with the pattern template (see Chapter 16) facedown. When making a quilt, always mark the long border pieces before marking the smaller patchwork pieces. When you mark templates on the back of your fabric, leave at least ½ inch between shapes for the seam allowance when you cut out each piece. Mark templates for appliqué with a light pencil on the front of the fabric so you can easily see the turn-under line (see Chapters 15 and 16).

The hard facts about cutting

Where you cut your fabric is as important as how you cut your fabric. Cutting fabric requires a hard, flat surface large enough to hold the entire length of the cloth. If you don't have a table or countertop large enough, you can cut the fabric on the floor. Whatever surface you cut your fabric on, make sure you protect it with a table pad, a dressmaker's cutting board, or a piece of foamboard from an art supply store.

After you master cutting fabric, you can begin to cut several layers of fabric at once. This layer method of cutting is useful, for example, when you make a patchwork quilt that requires identical pieces of different fabrics. To cut several layers of fabric at once, use a rotary cutter — a circular cutting device (see Chapter 2) that looks like a pizza-cutting wheel.

If a pattern calls for large or small triangles, rectangles, or squares, you can pin and stitch together two large pieces of fabric. Then mark only the top piece of the fabric and cut both layers at one time.

Basting stitches

Making a quilt (see Chapter 15) requires that you temporarily hold three layers of material together until you can complete all of your stitching. Use *basting stitches* (very long, loose stitches that you make through all the material) to do so. Start basting at the center of the fabric and move outward in a starburst pattern to temporarily hold your fabric and keep your material from shifting while you quilt.

Make sure to leave approximately 6 inches between the basted lines at the edges of the patchwork top's edges, and be sure to baste from the top only. Cut away the basted stitches as you quilt.

Pressing matters

Every time you stitch two pieces of fabric together, you use an iron to press the seams apart or to one side of the seam line. (See "The Well-Equipped Sewing Basket" earlier in this chapter). Because pressing is done often, many sewers find it handy to pad the seat of a stool to place next to the sewing table. With a padded surface and iron next to you, you can stitch and then press without continuously getting up and down each time you need to press your fabric pieces.

Needlepoint

Needlepoint is embroidery that you work with a needle to create a design on an even-weave material called *canvas*. Aside from the basic materials in your craft kit, you need a tool to stretch the canvas taut so you stitch evenly and smoothly. Stores that sell needlepoint canvas also sell *embroidery hoops* and *frames* that hold your needlepoint project while you work with it. A small hoop or frame works well for work you can do in your lap, but the required size graduates to a full-size hoop or frame that rests on a stand if your canvas is quite large.

Working on a needlepoint canvas is easy. Thread the needle with the appropriate thread (according to the project directions) for your project. Needlepoint stitches go in only two directions, either diagonally across or parallel to the canvas threads (known as the *mesh*). Following the project's chart, known as the *pattern,* you work each stitch in the color that the pattern indicates to form the design or illustration. When the canvas mesh is fine (a tight weave), you make smaller stitches and your work takes longer than when you use loose canvas and make larger stitches.

Chapter 17 has small needlepoint projects to get you started on this satisfying craft.

Counted Cross-Stitch

Perhaps you've seen early American samplers that date back to colonial days. These samplers were done in *cross-stitch. Counted cross-stitch* is another embroidery technique that's popular because it's easy to do and always looks perfect. All cross-stitch creates neat geometric rows that form patterns that range from borders, numbers, and letters to sayings, scenes, and everything in between. The difference between cross-stitch and counted cross-stitch is that the first has the stitches already printed on the fabric for easy placement on the fabric. Counted cross-stitch is more popular today. The counted cross-stitch patterns come with a chart indicating the placement of the stitches on the fabric with a symbol for each color of floss to be used.

To create a cross-stitch illustration, you need embroidery floss, a blunt tapestry needle (see Chapter 18), a hoop to hold the even-weave fabric (also called *canvas* and made especially for this craft), and a charted design. Counted cross-stitch fabric looks like little squares. You fill each square with an X-shaped stitch in the color that the chart indicates. (See Chapter 18 for how to work counted cross-stitch.)

Counted cross-stitch is inexpensive to produce, and because it doesn't require many materials, you can do it almost anywhere. Your work-in-progress fits easily into a purse or briefcase, and design possibilities are endless. Add to this convenience a perfect-product guarantee, and you have the ideal leisure-time craft. Check out some good cross-stitch projects for beginners in Chapter 18.

Child's toy bin.
See Chapter 5.

Paper bag planter. *See Chapter 5.*

Elegant boxes. *See Chapter 5.*

Top left
Recycled cookie tins. *See Chapter 9.*

Top right
Découpage light-switch plate. *See Chapter 9.*

Bottom right
Photo memory box. *See Chapter 7.*

Bottom left
Twig frame. *See Chapter 7.*

Left
Dressed-up dresser. *See Chapter 9.*

Bottom left
Children's découpage boxes. *See Chapter 9.*

Bottom right
One-color stenciled boxes. *See Chapter 11.*

Above
Five easy pieces.
See Chapter 11.

Right
Faux-marble side
table. *See Chapter 12.*

Left
Painted and stenciled dresser.
See Chapter 11.

Bottom left
Two-color stenciling.
See Chapter 11.

Bottom right
No-sew pillows. *See Chapter 14.*

Whimsical jelly cabinet.
See Chapter 12.

Top left
No-sew curtains. *See Chapter 14.*

Top right
Patchwork pillow. *See Chapter 15.*

Right
Sponge-painted country table ensemble.
See Chapter 12.

Left
Country patchwork potholders. *See Chapter 15.*

Below right
Patchwork cat. *See Chapter 15.*

Bottom
Pinwheel baby quilt. *See Chapter 15.*

Above
Ducky place mat and bib.
See Chapter 16.

Left
Cookie cutter appliqués.
See Chapter 16.

Above
Appliqué accent pillows.
See Chapter 16.

Right
Needlepoint eyeglass case. *See Chapter 17.*

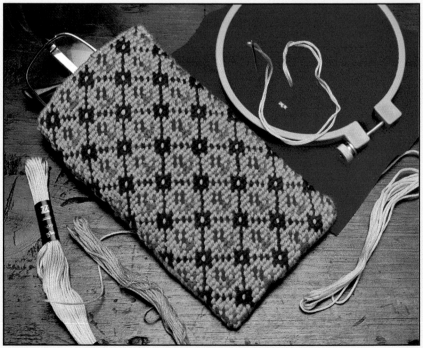

Above
Friendship frame. *See Chapter 17.*

Right
Monogrammed needlepoint gift tags. *See Chapter 17.*

Below
Cross-stitch pictures for baby's room. *See Chapter 18.*

Above
Juicy fruit pictures and coasters. *See Chapter 18.*

Left
Dried-flower wreath. *See Chapter 20.*

Below
Flowering candles. *See Chapter 20.*

Above
Seashell frame. *See Chapter 21.*

Right
Dynamo dinosaur ornaments. *See Chapter 23.*

Above
Sensational stenciled wraps. *See Chapter 25.*

Right
Cross-stitch cuties. *See Chapter 23.*

Left
Snowman holiday card holder. *See Chapter 26.*

Bottom left
Painted glass hurricane lamp. *See Chapter 26.*

Bottom right
Recycled découpage jewelry box. *See Chapter 28.*

Toyland stocking, ornaments, and gift tags. *See Chapters 23, 24, and 25.*

Chapter 14

No-Sew Crafts

*W*hat do linen napkins, a lacy tablecloth, dish towels, scarves, and pillowcases have in common? You can use them all to make curtains, lampshades, and window valances, quickly and without making a stitch. In this chapter, I show you creative ways to combine scraps of fabric with self-fusing material such as glue, staples, ribbons, and other readily available and inexpensive components. You can find all the materials for the crafts in this chapter in fabric stores.

Fabric is the basic ingredient in no-sew projects. The only skills necessary for making no-sew projects involve fusing fabric to fabric with the use of an iron and fusing material or tying fabric together with ribbon and other decorative trims. Other no-sew projects, like making curtains, use self-hemmed fabric that has pre-finished edges and special clips that attach to fabric without stitching. Choosing the fabric that you like best is the biggest challenge of no-sew projects — it's also a lot of fun.

With no-sew projects, you can make new pillows for your living room sofa, put up a new kitchen curtain, decorate a lampshade for your bedroom, make a valance for a powder room window, and re-cover an old chair seat — all without breaking open the sewing machine. The projects in this chapter show you how to make any and all of these projects.

Putting Your Scraps to Good Use

Because fabric is the basis for a no-sew craft project, the first thing you need to know is the language of fabric. A piece of fabric that seems too small to use on its own to make a project is called a *scrap.* You probably have leftover pieces of fabric in your scrap basket. Don't throw the scraps away! That's gold in your scrap basket.

If you don't have a basket filled with fabric scraps, you can buy small pieces, called remnants, from your local fabric shop. A *remnant* is a small, leftover piece of fabric that's usually under a yard long. (Most fabric is sold by the yard and is 45 inches wide.) Upholstery or large-project fabric, on the other hand, is usually 54 or 60 inches wide. Upholstery fabric is larger because people use it to cover large areas, such as a sofa or chair. The fabric's larger width eliminates the need for piecing fabric together and unsightly seam lines on your furniture.

You can purchase fabric in amounts as small as a quarter of a yard. Very often, fabric shops have a container filled with rolled-up quarter-yard fabric pieces that sell for about a dollar apiece. These remnants are perfect for many craft projects, especially when your project requires a small amount of many different fabric colors or patterns. These fabric bargains mean that you can buy a piece of fabric measuring 9 x 45 inches to make a variety of projects, including a pillow, several sachets, a Christmas stocking, tree ornaments, two potholders, or a window valance, just to name a few, for about a dollar. Because a no-sew project doesn't require much time or money, it represents quite a bargain. And if you're ready to discard an old bedspread, blanket, curtains, a favorite shirt, skirt, or other article of clothing, consider cutting it into scraps for use in a no-sew project. See what I mean about finding gold in the scrap basket?

Sticking Fabric Together Without Needle and Thread

With no-sew projects, you don't need a needle and thread, but you do need some method to hold your scraps or remnants to each other or to other parts of your project. You may be surprised to discover that you have a wide variety of ways to secure your material. Some securing methods are more suitable for specific uses, but all the methods come in handy sooner or later.

An iron is a necessary tool for no-sew crafts. An iron is also used with fusible webbing (see "Amazing feats of fusible webbing," later in this chapter) to fuse fabric pieces together. An iron allows you to press unfinished fabric edges. By turning under the *selvage* (raw or unfinished) edges and ironing them down, you can create a finished edge for your project's fabric.

Taking the hard line

Creating no-sew projects often requires tools such as a glue gun (see Chapter 2) or staple gun. You can easily use a glue gun to glue the edges of fabric together. You can find staple guns in hardware stores. A staple gun is much sturdier than a regular paper stapler. The industrial staples that the staple gun uses can penetrate wood. You can also use thumb tacks, upholstery tacks, and double-sided tape to make no-sew crafts.

Amazing feats of fusible webbing

Crafters use *fusible webbing*, a certain type of material, to attach fabric to fabric. Fusible webbing is, in a word, amazing. In a pinch, you can use fusible webbing to turn up a hem, fix a tear, and cover a hole in your jeans — no stitches required. You can buy fusible webbing in sheets, by the yard (like fabric), or in thin strips on a roll like tape. It isn't sticky to the touch, and it looks like thin, gauzy paper. You can find fusible webbing in all fabric shops.

A common brand name for fusible webbing is Stitch Witchery.

When a project requires you to join two pieces of fabric, cut a piece of fusible webbing to match the shape of the fabric pieces. Sandwich this piece of webbing between the fabric pieces and then hold a warm iron on top of the fabric for a few seconds. The iron's heat melts the webbing, and the melted webbing fuses the fabric pieces together. For example, if you want to add a strip of ribbon trim to the hemline of a pillowcase, cut a strip of fusible webbing slightly narrower than the width and the same length as the trim piece. Place the webbing on the pillowcase, position the ribbon on top of the webbing, and fuse it with a warm iron.

Crafters also use fusible webbing to attach appliqués (see Chapter 16) to background fabric. Fusible webbing is an invaluable tool for decorating Christmas ornaments and stockings with felt designs (see Part VI). You can pin a piece of felt to the fusible webbing and cut both pieces out in different holiday shapes, like holly leaves and berries or candy canes and trees. You then place the felt shapes in position on a stocking or ornament, remove the pin, and fuse the design to the background with a warm iron. The technique is simple — fusing is never confusing.

Velcro is a brand name for another material that you use to attach one piece of fabric to another. Velcro comes in strips and is an effective substitute for buttons and zippers. Velcro consists of two pieces of material that grip together with a positive and negative side. If you buy self-adhesive Velcro, you can position each negative and positive piece on either piece of your fabric. After you align one piece of fabric with the other, press the fabric pieces together. The fabric pieces now stick to one another where you've attached the Velcro.

Ribbons to the no-sew rescue

Ribbons come in many colors, designs, widths, and materials. The most common sizes of ribbon are ¼ inch and 1 inch. *Grosgrain* ribbon is ribbed and has a flat, matte finish. *Satin* ribbon is shiny and is softer and more pliable than grosgrain ribbon. Ribbon that has very thin wire rolled into the edges is called *French wired* ribbon. It can be made of satin, organdy, grosgrain, taffeta, or velvet. The wire enables the ribbon to hold its shape. *Taffeta* ribbon is often used when making holiday projects because you can find it in beautiful tartan plaids.

You can use ribbon to dress up plain items — add a ribbon edge to plain pillowcases, along the hem of plain sheets, or to the edge of plain towels. The simple addition of ribbon trim enhances all of these items. If you don't want to do any sewing, you can still apply ribbon in other ways: You can fuse it to the background fabric with fusible webbing (see the preceding section), or you can glue it — around the edge of a plain lampshade, for example.

Because ribbon comes in many widths, you can use wide ribbon to trim the side edge of curtain panels and narrow ribbon to trim the edge of café curtains.

Pillows from Scraps

Freshen up your bedroom and add instant pizzazz to a tired old sofa with no-sew pillows, shown in the color section of this book. All you need to make no-sew pillows is a pillow form (available in fabric stores) and a piece of fabric. Pillow forms come in standard sizes from 9-inch squares to 22-inch squares, as well as round, rectangular, and oblong shapes.

Ribbons and bows

Tools and Materials:

2 pieces of fabric, approximately 5 inches wider and longer in each direction than the pillow form

1 square or rectangular pillow form in any size

Iron

1 ½ yards of 1-inch-wide grosgrain ribbon

Rubber bands

1. Cut two pieces of fabric about 5 inches larger than the dimensions of the pillow form.

2. Turn ¼ inch of each fabric piece's unfinished edge to the wrong side and press with your iron.

3. Place the pillow form in the center of the wrong side of one piece of fabric. Place the second piece of fabric, wrong side down, on top of the pillow form. Make sure that the pressed, raw edges face the pillow form.

4. Gather the fabric tightly at each corner and secure with rubber bands. Tie a length of the grosgrain ribbon around each rubber band.

The open side edges of the fabric bunches together in folds and holds securely along the sides of the pillow form.

Package wrap

Tools and Materials:

1 piece of fabric (satin, taffeta, or velvet), about 2 ½ times larger than the pillow form

1 square pillow form any size

1. Place the pillow form diagonally in the center of the wrong side of the fabric.

2. Bring two opposite corners of the fabric together and tie a knot in the center of the pillow.

3. Bring the remaining two corners together and tie them in a knot on top of the first knot.

4. Tuck all the fabric ends under the center knot.

Neck roll pillow

You use an oblong pillow for this project. You can use ribbon or strips of the pillow's cover fabric to make bows on each end.

Tools and Materials:

1 piece of fabric, 6 inches longer and 2 inches wider than the pillow form

Pinking shears

Two 2-x-12-inch-long strips of fabric (cut with pinking shears) or ribbon in the same dimensions

Iron

1 oblong pillow form in your choice of size

Rubber bands

Note: If you don't have pinking shears, cut four strips of fusible webbing, one for each long edge of the fabric strips. Place the fusible webbing on the fabric's wrong side, along the edges of the strips of fabric. Turn the fabric's raw edges over the webbing and press with your iron. This gives the fabric edges a smooth finish, without any stitching.

1. **Turn the raw edges of the pillow fabric under ½ inch and press with your iron.**

2. **Place the pillow form in the center of the fabric's wrong side. Wrap the fabric around the pillow so that the fabric's open edges overlap.**

3. **Tightly gather the fabric at each pillow end and secure with rubber bands. Tie the 2-x-12-inch strips of fabric (or ribbons) around each rubber band and make a bow.**

4. **Fan out the excess fabric that sticks out at each end above the bow and trim with pinking shears or regular scissors.**

Re-Covering a Chair Seat

You can easily re-cover fabric-covered chair seats, such as those you find on dining room chairs. Screws in each corner of the underside of the seat frame hold the chair seats in position. (Your chair's setup may differ slightly.) You need either a regular screwdriver or a Phillips screwdriver, depending on the type of screws that your chair uses, to remove the seat from your chair. You also need a staple gun for this project.

A regular screw has a straight slit at the top and the Phillips screw has a crisscross slit at the top.

Tools and Materials:

Screwdriver (size and type
depends on the screws in the
bottom of your chair)

A piece of fabric (any type) 3
to 4 inches larger than seat
top's perimeter

A piece of quilt batting (see
Chapter 15) slightly smaller
than the fabric

Staple gun

1. **Turn your chair upside down and remove the screws from each corner of the seat.**

2. **Turn the chair upright and remove the seat. Remove the old fabric and underpadding from the wooden base by lifting the old staples with the end of a regular screwdriver.**

   If the old fabric was glued to the base, it should pull away easily. If it can't be removed, simply cover it with the new fabric.

3. **Place the chair's new fabric right side down on a hard work surface, like a table or countertop. Center the piece of quilt batting on top of the fabric. Position the chair seat on top of the batting.**

4. **Grip the middle of one side edge of the fabric, bring it to the underside of the seat, and staple it in position. Repeat on the opposite side edge of the fabric, pulling the fabric so that it's tight and smooth before stapling.**

   Continue to staple all four sides of the fabric to the underside of the chair seat (but not the corners just yet), pulling the fabric so that it's tight and smooth as you do this. Staple all along the edge of the fabric on all sides to secure the fabric tightly on the underside of the seat.

5. **Pull each corner piece of fabric to the chair's underside and staple it in position.**

6. **Next, pull the fabric on both sides of each corner so that the fabric is tight and staple it.**

7. **Trim any excess fabric where bunching occurs.**

8. **Place the newly covered chair seat back in position on the frame and press down on it firmly. Turn the seat upside down and insert each corner screw.**

   As you apply pressure to the screwdriver while tightening each screw, the screw penetrates the fabric and batting.

   If you encounter resistance, remove the newly covered seat and use the point of a pair of scissors or craft knife to puncture a hole in the fabric at each corner where the screws need to go through. Replace the seat and the screws.

Easy Curtains

Linen napkins, dishtowels, table linens, pillowcases, and napkins make inexpensive and stitchless curtains and valances. Hang your curtains on spring-type tension rods that fit any standard-size window (available in the curtain departments of many stores), and you don't need hardware or tools. You have a window treatment in minutes.

Dish towel café curtains

Blue and white plaid linen dish towels make great country-style café kitchen curtains. You can see a photo of these curtains in the color section of this book.

Tools and Materials:

3 dish towels for the curtains and valance of a standard-size window

1 package of clip-on curtain rings (available wherever curtain rods are sold)

2 tension curtain rods to fit your window

1. **Evenly space the curtain rings across one end of two dish towels and then hang the towels on the bottom curtain rod.**

2. **Place the tension rod inside the window frame and adjust it (up or down) so that the bottom edge of the curtains just touches the window sill.**

3. **Turn the third towel lengthwise and drape it evenly over the top rod to serve as a valance.**

You can also use pillow cases instead of dish towels for curtains and a valance. For the café curtains, use pillowcases with decorative borders and a matching printed or solid pillowcase for the valance. Silk or rayon scarves also provide another option for café curtains. Use two scarves with clip-on curtain rings attached, following the directions for the dish towels. Fold a scarf lengthwise over a curtain rod (just as you did with the dish towel) to serve as the valance.

Table linen curtains

A lace-edged tablecloth makes a perfect window covering. The size of the tablecloth isn't crucial as you can easily adjust it to fit when hanging the cloth over the rod.

Tools and Materials:

*1 square lace-edged tea cloth
for a small window or tablecloth for a large window for
the curtain.*

*3 or 4 (depending on the size
of the window) floral or lace-
edged linen napkins for the
valance*

2 tension curtain rods.

1. **Fold the tablecloth diagonally and drape it over the lower tension curtain rod.**

   If the tablecloth is too wide for the window, simply fold the corners back
   over the cloth to create a folded, finished edge.

2. **Fold three napkins diagonally and hang them evenly over the top tension rod to create the valance.**

   If you use large napkins, fold two of them in half, on the diagonal, and
   hang them like you hang the smaller napkins.

Dressing Up Plain Lampshades

You can use fabric, ribbons, and decorative trim to give a plain paper lampshade a new look in less than an hour. Choose colors and fabric prints that
match other elements in your room.

Fabric appliqué lampshade

For this appliqué lampshade, choose fabric with a pleasing print, such as
flowers, whose print is easy to cut out. You may want to use fabric with a
juvenile print for a child's room. Be sure to use sharp scissors when cutting
out the appliqué shapes so that the fabric doesn't fray.

Tools and Materials:

*Fabric (a piece large enough
to cut enough appliqués to
cover your shade)*

Plain lampshade

Scissors

White craft glue

1. **Cut out several images from the printed fabric. You may cut out different size flowers, leaves, and buds.**

2. **Arrange the cutout fabric pieces around a plain lampshade. The friction enables the fabric to hold long enough for you to decide where you want to place each piece.**

3. **Remove one cutout at a time and spread craft glue over the back of it. Reposition the fabric appliqué on the lampshade.**

   With one hand inside the shade behind the glued piece and the other hand on the front of the fabric, press hard to adhere the appliqué to the shade.

4. **Continue to glue the fabric cutouts around the shade until you finish.**

Lampshade borders

You can use cutout fabric appliqués to create a border around the top and bottom rims of your lampshade. Ribbons, gold braid, and rickrack trim also make a beautiful finished border.

Tools and Materials:

Fabric appliqués (border material)

Plain Lampshade

Scissors

White craft glue

1. **Cut out enough fabric pieces to create a border of the desired width around your lampshade.**

2. **Spread glue onto the back of each fabric piece and apply it in position on the shade.**

   Continue to do this while you overlap similar size appliqués (such as small flowers) to create a border around the shade.

3. **After you apply the desired amount of cutouts to create a band around the lampshade, stand back to assess your work.**

   If you want a wider decorative border, simply add more cutouts wherever you think they're necessary around the shade.

Instead of using fabric cutouts to decorate your lampshade, add a simple band of ribbon, braid, or rickrack in the color that you desire. Measure the circumference of the shade and cut the length of trim to that measurement plus ½ inch. Spread a thin line of glue along the back of the strip of trim and attach it to your shade. You can overlap the ends where they meet or trim the ends so that they butt together.

Chapter 15

Patchwork and Quilting

● ●

In This Chapter

▶ Getting familiar with basic patchwork terms

▶ Finding out everything you need to start

▶ Acquiring technical information that you need to know

▶ Quilting basics

▶ Mastering quick and easy techniques

▶ Making simple projects

● ●

*J*oining pieces of fabric together to form a larger unit of fabric is the basic technique of patchwork. Most patchwork projects involve stitching together square, triangular, or rectangular pieces of fabric. In this chapter, I expose you to the wide world of fabrics, and you gather quick and easy techniques for making patchwork projects to enhance your home with warmth and personality and to give as treasured gifts.

Making the patchwork potholder, patchwork pillow, and patchwork quilt from the patterns and steps in this chapter gives you the experience you need to make any patchwork project, no matter how complicated the pattern may seem. The same principles for creating a potholder apply to creating a quilt — the only difference between the two is size.

Basic Patchwork Terms

Patchwork has its own language. Familiarizing yourself with the basic terms of the craft makes the patchwork technique easy to understand. Knowing what's involved before you begin patchwork helps you decide which project you want to make. Even if you start your fabric craft adventure with a patchwork potholder, eventually you may want to use your newfound skills to make a patchwork quilt. Some of the following terms relate only to quilting, a project that most fabric crafters make after they master the basics of patchwork.

✔ **Backing:** The piece of fabric used on the underside of the patchwork (front) piece of fabric.

✔ **Basting:** Long, loose stitches that you use to hold the top, batting, and backing of a quilt together before quilting. You remove these stitches after you quilt each section.

✔ **Batting:** Soft lining that you use between two layers of fabric that you quilt. Batting makes quilts puffy and gives them warmth. You can also use batting for potholder padding.

Most quilts are made with a thin layer of cotton or synthetic batting, but you can purchase batting in varying degrees of thickness, each appropriate for different kinds of projects. Batting also comes in small, fluffy pieces that you can use for stuffing projects, such as sachets, pin cushions, pillows, and ornaments.

✔ **Binding:** Use binding to finish the raw edges of fabric. You can use strips of contrasting fabric or packaged bias binding.

In place of using separate binding, many quiltmakers cut the project's backing slightly larger than the top piece so they can bring the extra fabric forward to finish the edges of the top piece of fabric. Or you can cut the backing the same size as the front and turn the front (patchwork top) to the back.

✔ **Blocks:** You sew together small pieces of fabric in a specified design to create a square or rectangular block. You can use individual blocks to make a patchwork pillow, or you can sew several blocks together to create a quilt top.

✔ **Borders:** Fabric strips that frame the pieced design. A border can be narrow or wide and can be made from one of your patchwork fabrics or from a contrasting fabric. Use borders to frame quilt blocks or to enlarge a quilt top so that it extends over the sides of a mattress. You can also use more than one border around a patchwork project.

✔ **Piecing:** Joining fabric patchwork pieces together in a design or pattern to form a block.

✔ **Quilting:** Stitching (by hand or machine) together two layers of fabric with a layer of batting between them.

✔ **Quilting patterns:** Lines or markings on fabric that make up the design for the quilting. When quilting, you make small hand or machine stitches along these lines. The quilting pattern can be straight, curved, or elaborate curlicue patterns; it may be a pattern of diamonds or a grid. You can also follow the seam lines where pieces of fabric are joined with small quilting stitches.

✔ **Sashes or strips:** Narrow pieces of fabric that you use to frame individual blocks and join the blocks together. Sashes or strips often appear in contrasting colors.

✔ **Seam allowance:** The specified measurement of fabric that lies between the stitch or seam line and the fabric edge. When directions state that you must sew two pieces of fabric together, begin stitching ¼ inch in from the fabric's raw edge, unless otherwise indicated.

✔ **Setting:** Sewing together quilt blocks to form a finished quilt top.

✔ **Top:** The front layer of a quilting project that shows the right side of the fabric. Patchwork or appliquéd pieces create the project's top fabric.

Materials That You Need

You need the following items to make patchwork projects:

✔ **Cutting board:** Use this handy item for quick measuring and cutting when making patchworks. You can find cutting boards in fabric stores or from mail-order sources.

✔ **Fabric:** Decisions about fabric is the main concern of any patchwork project; what kind, how much to buy, and deciding what colors or prints work together. You can never have too many different fabric patterns to choose from when you design a patchwork project. I always need ten times more variety to choose from than what I originally think I do.

Most fabric crafters prefer 100-percent cotton fabric, and all the fabric used in your patchwork project should be of the same weight. Most fabric is 45 inches wide with *selvage* (see Chapter 14). Be sure to wash the fabric before you use it to remove any *sizing* (a printing chemical) from the fabric, allow for shrinkage, and slightly fade the fabric. Slightly faded fabric produces a worn, old look that some crafters find desirable — especially quiltmakers.

While collecting a variety of fabric prints for your patchwork projects, collecting a selection of light and dark prints is a good idea. The colors and patterns of the fabric greatly affect the project's design. Calico works well with patchwork projects, because you can use the small prints effectively together and it comes in a wide variety of colors to choose from. Pretty floral prints work well with alternating solid colors that match the calico print colors.

You can use a sheet, muslin, or one of the fabrics that you used for the patchwork on the top of your project for the backing fabric. Unlike fabric that you buy in a store, which is generally only 45 inches wide, a bed sheet can cover the back of any size quilt without piecing. Most crafters prefer backing that is 100-percent cotton. A light color is usually better than a dark color for the backing because a dark backing color may show through the thin batting and light fabric on the top of the project.

✔ **Iron it right:** Working on any patchwork project without having an iron on a padded stool or chair next to the sewing machine is not practical. After each stitching step, you need to press the fabric and seams using the steam setting.

✔ **Marking pen:** Sometimes you may need to trace a pattern or design from a book and transfer it to the fabric. For example, when you want to quilt a design over a pillow top, you need pattern lines to follow. You can find water-soluble marking pens, made specifically for marking quilting lines on fabric, in fabric shops. After you finish quilting, you can remove the pen marks by spraying them with a plant mister or by patting over the lines with a damp sponge to make them disappear.

✔ **Needles:** Crafters sew most patchwork piecing with a sewing machine but do most of the quilting by hand. To hand quilt, you need #7 and #8 sharp needles (often called *betweens*). See Chapter 2 for more information about needles.

✔ **Rotary cutter:** This tool resembles a pizza cutter, allows you to cut several layers of fabric at once (see the how-to in Chapter 3), and cuts fabric more accurately than scissors.

✔ **Ruler and yardstick:** You can't work without these two tools. Use a metal ruler as a straightedge to accurately cut fabric. Use the yardstick to cut lengths of fabric on which you must mark and cut at least 36 inches at one time.

✔ **Scissors:** You need good scissors to cut your fabric. If you use your scissors to cut only fabric, they stay sharp, but if you use your scissors to cut paper, they dull quickly. Also, invest in a pair of small, pointed scissors to snip threads as you stitch and quilt.

✔ **Straight pins:** Use special quilting pins — extra-long 1¾-inch sharp pins — if you can. Regular straight pins are fine, but the extra long steel pins made especially for quilting work best for holding three layers of material together.

✔ **Template:** A template is a rigid, full-size pattern that you use to trace design elements. You can cut templates out of cardboard, manila paper, plastic, acetate, or sandpaper. When your project requires a repeat design, use acetate because it's transparent and it produces clean, crisp edges. Sandpaper's main advantage is that it doesn't slip when you place it facedown on the fabric. If you cut one paper design, pin the pattern to the fabric to use as a cutting guide for more efficiency.

✔ **Thimble:** I can't stand to work with one, but I try to use a thimble from time to time because my fingers get numb from pricking them with my needle so often. Try using a thimble for quilting by hand, but make sure that you get the right size. Without a thimble, you run the risk of bleeding on your fabric.

✔ **Thread:** Match thread and fabric colors. Cotton-blend thread works best for all piecing and quilting projects.

Technical Stuff You Need to Know

How do you calculate the amount of fabric to buy for your project? If the back of a patchwork pillow isn't patchwork, what is it? How do you enlarge or reduce a pattern that isn't the right size for your project? How do you make a template? Read on, and you can speed through this technical jargon to get to the hands-on part.

Estimating fabric yardage

If you follow project directions, the amount of each kind of fabric that you need is listed. However, when you make projects without directions, such as quilts, determining the amount of fabric that you need can be tricky. Estimating yardage for a quilt includes a few basic rules:

1. **Measure your bed fully made — this means with the bed pad, sheets, and blankets over the mattress. Measure the length, width, and depth of your bed, including the box spring.**

2. **Decide whether you want your quilt to overhang slightly, overhang to the top of the dust ruffle, or drop to the floor, and whether you want your quilt to extend up and over the pillows.**

3. **After you make your decision, add the appropriate number of inches to the measurements you took in Step 1 to make the quilt large enough to hang where you want it to.**

If you find a quilt pattern that you like but the quilt size doesn't fit your bed, you can add or subtract from the border measurements to make it fit. Changing the pattern's measurements usually doesn't change the quilt's basic design.

Piecing the backing

If you make a quilt, tablecloth, wall hanging, or other large patchwork project, you may have to piece panels together to make the correct backing size. Use the following steps to piece your project's backing.

1. **Cut two pieces of fabric to the appropriate length for your project.**

   Most fabric is 45 inches wide, so you now have two 45-inch wide lengths of fabric.

2. **Cut one of the pieces of fabric in half lengthwise to produce two narrow strips the same size.**

3. **Stitch one of these two matching panels to each long-sided edge of the second piece of fabric.**

Now you have a piece of fabric wide enough for your backing that doesn't have a seam down the middle. Two seams make the back of a quilt look neater than a seam down the middle of the back of the quilt, and a tablecloth lays flatter on the tabletop with two seams than with one down the middle. Also, working with three smaller pieces of fabric is more manageable than working with two large pieces of fabric.

4. **Press the seams open.**

If you use a bed sheet the same size as the patchwork top, you have a solid backing that doesn't require piecing.

Enlarging designs

Sometimes, you need to adjust your project's pattern size. A copy machine works best when you want to enlarge or reduce a design. However, if you don't have access to a copy machine, see Chapter 3 for directions on how to enlarge the design manually.

Transferring a large design

To transfer a large design, follow these steps:

1. **Trace the pattern pieces or a quilting design onto tracing paper.**

2. **Place a piece of dressmaker's tracing (carbon) paper on the right side of the fabric with the carbon side down. Lay the tracing paper on top and pin the tracing, the carbon, and the fabric together.**

3. **Trace all the pattern lines with a tracing wheel or ballpoint pen to transfer the design from the paper to the fabric.**

If you are using a ballpoint pen to trace your design, be careful not to poke through the tracing paper and mark up the fabric.

4. **Remove the dressmaker's paper and tracing paper.**

The transfer lines appear on the fabric so you can use these lines as a guide for cutting out the pattern from the fabric.

Making a template

If you use manila paper, cardboard, or acetate as template material, you need to first trace the design so you can transfer the pattern to the template. For more information on templates, see Chapter 16. Use these steps to make a template:

1. **Trace the design onto tracing paper.**

2. **Place the tracing face down on the cardboard and use a pen or pencil to rub over each traced line.**

   The outline transfers to the cardboard. (See "Transferring a large design" in this chapter for more information on tracing patterns.)

3. **Remove the tracing paper and go over the rubbed lines with a ball-point pen to make the lines more legible, if needed.**

4. **Cut the design outline from the cardboard. (If you use acetate, place it over the tracing and cut out the design shape.)**

Using acetate for template material has several advantages. You can use it many times without it losing its sharp edges, and because it's clear, you can trace a pattern piece directly onto it. Further, you can see through it when placing it on the fabric in order to position it where you want it. For example, if you are using a floral print, you may want to center a flower in the middle of the template piece.

Using the template

If you're making a patchwork project, determine which fabric you want to use for each template. When you place the templates on the fabric to cut out the pieces, place the templates at least ½ inch apart to allow for the ¼ inch seam allowance when you cut out each piece of fabric. Or you may want to allow for ⅜-inch seams for turning each of the edges to the underside of the fabric. The thickness of the fabric, whether the design has points, curves, and so on, determines how much of a seam allowance you need to leave. Try both space allowances to see which works best for you.

Hand Quilting 101

Quilting consists of sewing layers of fabric and batting together to produce a padded structure that straight, even, small stitches hold together. The quilting process (generally the final step in a patchwork project) makes the project interesting and gives it a textured look.

Follow these steps to hand quilt:

1. **Cut a length of thread approximately 18 to 20 inches. Thread the needle so that approximately 8 inches of thread goes through the needle. Make a small knot in the long end of the thread, leaving a 1-inch tail below the knot.**

   Make the knot in only one end of the thread so that you quilt with a single strand of thread.

2. **Bring the needle up through the back of the patchwork to the top front where you start the first line of quilting. Give the knotted end a good tug and pull it through the backing fabric into the batting.**

   You make all subsequent quilting stitches through all three layers of fabric. But each time you rethread the needle, pull the first stitch into the batting to avoid knots on the underside of your quilted project.

3. **Make small running stitches (see Chapter 13) and follow your pre-marked quilting pattern. Or make a line of stitches ¼ inch on each side of all the patchwork seam lines.**

   Make sure you don't stitch into the ¼-inch seam allowance that resides around the outside edge of the patchwork top.

4. **When you come to the last 3 inches of thread, take one last stitch into the patchwork fabric, but not out through the backing. Push the needle up again an inch from where you put it in, and pull the needle up through the patchwork top and away from the remaining thread. Snip the end of the thread (if a tiny end shows), close to the top of the fabric.**

   The thread is secure inside the batting.

5. **Rethread your needle (Step 1) and continue quilting as in Step 2.**

Quick and Easy Techniques

Because patchwork has been popular for such a long time, many different crafters have devised their own particular system of creating patchwork projects. Often, a crafter who succeeds with a pattern repeats that pattern with different fabrics. Repeating patterns produces shortcuts and new tricks that crafters pass to each other.

Quilting overview

When you need to fill large areas of a background (such as a border or large plain blocks between patchwork blocks) with quilting, choose a simple design. Background quilting should never interfere with patchwork or applique elements.

For a quick-and-easy way to make quilting grid patterns of squares or diamond shapes, use a yardstick or masking tape in the following way:

1. **Place a yardstick across the top edge of your fabric and use a marking pen to mark the material along the edge of the yardstick.**

   The marking pen washes out of the fabric easily. See Chapter 13 for more information about marking pens.

2. **Without removing the yardstick from the fabric, turn it over sideways and, once again, mark along the edge of the yardstick.**

3. **Continue across the fabric to the bottom edge.**

   This method creates perfect, 1-inch spaces between each yardstick line. You can use various sizes of masking tape instead of a yardstick to increase or decrease line spacing.

4. **Lay the yardstick along one side edge of the fabric and repeat the line-marking process to create a 1-inch grid across the fabric.**

5. **Stitch along the marked lines.**

Follow these steps to make a diamond grid:

1. **Place the yardstick diagonally across one corner of the patchwork fabric and mark the material with a marking pen.**

2. **Continue to turn the yardstick over and mark each line until you reach the opposite corner.**

3. **Repeat this process in the opposite direction.**

Nothing illicit about strip piecing

Strip piecing consists of sewing strips of different fabrics together and then cutting them into units that you arrange to create a patchwork top. The strip piecing method works well when you make a quilt whose pattern requires many fabric pieces. Instead of repeatedly cutting and sewing individual squares together, the strip piecing method allows you to sew two or more strips of fabric together and then cut those strips into equal pieces called units. You then arrange the equal pieces (units) and stitch them together in different positions (as in the project directions) to form your patchwork pattern.

Follow these steps (and keep an eye on Figure 15-1) to get in on the strip piecing act:

1. **Row 1: With right sides facing together and long edges aligned, sew equal-width strips of fabric together and mark off units (with a light pencil and ruler) equal to the width of the strips.**

2. **Row 2: Cut out each unit along the marked lines.**

3. **Row 3: Sew another group of strips (with three different fabrics) together in the same manner as row one and cut out the units as in row 2.**

4. **Row 4: By joining a unit from row 1 to each side edge of a unit from row 2, you can create a multi-colored quilt block quickly and easily.**

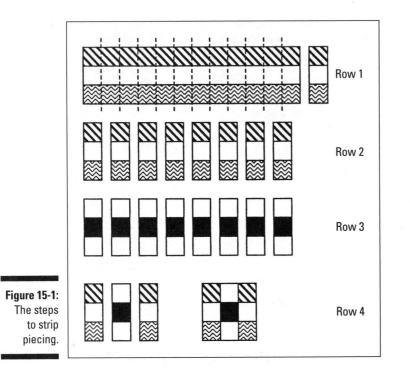

Figure 15-1:
The steps
to strip
piecing.

Even the mathematically challenged can get a triangle right

Follow these steps for a quick-and-easy way to join light and dark triangles to create squares of any size. The steps are illustrated in Figure 15-2.

1. **Determine the size of the patchwork squares that you want.**

2. **Add 1 inch to your determined patchwork square size and then mark that size off on the wrong side of the light fabric.**

   For example, if you want to create 2-inch squares, mark off 3-inch squares.

3. **Draw diagonal lines through each square, as shown in Figure 15-2a.**

4. **With the light and dark fabric's right sides facing and raw edges aligned, pin the marked light fabric to the dark fabric of the same size.**

5. **Stitch ¼ inch away from the diagonal lines, on each side of the lines, as shown in Figure 15-2b.**

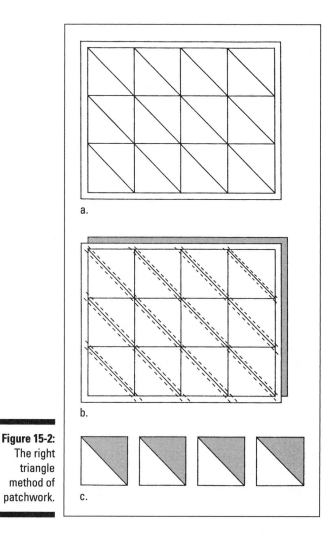

Figure 15-2:
The right triangle method of patchwork.

a.

b.

c.

6. **Cut all the solid lines of the squares to make individual squares of light and dark triangles.**

7. **Open the seams of the squares you cut out and press.**

   You now have 24 squares, each made up of a dark and light triangle patch.

Sewing small squares together

When you need to make patchwork pieces from small squares of fabric (approximately 1 to 1½ inches), use the easy method shown in Figure 15-3 to stitch them together.

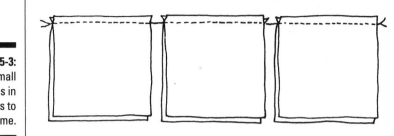

Figure 15-3:
Sew small squares in multiples to save time.

1. **With their right sides facing, pin together individual sets of two small fabric squares each.**

2. **With your sewing machine, stitch along one side of the pinned fabric edges of one set, but don't cut the thread when you finish stitching.**

3. **Run the sewing machine for two or three more stitches and then feed the next set of squares through.**

4. **Continue to stitch all the square sets with this method so that you end up with a string of patches connected by threads.**

5. **After you make enough pieces of patchwork for your project, cut the threads between the squares and separate them.**

6. **Open each set of squares and press with your iron.**

Country Potholders

Potholders make excellent patchwork projects for beginners because they teach you the basic fundamentals of patchwork and quilting and because making a potholder produces a useful kitchen tool. You can make potholders quickly and inexpensively, so you can use your newfound quilting and patch-work talent to make potholders to sell at fundraisers. Although you can stitch these small patchwork projects by hand, it's more practical to stitch the fabric together by machine, if you have a sewing machine.

The pastel potholders (see the photo in the color section of this book) that I make in this project consist of pink and green plaid homespun fabric. *Homespun fabric* is heavy woven cotton that looks and feels like linen. You can find this fabric in any fabric store. Homespun comes in many colors, so you can make these projects in colors that match your kitchen. Whatever colors you choose, you can piece together each of these 8-x-8-inch pothold-ers in a different patchwork pattern. You can make one pattern or all four patterns (see Figure 15-4).

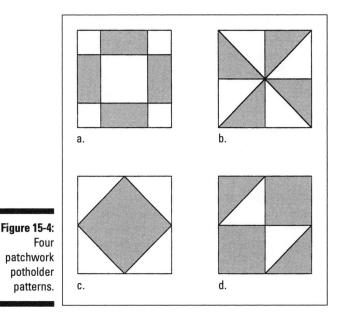

Figure 15-4:
Four
patchwork
potholder
patterns.

a.

b.

c.

d.

Tools and Materials:

Basic sewing craft kit (see the Cheat Sheet at the front of this book)

¼ yard of green plaid homespun fabric

¼ yard of dark solid coral homespun fabric

¼ yard of light coral plaid homespun fabric

16-x-16-inch piece of quilt batting for each potholder

Note: All measurements for each project include ¼ inch seam allowance.

Big square/little square potholder

Cut the following shapes from your fabric:

- 4 rectangles from the green plaid fabric, each 2½ x 4½ inches
- 1 square of the dark solid coral fabric, 4½ x 4½ inches
- 4 squares of the coral fabric, each 2½ x 2½ inches

1. **With the fabric's right sides facing and raw edges aligned, stitch a small coral square to each short end of a green rectangle. Open the seams and press with an iron.**

2. Repeat with the other three green rectangles and small coral squares.

3. Stitch, along the long edge, a green rectangle to each side of the 4½-inch coral square. Open the seams and press with an iron.

4. With the right sides facing and raw edges aligned, join the fabric rows together, placing the wide row between the two narrow rows, as shown in Figure 15-4a.

5. To finish your potholder, see "Finishing the potholders" later in this section.

Pinwheel potholder

1. Cut the following shapes from your fabric:

   • 2 squares of green plaid, each 5 x 5 inches, cut into two equal triangles.

   • 2 squares of light coral plaid, each 5 x 5 inches, cut into two equal triangles.

2. With the fabric's right sides facing and raw edges aligned, stitch a green triangle to a coral triangle along the long edges of each. Repeat this step to make four green and coral squares. Open the seams and press with your iron.

3. Stitch the green and coral squares together, alternating green and coral, as shown in Figure 15-4b. Open the seams and press with your iron.

4. To finish your potholder, see "Finishing the potholders" later in this section.

Square-in-a-square potholder

1. Cut the following shapes from your fabric:

   • 1 square of green plaid, 6⅛ x 6⅛ inches

   • 2 squares of dark solid coral, each 5 x 5 inches, cut into two equal triangles.

2. With the fabric's right sides facing and raw edges aligned, stitch each coral triangle, along the diagonal, to each side of the green plaid square to make a larger square. (See Figure 15-4c.)

3. Open the seams and press with your iron.

4. To finish your potholder, see "Finishing the potholders" later in this section.

Hourglass potholder

1. Cut the following shapes out of your fabric:

    - 1 square of green plaid, 5 x 5 inches, cut into two equal triangles

    - 2 squares, each of green plaid, 5 x 5 inches

    - 1 square of coral plaid, 5 x 5 inches, cut into two equal triangles

2. **With the fabric's right sides facing and raw edges aligned, stitch a green triangle to a coral plaid triangle along the diagonal. Open the seams and press with an iron.**

3. **With the fabric's right sides facing and raw edges aligned, stitch a green and coral plaid square to a plain green square on the coral side, as shown in Figure 15-4d. Open the seams and press with an iron. Repeat this step with the remaining squares.**

4. **To finish your potholder, see "Finishing the potholders" later in this section.**

Finishing the potholders

To finish your potholder, follow these steps:

1. **Cut a 1½-x-6-inch strip from any piece of remaining fabric to make a hanging loop for your potholder.**

2. **With wrong sides facing, fold the strip in half lengthwise and press with your iron. Turn the raw edges in ¼ inch, press with your iron, and stitch along the long edge of the fabric.**

3. **Fold the strip into a loop and overlap the raw ends. Pin the raw ends of the loop to one corner of the top of the potholder so that the loop lies on the front of the patchwork top.**

4. **Cut the batting in half so you have two 8-inch square pieces.**

5. **Cut an 8½-x-8½-inch backing piece from either the green or the coral fabric.**

6. **Pin one piece of batting to the back of the potholder top and quilt by hand or machine along all the seam lines of the potholder's design.**

7. **Pin the second piece of batting to the wrong side of the backing fabric.**

8. **With the fabric's right sides facing and all the edges aligned (make sure the hanging loop is between the two fabric sides), stitch around three sides and four corners of the potholder. Make sure you catch the raw ends of the loop as you stitch.**

9. **Turn the potholder right-side out and push the corners out with a**

10. **Turn the potholder's raw edges to the inside and stitch the opening closed.**

Patchwork Pillow

Making an oversized pillow requires patchwork and quilting techniques and is an easy sewing machine project. The generous 24-inch square size of this pillow project makes it ideal for your sofa, bed, or for lounging on the floor. The pillow's patchwork border frames a center panel of fabric that you quilt in a pattern of circles (see the photo in the color section).

When you stitch any two pieces of fabric together, always begin stitching at the seam allowance — ¼ inch in from the fabric's edge.

Tools and Materials:

Basic sewing craft kit (see the Cheat Sheet at the front of this book)

½-yard of 45-inch-wide blue calico (or color of your choice)

¾-yard of 45-inch-wide muslin

Needle and white thread

24-inch square piece of quilt batting

Compass

24-inch square pillow form (sold in fabric shops) or stuffing, such as Poly-Fil

1. **Cut the following shapes from the printed blue fabric:**
   - 1 square, 12½ x 12½ inches
   - 20 squares, 2½ x 2½ inches each
   - 4 strips, 2½ x 12½ inches each

2. **Cut the following pieces of muslin:**
   - 8 strips, 2½ x 12 inches each
   - 16 squares, 2½ x 2½ inches each

3. **Cut 1 backing piece of fabric (either muslin or printed), 24½-inches square.**

4. **With the fabric's right sides together and raw edges aligned, pin one 2½-inch muslin square to one blue calico 2½-inch square. Stitch along one side edge of the fabric. Open the seams and press with your iron from the wrong side.**

5. Join the two squares you've already stitched with another blue calico square on the opposite side of the muslin square in the same way as in Step 4. Stitching these three squares of fabric together creates a row of two printed blue square patches with a muslin square in between (see Row 1 in Figure 15-5). Open the seams and press with your iron.

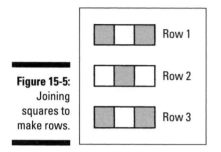

Figure 15-5:
Joining
squares to
make rows.

6. Repeat Steps 4 and 5 to make a row of one muslin square, one printed blue square, and a muslin square (see Row 2 in Figure 15-5).

7. Repeat Steps 4 and 5 to make a row of one printed blue square, one muslin square, and one printed blue square (see Row 3 in Figure 15-5).

8. Repeat Steps 4 through 7 until you have 12 rows of fabric; 8 rows like Row 1 and 4 rows like Row 2.

9. With the fabric's right sides together and raw edges aligned, pin Rows 1 and 2 together and stitch across the long edge on top. Open the seams and press the fabric's wrong side with your iron.

10. With the fabric's right sides together and the bottom raw edge of Row 2 aligned with a long edge of Row 3, pin Rows 2 and 3 together. Stitch along the long edges of the fabric to join Rows 2 and 3. Open the seams and press with your iron. You've created a patchwork block! (See Figure 15-6.)

Figure 15-6:
Joining
three rows
to make a
block.

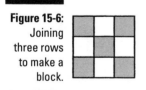

11. Repeat Steps 9 and 10 to make three more patchwork blocks. The patchwork blocks make up each corner piece of the pillow.

12. With the fabric's right sides facing and raw edges aligned, pin one of the 12-inch long muslin strips to one of the 12-inch long blue strips and then stitch along one long edge of the fabric. Open the seams and press with your iron.

13. Pin another 12-inch long muslin strip to the long edge of the blue strip (right sides facing) and stitch together. Open the seams and press with your iron.

14. Repeat Steps 12 and 13 to make three more borders.

15. With the fabric's right sides facing, pin one border to one edge of the printed blue 12 ½-inch center fabric square and then stitch the edges together (see Figure 15-7). Open the seams on the fabric's wrong side and press with your iron.

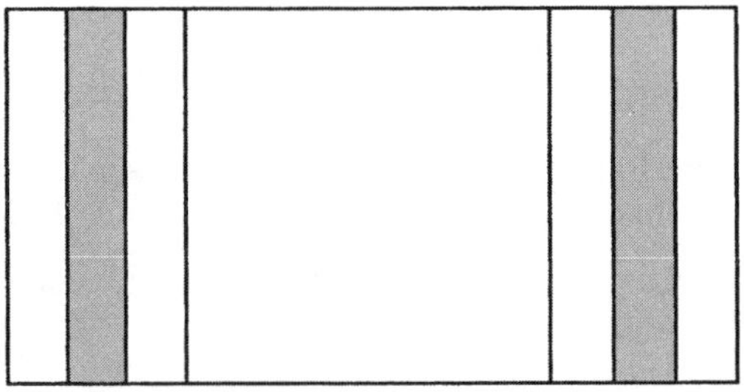

Figure 15-7: Joining borders to the center piece.

16. Repeat Step 15 on the opposite edge of the center square.

17. With the fabric's right sides facing and raw edges aligned, pin and then stitch one patchwork block to each short edge of the two remaining borders (see Figure 15-8). Open the seams and press with your iron.

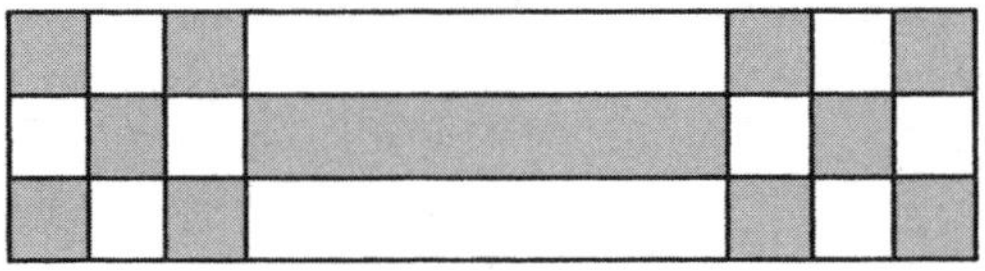

Figure 15-8: Joining corner pieces to borders.

18. With the fabric's right sides facing and raw edges aligned, pin and then stitch the pieces that you made in Step 17 to the top and bottom edges of the central square to complete the pillow top assembly, as shown in Figure 15-9. Open the seams and press with your iron.

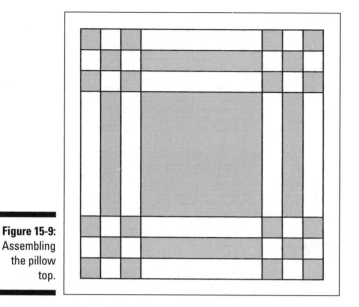

Figure 15-9:
Assembling
the pillow
top.

19. Place the pillow top on a hard surface. Use a compass and a light pencil to draw overlapping, 5-inch circles in the center square on the right side of the fabric. Look at the photo in the color section to see how to position the circles.

20. Use a ruler to make diagonal lines across the borders with ½-inch spaces between the lines.

21. With the front of the fabric facing up, pin the pillow top to a piece of quilt batting.

22. Sew running stitches (see Chapter 13) along the lines you drew in Steps 19 and 20 to quilt the pillow.

23. With the fabric's right sides together, pin the quilted pillow top and backing fabric together.

24. Stitch around three sides and four corners of the pillow, leaving a ¼-inch seam allowance.

25. Turn the fabric right-side out and press with your iron. Turn in the open edges ¼ inch and press with your iron.

26. Insert the pillow form, or stuff with the stuffing until the pillow is full to your satisfaction.

27. Slipstitch the opening closed, as shown in Figure 15-10.

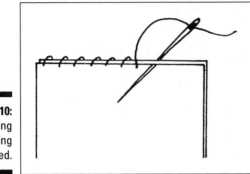

Figure 15-10:
Slipstitching
the opening
closed.

Stuffed Patchwork Cat

You can use this stuffed patchwork cat (see the photo in the color section) as a pillow, a child's toy, or a doorstop. (To use it as a doorstop, fill the finished cat with sand or weigh down the bottom with a brick.) You make this 13-inch high cat from 1-inch squares of light and dark and solid and printed fabrics that you stitch together. The patchwork cat's backing fabric is a solid piece of fabric that you cut from one of the fabrics you use on the front of the cat. You can make this project to use up the tiny leftover scraps from the other projects in this chapter. You quilt the grid pattern of this cat by hand.

Tools and Materials:

52 1½-x-1½-inch squares, made of assorted calico scraps

52 muslin squares, each 1½ x 1½ inches

Calico fabric, 8 x 13½ inches (for the project's backing)

Stuffing, such as Poly-Fil

Tracing paper

Note: All measurements include ¼-inch seam allowance.

1. **With the fabric's right sides facing and raw edges aligned, stitch a calico square to a muslin square along one edge. Open the seams and press with your iron.**

2. **Continue to join squares in this way, alternating a calico square with a muslin square, until you have 13 rows with 8 squares each. Press all the seams to the same side.**

3. **With the fabric's right sides facing and raw edges aligned, join all the rows so that the light and dark squares lie above and below each other. This creates a patchwork piece of fabric that is approximately 8½ x 13½ inches.**

4. **Enlarge the cat pattern shown in Figure 15-11 by 210 percent (to 13½ inches high) and transfer the enlargement to tracing paper. Make a separate enlargement of the cat's tail. (See Chapter 3 for more information on enlarging and transferring patterns.)**

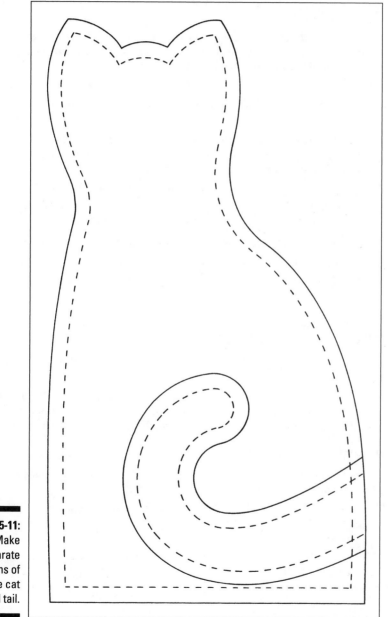

Figure 15-11:
Make
separate
patterns of
the cat
and tail.

5. Pin the enlarged pattern to the right side of the patchwork fabric and cut out the pattern of the cat only.

6. Pin the pattern of the tail to the remaining piece of patchwork fabric and then cut it out.

7. Cut the cat and tail pattern pieces from the 8-x-13½-inch solid calico backing fabric.

8. With the right sides facing and raw edges aligned, stitch the tail pieces together but leave the straight edge open so you can fill it with stuffing. Turn the tail fabric right-side out and use a pencil eraser or crochet hook to stuff the tail tightly with stuffing.

9. Pin the raw edges of the tail in position on the wrong side of the patchwork cat's front.

10. With the fabric's right sides facing and raw edges aligned, pin the backing to the front of the cat, with the tail between the two pieces of fabric. Stitch all around, leaving the bottom end open.

11. Use snipping scissors to make small, evenly spaced snips into the excess fabric of the seam allowance (but not into your stitches) around all the cat's curves, including all the corners.

12. Turn the cat right-side out. Press with your iron.

13. Stuff the cat tightly with stuffing. Turn the raw edges of the fabric's opening to the inside and slipstitch the opening closed (refer to Figure 15-10).

Pinwheel Baby Quilt

Quilts make great gifts for newborn babies and are easy to take care of. The more you wash a quilt, the softer it gets and the better it looks. The 24-x-32-inch baby quilt (shown in the color section) is the perfect size for a bassinet, carriage, or stroller and is an easy sewing-machine project. Finish the edge of the quilt with eyelet trim, which is available by the yard in fabric shops.

Tools and Materials:

Basic sewing craft kit (see the Cheat Sheet at the front of this book)

Tracing paper

Cardboard

¼ yard white fabric (cotton or polyester/cotton blend)

¼ yard pink fabric (cotton or polyester/cotton blend)

1 yard blue calico (includes backing)

1 yard quilt batting

3¼ yards of 2-inch wide eyelet

3¼ yards of 1-inch-wide eyelet

1 skein pink embroidery floss

Note: All fabric is 45 inches wide. All measurements include a ¼-inch seam allowance.

1. **Trace Patterns A and B in Figure 15-12, enlarge them by 125 percent, and transfer them to cardboard to make templates.**

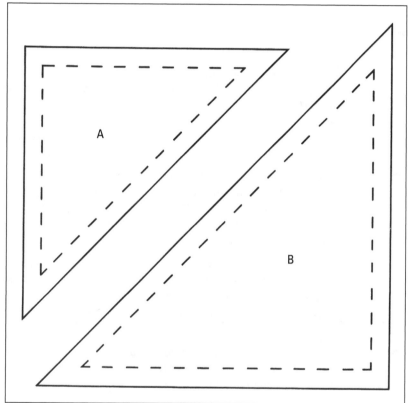

Figure 15-12:
Pattern pieces for pinwheel quilt.

2. **Cut the following shapes from the fabrics:**
   - 48 white pattern A triangles
   - 48 pink pattern A triangles
   - 48 blue calico pattern B triangles
   - 24½-x-32½-inch backing piece

   See Figure 15-13 for diagrams to help you assemble the pinwheel baby quilt as you follow the steps.

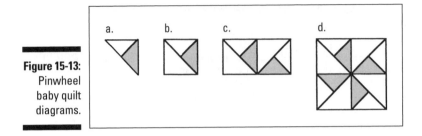

Figure 15-13:
Pinwheel
baby quilt
diagrams.

3. With the fabric's right sides together and raw edges aligned, pin a white pattern A piece to a pink pattern A piece and then stitch along one of the triangle's short edges to make a larger triangle, as shown in Figure 15-13a. Open the seams and press with your iron on the fabric's wrong side.

4. Repeat Step 3 to make 48 larger pieced triangles.

5. With the fabric's right sides together and raw edges aligned, pin a pieced triangle to a blue calico pattern B triangle and then stitch along the triangle's diagonal to make a square. (See Figure 15-13b.) Press open the seams on the fabric's wrong side.

6. Repeat Step 5 to make 48 patchwork squares.

7. With the fabric's right sides together and raw edges aligned, pin two of the 48 squares together, as shown in Figure 15-13c, to make half of the pinwheel block. Press open the seams on the fabric's wrong side.

8. Repeat Step 7 to make 24 pinwheel block halves.

9. With the fabric's right sides together and raw edges aligned, pin two pinwheel block halves together to form a block, as shown in Figure 15-13d. Stitch along the fabric's bottom edge. Press open the seams on the fabric's wrong side.

10. Repeat Step 9 to make 12 blocks.

11. With the fabric of the patchwork block's right sides together and raw edges aligned, stitch two blocks together along a side edge. Press open the seams on the fabric's wrong side.

12. Repeat Step 11 to make a row of three blocks, as shown in Figure 15-14. Press open the seams on the wrong side.

Figure 15-14:
Stitch three
blocks
in a row.

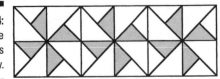

13. **Repeat Steps 11 and 12 to make three more patchwork block rows.**

14. **With the fabric's right sides facing and raw edges aligned, pin two patchwork block rows together and stitch across their bottom edges. Open the seams and press with your iron on the fabric's wrong side.**

15. **Repeat Step 14 to join all four rows to make the quilt's top, shown in Figure 15-15.**

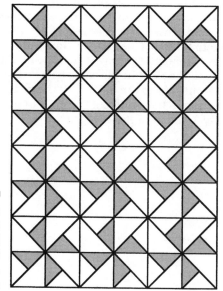

Figure 15-15:
The pinwheel baby quilt top.

Note: The quilt's eyelet trim is optional. If you prefer not to trim your quilt, skip to Step 19.

16. **With the raw edges matching, pin the 1-inch-wide eyelet to the front of the 2-inch-wide eyelet and stitch across the bottom edge to join the two eyelet fabrics.**

17. **With the right sides of the eyelet facing the front of the quilt, pin the raw edges of the eyelet all around the quilt top. Overlap the eyelet ends where they meet.**

18. **Stitch the eyelet all around the quilt top, ¼ inch from the edge of the patchwork top.**

19. **With right sides facing, pin the backing fabric and the quilt top together.**

20. **Center the pinned fabric over the quilt batting and re-pin all three layers together.**

21. Use fabric shears to trim the excess batting to the quilt's size.

22. Stitch around three sides and four corners of the quilt, leaving one edge of the quilt open. Turn the quilt right-side out.

23. Turn the raw edges of the fabric's opening to the inside ¼ inch and press the quilt with your iron.

24. Slipstitch the quilt's open edge closed.

25. Use the embroidery floss to tie the center of each block: Cut a 12-inch piece of embroidery floss and thread your needle with it. (Don't make a knot at the end of the floss.) Insert the needle through the top of the quilt in the center of the first block (the intersection of the four triangles), without pulling the thread all the way through, and then bring the needle back up through the quilt in the same spot so that both ends of floss are on the front side of the quilt. Pull the needle off the thread. Make a knot and then a bow, and cut the ends of the floss. (You need approximately 6 inches of floss for each bow.)

Chapter 16

Appliqué

- -

In This Chapter

▶ Discovering the basics of appliqué

▶ Applying appliqué by hand, with a sewing machine, and by pressing

▶ Making appliqué projects

- -

Appliqué is the craft of applying pieces of one fabric onto a background fabric to create a pattern or design. This chapter clues you in to the language of appliqué (easier to master than French or Italian), shows you how to cut templates, gives you the ins and outs of making smooth curves, tells you how to cut corners (quite literally), and shows you how to appliqué with and without stitches. After you absorb the how-to-do-it information in this chapter, you can create all sorts of accessories with appliqués.

Learning the Language: Basic Appliqué Terms

Appliqué is a fabric craft that many people associate with patchwork and quilting. With appliqué, you use the same basic materials and terms as those you use with patchwork (see Chapter 15), with a few more terms thrown in for good measure.

✔ **Appliqué:** Layering one fabric over another to create a design, picture, or decoration.

✔ **Bias:** Diagonal to the grain of fabric. Directions for cutting a pattern piece "on the bias" mean that you need to cut the pattern on the diagonal of the fabric's grain.

✔ **Bias tape:** Prepackaged fabric cut on the bias with both raw edges folded under. Single-fold bias comes in ½-inch and ⅞-inch widths. Double-fold bias tape comes in ¼-inch and ½-inch widths. You use bias tape to bind raw edges around a finished project.

✔ **Dressmaker's carbon:** Thin paper with a special finish on one side that allows you to transfer design lines onto fabric. The transferred design lines disappear within 24 to 72 hours, or you can remove them by dabbing the lines with a damp cloth (check manufacturer's directions on the package).

✔ **Freezer paper:** Often used to cut templates, this paper is available in your supermarket. Be sure to purchase poly-coated paper, not waxed paper, because you use a hot iron to press the paper temporarily in position on the fabric.

Poly-coated freezer paper peels off the fabric, but waxed freezer paper doesn't.

✔ **Grain:** The direction that threads run in woven fabric.

✔ **Markers:** Any writing instrument that you use to trace and transfer designs onto your fabric. A soft pencil works well for tracing and transferring designs to the fabric. Many crafters also use chalk to mark dark material.

Always use water-soluble markers on fabric.

✔ **Motif:** Shapes to be applied to a background fabric.

✔ **Template:** A rigid, full-size pattern that you use to make appliqués. You can cut templates from freezer paper, manila paper, acetate, sandpaper, an index card, cardboard from a new shirt, or even a plastic coffee can lid. Templates enable you to make multiple copies of the same appliqué piece accurately.

✔ **Zigzag stitch:** Almost every sewing machine, no matter how basic, includes an adjustment for making zigzag stitches. A zigzag stitch looks exactly the way it sounds, and you use it to cover the edges of the fabric appliqués while stitching them to the background fabric. You can adjust the length and width of the zigzag stitch on your sewing machine. You use the zigzag stitch most often when you're working with small appliqués, when there isn't enough fabric all around the appliqué shape to turn under.

Use a scrap piece of fabric to try different-size zigzag stitches to determine which size you like best. Keep in mind the smaller the appliqué piece, the shorter and closer the zigzag stitches should be.

Using Templates to Cut Out Your Design Pieces

The template is the heart of appliqué. You use the template pattern to make the pieces for your design. If you can cut a simple shape from cardboard, you can begin the first steps of making appliqué. The rest of the appliqué steps are clear sailing. You'll find designs for making templates with each project in this chapter. Quilt shops often sell packages of templates in a variety of shapes for doing appliqué projects, but making your own is easy, and then your projects are one-of-a-kind.

Cutting out templates

Trace the appliqué design provided with the project you are making and transfer (see Chapter 15) the design to template paper. Using sharp scissors, cut out your design's outline from cardboard. If you use acetate for your template, place it over the traced design to cut out the exact shape. You can also mark a pattern on paper to cut out a template. Just glue the paper pattern to a stiff piece of cardboard, freezer paper, or plastic; let it dry; and then cut along the traced outline.

Drawing around the template

After you make a template, place it on the back of your fabric and draw around it to create a design element.

Before you start drawing around your templates, however, read the next two sections about cutting and allowing enough fabric around each template for the type of appliqués you need for each project. If you start drawing templates without planning the layout first, you may end up without enough fabric.

Cutting appliqué pieces

Cutting out appliqué pieces requires accuracy, unlike many other crafts that require the use of scissors.

After you decide which fabric you want to use for each template, figuring out the best layout for getting the most appliqué pieces from your fabric is easy. For example, if your design calls for triangles, place the triangles on the fabric so they form squares to minimize the amount of fabric that you waste. Mark each template on your fabric and then use sharp scissors to cut out each pattern piece from your fabric.

Allowing for seams

If you are planning to appliqué by hand, you need to add a ¼-inch seam allowance beyond the drawn lines when cutting out the fabric around the drawn lines of the template. The line that you've drawn around the template (on the fabric) indicates where you turn the edges of the fabric under when you apply the appliqué to the background fabric.

If you plan to appliqué by machine (with a zigzag stitch) or with fusible webbing, cut each template piece without the ¼-inch extra fabric for turning. Cut directly on the drawn lines.

Enlarging designs

You must enlarge some of the designs for the projects in this book before you draw them on the fabric. Enlarge the designs to the size indicated on a copy machine. If you don't have access to a copy machine, see Chapter 3 to find out how you can enlarge any design.

Throwing curves: inner and outer

Some appliqué pieces curve. After cutting out curved pieces, make small, evenly spaced cuts in the seam allowance around the fabric piece. Clipping into the seam allowance of curves enables you to easily turn the cut edges of the appliqué pieces under to the wrong side of the fabric so that the appliqué lies flat on the background fabric.

Smooth turning

Place the template in position where you drew the template outline on the back of the fabric. Carefully fold up the ¼ inch of extra fabric (the seam allowance) all around the template. With an iron, press all the fabric's edges over the template's edges. If your appliqué is curved, don't forget to clip all the edges to the seam line before turning (see the preceding section).

How to Appliqué

You can appliqué by hand-stitching, machine-stitching, or by using fusible webbing. The next sections show you how to appliqué using all three methods.

Regardless of which technique you use, you have to pin each appliqué piece to the background fabric with straight pins. First, attach the appliqué piece with a pin through the center. When you pin the fabric edges, whether they are turned or raw, place the pin perpendicular to the edge of the appliqué piece. A sewing machine needle can stitch right over the pins in this position.

Appliqué by hand

If you hand-stitch an appliqué to the background fabric, you must turn the appliqué's edges (see "Smooth turning," earlier in this chapter) for a smooth, neat finish. After you securely pin each appliqué to the background fabric, you can begin to stitch the appliqués in place.

1. **Using thread in a color that matches the appliqué fabric, thread a needle and make a knot at one end (see Chapter 13).**

2. **With the needle on the underside of the background fabric, bring the needle up through the background fabric, under and through the edge of the appliqué.**

3. **Stitch around the edge of the appliqué piece with a slip stitch (see Chapter 15).**

4. **When you finish stitching, bring the needle to the underside of your fabric, make a small knot, and cut the end of the thread.**

Appliqué by machine

Stitching an appliqué on a sewing machine requires a zigzag stitch (see "Learning the Language: Basic Appliqué Terms," earlier in this chapter). Remember, to machine appliqué, you need to cut the fabric without a seam allowance. With the appliqué piece pinned in position and the sewing machine threaded with a color that matches the fabric piece, machine-sew a zigzag stitch around the appliqué's edges. When you appliqué a pointed piece, gradually narrow the zigzag width just before you reach the point on each side of the fabric.

Fusing is a pressing matter

You can also use fusible webbing (see Chapter 14) and an iron to create beautiful appliqué. For fusible appliqués, you don't need any seam allowance. Before you pin your appliqué shapes to the background fabric, follow these steps:

1. **Pin the cutout appliqué to the fusible webbing and cut around the appliqué's outline.**

2. **Heat a dry iron to medium hot.**

3. **Pin the appliqué to the background fabric with the fusible webbing between the appliqué and the background fabric.**

4. **Place a dry cloth (such as a piece of cotton fabric) over the appliqué and then press the iron on top of the dry cloth. Hold for four or five seconds to fuse the appliqué to the background fabric.**

5. **Remove the dry cloth and pin(s) and then replace the dry cloth and reapply the hot iron to the area where you removed the pin(s).**

The fused appliqué remains through repeated washings.

You can add zigzag stitches around the edges of the fused appliqué to give the edges a finished look and to make the appliqué more permanent. Experiment with your zigzag stitch sizes and use contrasting thread color to vary the look. Large zigzag stitches in brightly colored thread might be fun for a project made for a child, such as the ducky bib and place mat shown in the color section of the book.

For quick appliqué projects, use the fusible webbing method. However, if hand-sewing intrigues you, nothing looks more attractive than a hand-stitched appliqué.

Cookie Cutter Appliqués

Simple shapes like hearts and gingerbread men are traditional country appliqué motifs. I call these designs "cookie cutter appliqués" because you can use your cookie cutters to make the shapes. Although I've provided you with the shapes in the exact sizes that the projects in this chapter require, you can open your kitchen drawers to expand your designs for other projects.

Pine-scented pillow sachets

You can use these little pine-filled sachets (see a photo of them in the color section of this book) for sweet dreams or in your linen closet to make your sheets and towels smell great. Sachets keep clothes closets fresh, they look attractive in a basket, or you can use them to accent larger pillows on your chair or sofa.

The background fabric for the sachets consists of blue and white ticking material (similar to that used for covering mattresses, sometimes referred to as *mattress ticking,* but softer) and red-plaid homespun fabric. The appliqués are cut from red and white homespun plaids or solid red fabric. You make the *piping* (trim) around each sachet from one of the background fabrics (or you can use pre-made piping that comes in a package in many colors, such as red or blue). The largest sachet measures 7 x 11 inches and the smaller sachet measures 6 inches square.

If you're making the pillow sachets by hand and not using a sewing machine, stitching the pre-made piping by hand is easier than making the piping from the matching fabrics, as I did for the pillow sachets shown in the color section.

Note: All yardages are figured for fabric that's 45 inches wide.

Tools and Materials:
(for all three pillow sachets)

Basic sewing craft kit (see the Cheat Sheet at the front of this book)

¼ yard blue and white ticking fabric

¼ yard red plaid, homespun fabric

Three 4-x-4-inch pieces of solid red , bold red plaid, and red calico or small checked fabric (one for each appliqué)

2½ yards of cording (or 1 package of narrow piping)

Stuffing, such as Poly-Fil

Pine needles (or pine-scented potpourri)

1. **Cut two 6½-x-6½-inch pieces of ticking fabric for the front and back of one pillow.**

2. **Cut two 6½-x-6½-inch pieces of red checkered fabric for the front and back of the second pillow.**

3. **Cut two 7½-x-11½-inch pieces of ticking fabric for the front and back of the third pillow.**

4. **Trace the heart pattern (see Figure 16-1) on tracing paper and then pin the paper pattern to a 4-x-4-inch piece of solid red fabric. Cut out the fabric heart.**

5. **Cut another heart from the red plaid and one from the red checked or calico fabric.**

   If you don't have a zigzag attachment on your sewing machine, cut each heart appliqué ¼ inch larger than the pattern size (see "Appliqué by hand" earlier in this chapter).

6. **Position and then pin each appliqué heart on the top piece of each sachet.**

   You can place the appliqués in the center of the fabric, as I did with one small sachet, or in one corner, like the other two sachets (see the photo in the color section).

7. **Use red thread and a narrow zigzag stitch on your sewing machine to stitch around the edges of each heart.**

   You can also apply the appliqués with fusible webbing or hand-stitching (see "How to Appliqué" earlier in this chapter).

Figure 16-1:
Heart
pattern.

8. **With the fabric's right sides facing and raw edges aligned, pin the piping around the edge of the sachet top, overlapping the finished strip end with the raw strip end.**

9. **Using the zipper foot, stitch the piping around the sachet, as close as possible.**

10. **With the fabric's right sides facing and raw edges aligned, pin the backing piece of fabric to the sachet top, with the piping between the two pieces.**

11. **Turn the sachet over so that the back faces up, and (still using the zipper foot), use the piping stitches to guide yourself as you stitch around three sides and four corners of the sachet.**

12. **Trim the seam allowance and cut off the corners.**

13. **Turn the sachet right-side out and press with your iron.**

14. **Stuff your sachet firmly with a combination of stuffing and pine needles.**

    The stuffing cushions the pine needles so they don't stick through the fabric, and the pine needles add a wonderful scent to your sachet.

15. **Use a slipstitch (see Chapter 15) to stitch the sachet's opening closed.**

Making the piping

You can find packaged piping in narrow sizes that are perfect for this project. However, using prepackaged piping restricts you to basic solid colors. If you'd like to use patterned fabrics for your piping (as I did with the homespun and the ticking for the smaller sachets), follow these directions:

1. Cut a 1½-x-25-inch strip of fabric for each small sachet and a 1½-x-37-inch strip for the larger sachet.

2. Place thin (⅛-inch diameter) cording in the center of the fabric strip's wrong side. (Make sure that the fabric strip is 1 inch longer than the cording.) Fold the fabric over the cording.

3. Align the raw edges of the fabric and temporarily secure them with evenly spaced pins placed perpendicular to the edge of the fabric.

4. Use a zipper foot (a sewing machine attachment — see Chapter 13) to stitch along the fabric's edge, close to the cording.

5. Turn one raw end of the fabric strip under ⅛ inch and press with your iron to finish it.

You use the finished end to overlap the raw end when you attach the piping to the sachet top.

Gingerbread boy dish towel trims

For the appliqués on this quick and easy project (see the photo in the color section), you don't need to make a template if you use gingerbread boy cookie cutters for the pattern — just draw around the cookie cutters. If you don't have a similar cookie cutter, you can use any cookie cutter you have. (I provide a gingerbread boy pattern for you in Figure 16-2.) The brown gingerbread boys look adorable on red and white plaid linen dishtowels. You can use this design to make no-sew café kitchen curtains (see Chapter 14).

Note: You can fuse the appliqués (see "Fusing is a pressing matter" earlier in this chapter), or you can machine-stitch the appliqués with a zigzag attachment on your sewing machine (see "Learning the Language: Basic Appliqué Terms" earlier in this chapter).

Tools and Materials:

Basic sewing craft kit (see the Cheat Sheet at the front of this book)

Red plaid linen dishtowel

Tracing paper

¼ yard brown calico fabric

Small piece of fusible webbing

4 small white buttons

½ yard of red embroidery floss

White craft glue

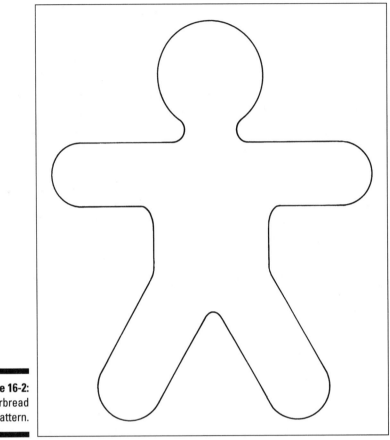

Figure 16-2:
Gingerbread
boy pattern.

1. **Trace the gingerbread man pattern (see Figure 16-2), pin it to the brown calico fabric and fusible webbing, and cut out two gingerbread men.**

   If you want to place the gingerbread men completely across the towel, cut out as many gingerbread men as you need to fill the space. If you're going to machine-stitch the appliqués, you don't need to cut out the fusible webbing pieces.

2. **Find and then mark with a pin the center of the towel's bottom edge.**

3. **Pin a gingerbread cutout on either side of the center pin, with the fusible webbing between the cutout and the towel.**

4. **Fuse the appliqués to the towel. (See "Fusing is a pressing matter" earlier in this chapter.)**

   If you decide to apply the appliqués with your sewing machine, use a zigzag stitch and brown thread to stitch around the edges of each appliqué.

5. **Stitch two buttons, evenly spaced in a row, down the front of each gingerbread man, as shown in the photo in the color section.**

6. **Make a small bow from the red embroidery floss and glue it to the neck of each applique.**

   To make the bow more secure, you can tack the bow in place on the appliqué with a stitch or two through the center of the bow.

Just Ducky

You can start with a plain bib and place mat and add the decorative ducky appliqués to create quick and easy projects that make perfect gifts for a new baby or good items to sell at a bazaar. Both of these sewing projects are easy to make and then decorate with the appliqués you apply by hand or by using the zigzag attachment on your sewing machine.

Ducky place mat

Brighten up a child's eating area with a fun fabric place mat decorated with three little ducks (see the photo in the color section). The place mat's finished size is 11 ½ x 15 ½ inches.

Tools and Materials:

Basic sewing craft kit (see the Cheat Sheet at the front of this book)

⅓ yard of 45-inch-wide blue and white fabric

Scraps of white fabric (large enough to cut out duck body pattern pieces)

Scraps of yellow fabric (large enough to cut out the duck's bills and feet pattern pieces)

Tracing paper

Heavy paper

Polyester quilt batting

White and yellow thread

1. **Cut two 12-x-16-inch pieces of blue and white fabric.**

   Use one piece as the front of the place mat and the other as the backing material.

2. **Separately trace the duck's body, bill, and feet from Figures 16-3 and 16-4 and transfer them to heavy paper to make templates (see "Using Templates to Cut Out Your Design Pieces," earlier in this chapter).**

3. **Place the template for each duck body on white fabric and trace one pattern A duck and two pattern B ducks.**

4. **On the yellow fabric, draw three feet triangles, one pattern A bill piece, and two pattern B bill pieces.**

5. **Cut out each appliqué fabric piece without a seam allowance.**

   If your sewing machine doesn't include a zigzag attachment, you can use fusible webbing to attach the appliqué pieces of fabric. Before cutting out the appliqué fabric pieces, pin the fabric to the fusible webbing and cut out each appliqué fabric piece with the fusible webbing.

6. **Pin one 12-x-16-inch piece of fabric to the quilt batting around the edges and in the center to hold the material together temporarily.**

7. **Pin each duck piece in position on the place mat, as shown in Figure 16-5, tucking the edge of the duck bills under the body by about ⅛ inch.**

8. **Use a narrow zigzag stitch and thread in the appliqué's color to stitch around the edges of the appliqués.**

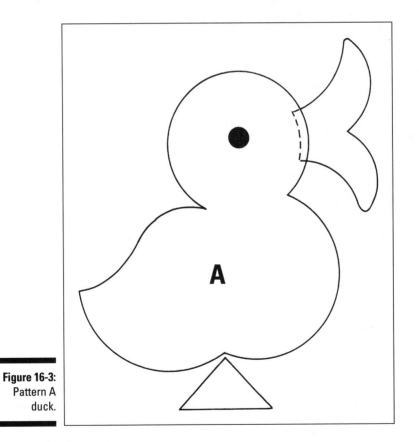

Figure 16-3:
Pattern A
duck.

A

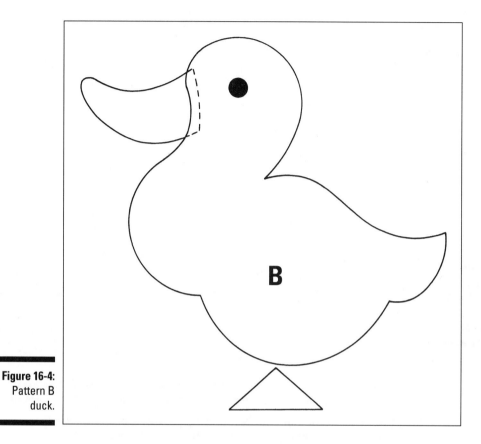

Figure 16-4:
Pattern B
duck.

If you are using fusible webbing to attach the appliqué pieces, pin the appliqué to the front of the place mat with the fusible webbing between and fuse with a warm iron (see "Fusing is a pressing matter," earlier in this chapter).

9. **If you desire, use running stitches (see Chapter 13) to illustrate rain on the place mat. Use either a backstitch (see Chapter 18) or a running stitch (see Chapter 13) to outline a fat cloud in one corner of the place mat.**

10. **Remove the pins from the place mat.**

11. **Place the backing fabric piece facedown over the appliquéd front piece, align the unfinished edges all around, and pin the two pieces of fabric together.**

12. **Stitch around three sides and four corners of the place mat, but be sure to leave a ¼-inch seam allowance. Leave 6 inches open for turning the place mat right side out.**

Figure 16-5:
Placement
diagram
for ducky
place mat.

13. **Clip off the corners to the seam line and trim the excess fabric and batting on each side to the seam line; turn the place mat right side out.**

14. **Press around the back of the mat's edges with your iron. Press the open edges to the inside and stitch the opening closed with your sewing machine or by hand with a slipstitch (see Chapter 15).**

Ducky bib

Two little ducks on a bright blue bib (see the photo in the color section) will delight any baby. You make these simple duck appliqués with the zigzag attachment of your sewing machine, because the appliqué fabric pieces are quite small and difficult to make by hand. If you don't have a zigzag attachment on your sewing machine, you can attach them with fusible webbing (see "Fusing is a pressing matter" earlier in this chapter).

Tools and Materials:

Basic sewing craft kit (see the Cheat Sheet at the front of this book)

Scrap of white fabric (large enough to cut out duck body pattern pieces)

Two 12-x-14-inch pieces of bright blue fabric

Scrap of bright yellow fabric (large enough to cut out the duck's bills and feet pattern pieces)

Tracing paper

Heavy paper

A 12-x-14-inch piece of thin quilt batting

Yellow and white thread

2¼ yards of extra wide, double-fold yellow bias binding (available in fabric shops)

1. Trace and enlarge the outline pattern in Figure 16-6 for the bib 230 percent.

2. Pin the pattern to the two 12-x-14-inch pieces of bright blue fabric.

3. Cut out the bib pattern, adding a ¼-inch seam allowance around the fabric.

4. Use the same bib template to cut a piece of thin quilt batting, but without a seam allowance.

5. Trace the elements of the duck's body patterns and transfer the patterns to heavy paper to make templates for both duck bodies.

6. Trace the patterns for the duck's bills and the triangles for the duck's feet.

   No templates needed for these small pieces — just pin the traced pattern directly onto the fabric.

7. Place templates A and B on the white fabric, draw around the templates, and cut out the pieces.

8. Pin the bill and triangle patterns to the bright yellow fabric, and cut one bill and one triangle for each duck.

9. Pin one of the bib fabric pieces to the batting piece.

10. Pin each duck piece in position on the bib front, as shown in Figure 16-6.

11. Use a narrow zigzag stitch and thread, in a color that matches each appliqué, to machine-sew around the edges of the appliqués.

12. With the wrong sides of the bib together, and the batting between, pin the back of the bib fabric to the appliquéd bib front.

13. Beginning at one outer neck edge, pin the bias binding around the raw outer edge of all three layers of material.

14. Leaving 8 inches at each end of the bias binding for the bib's tie, pin the bias binding around the inside neck opening. Tuck the raw ends from the binding around the bib into the binding for the neck/ties to cover the unfinished ends.

15. Stitch all the binding edges by hand or machine.

16. Turn the raw edges of the tie ends to the inside and stitch across the binding ends to finish the bib.

Figure 16-6:
Outline pattern for the ducky bib.

Appliqué Accent Pillows

Country pillows add warmth and charm to any area of your house. These decorative pillows are smaller in size than the decorative pillows that you normally use for backrests or sofas and chairs. These pillows work well as accents to place in front of another pillow or in the crook of the arm of your chair. Calico fabrics, which remain a staple in quilting and country-charm projects, make up the main ingredient of this project. You can apply these simple appliqués by hand or with the zigzag stitch on your sewing machine (see "Learning the Language: Basic Appliqué Terms" earlier in this chapter), or by attaching them with fusible webbing (see Chapter 13). Because of their relatively small size and the inexpensive material used in these projects, these pillows make great bazaar items, gifts, or home accessories.

Watermelon pillow

This pillow measures 8 x 10 inches when completed. See a photo of it in the color section.

Tools and Materials:

Basic sewing craft kit (see the Cheat Sheet at the front of this book)

Tracing paper

Heavy paper

White pencil

Scraps of black fabric (for watermelon seeds)

Small piece of red fabric (approximately 6 x 10 inches)

Small piece of green fabric (approximately 6 x 10 inches)

¼ yard of 45-inch-wide red and white calico print that is pre-dominately white

fusible webbing

1¼ yard of green piping

Green and red thread

Stuffing, such as Poly-Fil

1. **Enlarge each element of the watermelon design (the rind, the wedge, and the seeds) from Figure 16-7 by 200 percent, trace each element, and cut out each traced pattern individually.**

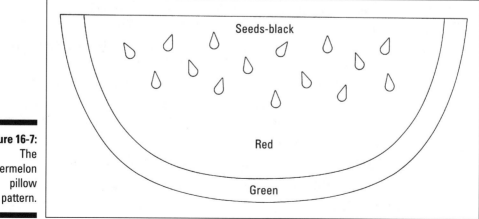

Figure 16-7:
The watermelon pillow pattern.

2. Pin the watermelon rind pattern to the green fabric and cut one piece; do the same with the watermelon wedge pattern and the red fabric.

3. Use the watermelon seed pattern to make a template and use this template and the white colored pencil to draw l5 seeds on the black fabric.

4. Pin the seed fabric to fusible webbing and cut out all the seeds from the fabric. (The seeds are too small to attach with zigzag or hand stitching.)

   If you want to use fusible webbing to attach the watermelon rind and wedge appliqué pieces, pin each appliqué pattern piece to the fabric and to the fusible webbing and cut out each pattern piece from the fabric and fusible webbing at one time, like you did for the seeds.

5. Cut two 8½-x-10½-inch pieces of the white and red calico for the top and back of the pillow.

6. Pin the watermelon appliqué pieces (the rind, wedge, and seeds) in position in the center of the front of one piece of the red and white calico fabric.

7. Using a zigzag stitch and matching thread, machine-sew around the edges of each appliqué piece.

   Use green around the outside edge of the rind, as well as around the inside edge of the rind where the red and green fabrics meet. Use red thread across the top part of the watermelon wedge. (To attach the appliqué fabric pieces using fusible webbing, see "Fusing is a pressing matter," earlier in this chapter.)

8. Place the seeds at random on the red wedge fabric (see the photo in the color section) and press each seed with a medium hot iron for three seconds to fuse the black appliqués to the watermelon wedge fabric.

9. With the piping and pillow top's right sides facing and raw edges aligned, pin the piping around the edge of the pillow top, overlapping the raw ends.

10. Stitch the piping and pillow top together, stitching as close to the cording (which is inside the piping) as possible.

11. With their right sides facing, pin the backing piece to the top piece, sandwiching the piping between the two pieces.

    Make sure that the raw edges of the back, piping, and top are even.

12. With the backing of the pillow facing up, use the piping stitches as guides and machine-sew three sides and four corners of the pillow.

13. Trim the seam allowance and clip corners.

14. Turn the pillow right-side out and press with your iron.

15. Stuff the pillow and turn the raw edges to the inside.

16. Slipstitch (see Chapter 15) the opening closed.

Apple pillow

This completed pillow measures 10 x 10 inches with a 2-inch ruffle. You can appliqué the apple fabric by hand or machine or use fusible webbing (as I did when making this project) to apply the appliqué pieces to the background fabric. See a photo of this pillow in the color section.

Note: All yardages are figured for fabric that's 45 inches wide.

Tools and Materials:

Basic sewing craft kit (see the Cheat Sheet at the front of this book)

Scraps of green calico (large enough to cut out leaves and stem appliqués)

⅓ yard of red calico

⅓ yard of white calico

1¼ yards of red piping

Tracing paper

Fusible webbing

Red and green thread

Stuffing, such as Poly-Fil

1. **Enlarge each element of the apple design (the apple, leaves, and stems) in Figure 16-8 by 135 percent, trace them, and then cut out each pattern piece.**

2. **Pin the apple pattern to the red calico fabric and pin the stem and leaves to the green calico. Cut out each piece.**

   If you want to hand-stitch the apple appliqué, cut out the red calico fabric for the apple with an extra ¼ inch of fabric all around the pattern piece. The leaves and stem are too small to apply with hand stitching and must be applied with fusible webbing or a zigzag machine stitch.

3. **Cut two 10½-x-10½-inch squares from the white calico for the front and back of the pillow.**

4. **Pin the apple, stem, and leaf fabric pieces in the center of the top piece of white calico.**

5. **Use a zigzag stitch and matching thread to stitch around each raw edge of the apple pieces, or fuse with a medium hot iron (see the steps in the "Watermelon pillow" section, earlier in this chapter).**

6. **With the right sides of the piping and pillow top facing and raw edges aligned, pin the piping around the perimeter of the pillow top, overlapping the ends, and then machine-sew as close to the cording (which is inside the fabric) as possible.**

7. **Cut, pin, and sew two strips of red calico together to make a 2¾-x-80-inch long strip for the pillow's ruffle.**

8. **With right sides of the calico together facing and short ends together, stitch across the ends to create one continuous piece of fabric.**

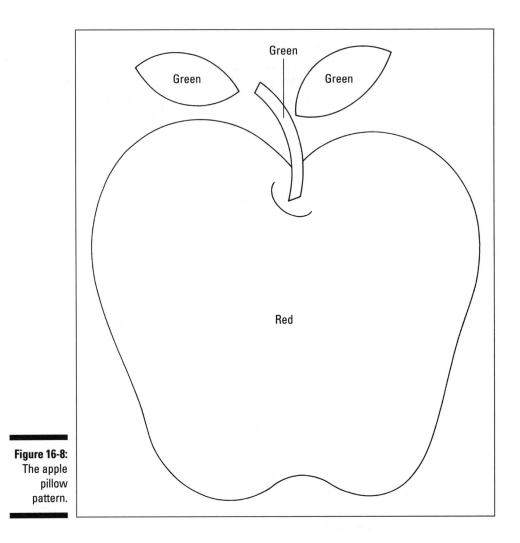

Figure 16-8:
The apple
pillow
pattern.

 9. **Turn one long edge of the strip under ¼ inch and press with an iron.
    Turn the strip another ¼ inch under, press with an iron, and machine-
    sew all around the turned edge of the fabric to create a finished edge.**

10. **Divide the ruffle into four equal parts and then mark the four parts
    with pins.**

11. **With the strip and pillow top's right sides facing and raw edges
    aligned, pin the ruffle strip to the pillow top.**

    Make sure that you gather the fabric between the pin markings so that
    the ruffle fabric is evenly distributed and fits each side of the pillow.

12. Using the piping stitches that you made as a guide, stitch around the pillow top to attach the ruffle.

13. With the backing and pillow top's right sides facing and raw edges aligned, pin the backing piece to the pillow top with the ruffle and piping between. Machine-sew around three sides and four corners of the pillow.

14. Trim the seam allowance and clip the four corners.

15. Turn the pillow right-side out and press with an iron.

16. Stuff your pillow firmly.

17. Fold the pillow's raw edges inside and slipstitch (see Chapter 15) the opening closed.

Chapter 17

Needlepoint

• •

In This Chapter

▶ Reviewing materials that you need

▶ Understanding needlepoint basics

▶ Creating needlepoint projects

• •

*N*eedlepoint involves using a needle and yarn to fill in an area of a special open, even-weave fabric called *canvas* with hand stitches to create designs. Needlepoint supplies can be found in craft stores and some fabric shops. Many craft stores specialize exclusively in needlepoint. In fact, needlepoint shops offer a vast array of printed and hand-painted canvases that include the needlepoint's design in color. But before you go into a needlepoint store, this chapter tells you all about the materials you need for needlepoint.

Many beginning crafters select needlepoint designs that are too advanced for them, and as a result, they never finish their products. This chapter includes simple projects that I've designed for first-time needlepointers.

Gathering Your Materials

Needlepoint crafts require only basic materials: You need yarn, a canvas background, a needle, a charted design to follow, and, optionally, a frame or holder.

All about yarn

Almost all needlepoint projects today use Persian yarn, which comes in 12 ½-yard skeins. Persian yarn is available in wool and acrylic, is washable and usually colorfast, and is made up of three strands. If you work with fine-mesh canvas and use Persian yarn, you can separate the yarn and use only one or two strands in your design (according to the directions given with a project). Custom needlepoint kits include Persian yarn more often than any other type of yarn. Hundreds of colors and shades of colors are available.

When purchasing yarn, make sure you get enough of each color needed to complete your project. If you have to go back to buy more of the same color, it may not always match exactly. Dye lots differ, and finding colors that match exactly can be difficult.

Crafters also use *crewel yarn,* a fine wool yarn, for needlepoint. Crewel yarn used for needlepoint projects is usually two-ply, single-strand yarn. It is slightly finer than one strand of Persian yarn.

You can't separate tapestry yarn; it's made of four-ply and is slightly finer than three strands of Persian yarn. It comes in both acrylic and wool. Because it's difficult to separate the strands, you use it when all four strands are indicated on a pattern.

Most needlepoint patterns include information about how many strands of yarn you need to use for the stitches that the design indicates.

Considering canvas

Many different types of needlepoint canvas exist, but the most common needlepoint canvas that crafters use is made of white or ecru cotton material that has been stiffened with *sizing* (a printing chemical). The weave (referred to as the *mesh*) of the canvas forms a grid, with a specific number of threads per inch, on which you work your needlepoint stitches.

Crafters use a 10-, 12-, 14-, or 18-inch-size mesh canvas most often. The higher the mesh number, the tighter the canvas weave, and the tinier the stitches you need to make. The size of the canvas mesh also corresponds to the number of stitches you make. If the canvas is 10-inch mesh, for example, you make 10 stitches in an inch.

Always cut your canvas 2 inches larger around than you need for your finished project. Doing so provides enough background fabric for finishing the project after you complete the stitching, such as making the needlepoint into a pillow. Protect the edges of your canvas from unraveling with 1-inch wide masking tape while you work on your project.

Plastic canvas is another type of canvas that many crafters use. Plastic canvas is stiffer than cotton canvas, and you can purchase it in sheets or packages of shapes, such as squares, circles, and triangles. Plastic canvas comes in 5-, 7-, and 10-count mesh. You can use plastic canvas to make items such as coasters, bookmarks, boxes, picture frames, and other small projects that require a more sturdy material. Cutting plastic canvas to the sizes and shapes that you need is easy, and it doesn't unravel because it's molded rather than woven.

Threading a needle

Here's the easiest way to thread a needle for needlepoint:

1. Wrap the yarn or thread once around the eye of the needle.

2. Hold the loops of yarn or thread tight and close to the needle. Pull the needle out of the loop of yarn or thread.

3. Squeeze the yarn as tightly as possible between your thumb and forefinger and use your other hand to press the eye of the needle onto the loop of the yarn (instead of trying to push the yarn into the eye of the needle).

4. Pull the looped end of the yarn through the eye until you have pulled the entire loop through the eye of the needle.

Necessary needles

Needlepoint needles are also known as *tapestry* or *embroidery needles*. They are short and blunt and have a large eye that makes threading the needle a cinch. Crafters refer to different needlepoint needles by their size number. For example, crafters most often use a #18 needle on the popular 10-count meshes. Generally, the higher your needle number, the higher the number of mesh you need.

Using a charted design

The needlepoint's charted pattern tells you which count canvas you need, the types of stitches that you make, the color of yarn that you need, and where you place each stitch to complete the design.

Frames and holders

When working on a canvas, it's helpful to put the canvas in a frame or holder. These devices, made especially for needlepoint and available through needlepoint shops, keep the canvas from becoming distorted by the stitches. However, many crafters prefer to hold the canvas in their laps so that the work is easy to roll up and take along in a purse or tote.

Mastering the basic stitch

The most common needlepoint stitch is a slanted one, called the *continental stitch* (see Figure 17-1). Follow these steps to master it:

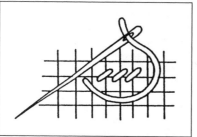

Figure 17-1:
How to make a continental stitch.

1. **Pull the needle up through one hole in the canvas from the back.**

2. **Insert the needle diagonally across to the upper right, through the hole in the front of the canvas.**

3. **Always work the continental stitch from right to left, so the next stitch you do is to the left of the first stitch (see Figure 17-1).**

4. **When you come to the end of a row, turn the canvas completely around and restart your stitch (see Step 1) in the next row according to the design, always working from right to left.**

Advanced needlepoint includes many more stitches, but for basic needlepoint projects, the continental stitch is the most commonly used for beginner projects.

Blocking the canvas

Stitching canvas usually distorts the fabric, making it slightly askew, even when you've used a frame (which helps but doesn't eliminate the problem altogether). However, you can steam-press your finished canvas project to restore its shape. Crafters refer to this process as *blocking* the canvas. Use the following steps to block your canvas:

1. **Lay your finished canvas facedown on a well-padded ironing board.**

2. **Dampen a Turkish towel and place it over the back of your canvas.**

3. **Press a warm iron over the damp towel.**

   As you press your finished canvas, pull your canvas from left to right and top to bottom to align the weaves in the material.

4. **Press your canvas again.**

   Make sure that you keep the towel over the back of the canvas so you don't scorch your project.

5. **Allow your canvas to dry.**

Small Needlepoint Projects

Needlepoint is the perfect craft for making small, elegant-looking gifts. After you stitch an eyeglass case, monogram tags for packages, and make a picture frame (these are projects in this chapter), you'll know everything you need to make a needlepoint project. Projects like making a needlepoint pillow or covering chair seats are just as easy — they just require more time.

Gift tags

Making attractive needlepoint gift tags (see them pictured in the color section of this book) with plastic canvas is easy. Plastic canvas, which is available in craft and fabric shops, makes this project quick and easy because you don't need to block the material. You can use needlepoint tags for tree ornaments, luggage tags, and bookmarks. You can also attach a lapel pin (available in craft stores) to the back of the tag before you tie the tag to the gift, and the recipient can use the tag as a lapel pin.

Tools and Materials:

Basic sewing craft kit (see the Cheat Sheet at the front of this book)

1 sheet of 7-count plastic canvas

Ruler and fine-point felt-tip marker (water-soluble)

1 skein each of red, green, and blue four-ply acrylic yarn or Persian wool

Tapestry needle #16

Iron-on felt scraps for backing (you can also use regular felt and craft glue)

Lapel pin backings (optional)

Ribbon for bookmarks (optional)

1. **Regardless of whose name or initials you want to put on your gift tag, you need to chart the letters you want to use. To do so, use graph paper (ten squares to the inch is a good size) and, using the alphabet chart in Figure 17-2 as a guide, chart the letters in the center of the graph paper. Draw a line around the letters on the graph paper to the size you want the tag to be (leave two or three rows around each of your designs).**

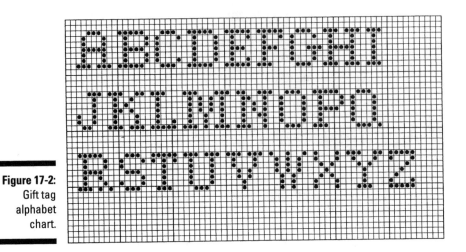

Figure 17-2:
Gift tag
alphabet
chart.

2. **Using the outline that you drew on the graph paper as a guide, count the number of squares up and the number of squares across to determine the size to cut out of the plastic canvas.**

3. **With a ruler and marker, draw the outline on the canvas and cut out the canvas through the middle of a row.**

Before cutting the plastic canvas, recount the number of holes on the canvas across and the number of holes up to be sure that the numbers match the number of squares on the graph paper within your outline.

Following the chart that you made in Step 1, you fill in the letters with cross-stitches in the color yarn of your choice as described in the following steps.

4. **Leaving an inch of yarn at the back of the canvas, bring your needle up through the first hole.**

5. **Bring your needle down through the hole diagonally to the upper right from where you brought the needle up through the canvas, to create a slant. (This is the continental stitch shown in Figure 17-1.)**

If you want to fill in more of the canvas area with your yarn, bring the needle up through the hole directly below the last stitch and then cross over diagonally to the upper-left hole to form an X. (This is a cross-stitch, as described in Chapter 18.)

6. **Use either the continental stitch or the cross-stitch to fill in the background with a second color yarn.**

7. **To bind the cut edge of canvas, follow Step 5 and bring the yarn up from the back to the front of the canvas, through the last hole that you stitched. Bind the unfinished edge of the canvas all around with a slip-stitch (see Chapter 15).**

8. When you have finished the last stitch, weave the yarn under the yarn at the back of the canvas and cut the yarn end.

9. Cut a piece of iron-on felt the same size as your needlepoint tag and fuse the felt to the back of the finished tag with a hot iron (hold in place for two seconds).

    If you can't find iron-on felt, attach a piece of plain felt to the back of your needlepoint with craft glue.

10. If you desire, stitch or glue a lapel pin backing to the center of the back of the needlepoint tag.

11. Thread a loop of yarn through the top center of the tag and then tie it to a gift, piece of luggage, or hang it on a tree.

Making a bookmark

If you prefer to make a bookmark instead of a tag, follow Steps 1 through 7 of the gift tag instructions, making two tags; and then follow the next steps. They can be the same design or different designs. Attach the needlepoint tags to the ends of a length of ribbon that becomes the bookmark. Place the ribbon between the pages, and the needlepoint tags extend beyond the top and bottom of the book.

1. Cut a length of ribbon approximately 8 inches long and place one end of the ribbon in the center of the back of the needlepoint canvas so that it extends below the design.

2. Cut a piece of felt the same size as the tag and glue or fuse the felt to the back of the canvas, with the ribbon between.

3. Place the remaining end of the ribbon on the back of the remaining needlepoint tag so that the ribbon extends above the design.

4. Glue the ribbon in place and finish as you did for the first tag.

Friendship frame

Frame your favorite 3-x-5-inch snapshot in a needlepoint heart frame. You can make this easy frame with a small number of materials. Use Figure 17-3 as the pattern for your stitches. The ×'s indicate red stitches for the background; the blank squares indicate white stitches for the hearts and borders. You can see a photo of this frame in the color section of this book.

Figure 17-3:
The friend-
ship frame
pattern.

Symbol	Color
×	Red
□	White

Tools and Materials:

Basic craft kit (see the Cheat
Sheet at the front of this book)

10-count, 6-x-8-inch piece of
plastic canvas

One 12½ yard skein of red
1-2-3 ply Persian yarn

One 12½ yard skein of white
1-2-3 ply Persian yarn

Tapestry needle #18

6-x-8-inch piece of cardboard

Tracing paper

Self-adhesive picture hanging
tab (available in photo stores)

A 3-x-5-inch snapshot photo of
your choice

1. **Leaving two rows unstitched all around the outside of the canvas,
   locate the placement of the first stitch in the top-left corner of the
   canvas.**

2. **Follow the chart (see Figure 17-3) to continental stitch one row of white
   yarn across to the right edge, down to the lower-right corner, across to
   the bottom-left corner, and up to the top-left corner where you began.**

3. **Follow the chart for the placement of the stitches and colors you need
   to create the project's white heart patterns and red background.**

Use the continental stitch for all stitching. Work all the white stitches first and then fill in the background with red stitches.

4. **To change yarn color, weave the last inch or two of yarn under the last stitches you worked on the back of the canvas. Cut the yarn end close to the canvas back.**

5. **Leaving one row unstitched all around the inside of the frame, cut out the center rectangle with a straightedge and craft knife.**

6. **Leaving one row unstitched all around the outside of the frame, cut out the frame with scissors or a straightedge and craft knife.**

7. **Using red yarn, finish the inside and outside edges of the frame following Steps 7 and 8 of the "Gift tags" project earlier in this chapter.**

   Note: Blocking isn't necessary with plastic canvas.

8. **Measure the outside of the frame and draw this measurement on the piece of cardboard.**

9. **Cut out the cardboard backing with scissors or with the straightedge and craft knife.**

10. **Position the needlepoint frame over the snapshot and then tape the snapshot to the back of the frame with masking tape.**

11. **Spread craft glue evenly on the cardboard and attach the cardboard backing to the back of the framed photograph. Set aside to dry.**

12. **Attach the hanging tab 1 inch down from the center of the top of the back of the cardboard frame backing.**

   This is a permanent project. Be sure to choose a photograph you love before framing it.

Eyeglass case

This needlepoint eyeglass case, shown in the color section of the book, is a perfect weekend project. A small print of red flowers on a bright blue background makes for an attractive 3½-x-6½-inch case.

Tools and Materials:

Basic craft kit (see the Cheat Sheet at the front of this book)

9-inch square piece of cotton 10-count needlepoint canvas

2 skeins of navy blue Persian yarn

2 skeins of red Persian yarn

2 skeins of green Persian yarn

1 skein of yellow Persian yarn

4 skeins of light blue Persian yarn

Tapestry needle #18

7-x-7-inch piece of fabric for the glass case's lining, in one of the Persian yarn colors

Sewing needle

Thread to match the lining fabric's color

1. Fold the canvas in half and press with the iron.

2. Open the canvas, place it on a flat surface, and draw a 6½-x-7-inch rectangle with a light pencil in the center of the canvas.

3. Following the chart in Figure 17-4, continental stitch (see "The basic stitch" earlier in this chapter) each row on one side of the canvas's folded line until you finish that side of the case.

   Work the yellow first, the navy blue second, the red third, the green fourth, and the background light blue last. (See Step 4 of the friendship frame project, earlier in this chapter, for how to change yarn colors.)

4. Continue stitching the design on the remaining side of the canvas until the needlepoint area measures 6½ x 7 inches.

5. Block (see "Blocking the canvas," earlier in this chapter) your needlepoint work with a steam iron. Allow the canvas to dry thoroughly.

6. Trim the canvas so you have a ½-inch border around the finished work.

7. Clip off the unstitched canvas corners and fold to the underside of the project all the unstitched canvas edges.

8. With the fabric's wrong sides together, fold the case at the center line of the canvas.

9. Use a slipstitch (see Chapter 15) to join the back and front of the needlepoint canvas along the bottom and side edges only. Make an extra stitch in the top corner hole (on top of the existing stitch) to reinforce the top of the seam.

10. With the fabric's right sides together, fold the fabric for the lining in half lengthwise.

11. Use a sewing machine or needle and thread to stitch across the bottom and side edges of the fabric, leaving a ½-inch seam allowance. Trim the seam allowance with scissors.

12. Fold the top ½ inch all around over onto the outside of the fabric and press with an iron.

13. Slip the lining inside the needlepoint case. Line up the side seams of the lining and needlepoint case and slipstitch the lining to the eyeglass case along the top edge.

Figure 17-4:
The design
pattern
for an
eyeglass
case.

Symbol	Color
■	Red
●	Green
✕	Navy blue
○	Yellow
□	Light blue

Chapter 18

Counted Cross-Stitch

● ●

● ●

Cross-stitch is a type of embroidery that uses only one stitch — an X stitch. With the X cross-stitch and colored thread, you can create a variety of designs.

The design, the most important element in counted cross-stitch, is charted on a graph. Each square of the graph represents a square on the fabric. Fill in each square with a cross-stitch, and your design is complete. As soon as you know how to make an X, you can start a cross-stitch project. The technique for creating counted cross-stitch is the same for making a small picture as it is for a large picture. You don't need to know any fancy stitches — the larger projects just take longer to make than the smaller ones.

This chapter gives you a description of the materials you need, tells you where to find them, and shows you how to use them. You find out how to make perfect stitches (you only have to know how to count) and how to avoid errors. This chapter contains nine cross-stitch projects, each of which you can complete in a weekend.

Picking Out the Materials

The materials that you need to create counted cross-stitch projects are simple and few. You can find everything you need in craft stores and fabric shops.

Even-weave fabric

Even-weave fabric is made up of tiny squares with holes at each corner in which you insert the embroidery thread and needle. Each X stitch that you make covers one square. The size of the fabric's checks determines how large the design is.

Crafters most commonly use *Aida cloth* fabric. This 100-percent cotton cloth is washable and comes in 18, 14, and 11 squares to the inch. Aida cloth usually comes in packages of pre-cut sheets; the most common size is 12 x 18 inches. Most crafters use white and ecru for their projects, but you can purchase Aida cloth in a variety of colors.

You can interchange the 11-inch and the 14-inch Aida cloth in projects. The 14-inch produces a smaller version of the same design done on 11-inch count, and vice versa.

If you want to create a project with a colorful background, you can use a small-checked, gingham fabric. Count the squares on the gingham to determine the placement of the stitches as you would the small squares on an even-weave fabric.

Embroidery hoop

Embroidery hoops hold the fabric taut as you work the embroidery stitches, one area at a time. A hoop consists of two rings; one fits tightly inside the other. To use a hoop, spread the area of the even-weave cloth over the inner hoop. Then fit the outer hoop over the fabric-covered inner hoop to hold the fabric taut while you stitch. Hoops come in various sizes and styles, are made of plastic or wood, and are sold in fabric or craft stores.

Each time you put your project aside, remove the fabric from the hoop to avoid a permanent crease in your fabric. When you finish your project, press the fabric with your iron to eliminate any wrinkles and creases.

Embroidery floss

A *skein* of embroidery floss consists of six strands of thread. Cross-stitch directions usually include the number of strands that you need to use for that particular project. Embroidery floss comes in the widest range of colors and shades that you can imagine. The instructions for most cross-stitch projects (including the ones in this book) list the color names and numbers for DMC brand cotton floss, but you can use similar colors from any brand of embroidery floss.

Tapestry needle

You use a tapestry needle for counted cross-stitch. This needle doesn't have a sharp, pointed end such as you would find on a quilting needle. The end of a tapestry needle is blunt, and therefore you don't need to use a thimble with the tapestry needle because the needle isn't sharp enough to prick your finger.

Embroidery scissors

Sharp little snipping scissors, embroidery scissors are invaluable for any needlework. Keep them next to you while you work — each time you finish a length of floss or need to trim excess fabric around a hoop frame, your scissors are handy for snipping.

Working Counted Cross-Stitch

Working the stitches begins with an 18-inch length of embroidery floss in the color indicated for the first stitch, which is the one in the middle of the chart. Separate all six strands of floss and then rejoin the number of strands that you need for the project that you've chosen — the directions for the project tell you how many strands you need. Thread the required strands through the needle (see Chapter 17 for tips on threading the needle).

Even if your project requires all six strands of floss, separating and rejoining them keeps the floss from tangling and knotting.

To determine where the stitches go, count each row on the project's graph and then count to the corresponding square on the fabric. Therefore, wherever the graph indicates a stitch — row 1 square 3, for example — you find the same square in the same row on the canvas.

You work the cross-stitch one area at a time. The area is defined within the embroidery hoop.

Here's how to begin your counted cross-stitch project:

1. **Find the center of the your project's charted design by measuring the height and width of the design and then finding the center of those two measurements.**

   The point at which these two measurement come together is the center of the design.

2. **Fold the fabric in half horizontally and then vertically to find the center of the fabric.**

3. **From the center of the design, count up to the top row and out to the left to the first X, which is your starting point.**

4. **Count up the same number of rows and out to the left the same number of squares on your fabric to find the corresponding starting point.**

Temporarily mark the starting square with a pin across it on the fabric until you're ready to begin stitching the design. You may be happy to know that it isn't absolutely crucial that you start on that exact square, but the marking of the beginning square (give or take a square one way or the other) helps to ensure that you allow enough fabric all around the design to complete it without running out of fabric on one edge of the design.

Remember that each square on the charted design represents a corresponding square on the fabric — even if the squares on the chart are a different size than the squares on your fabric.

Now you can begin working your stitches in horizontal rows.

5. **Secure the fabric in the hoop so that your starting point is within the area defined by the hoop. Tighten the hoop so your fabric is as taut as possible.**

6. **Thread your needle with embroidery floss of the appropriate color. Don't make a knot at one end of the floss like you do for regular sewing.**

You never make knots in the thread when doing counted cross-stitch; knots make your work lumpy. The weave of the fabric is tight enough to hold the embroidery floss securely in place.

7. **Locate the first square and, from the underside of the fabric, insert your needle up through the fabric's hole. Pull your needle through the fabric until you have a 2-inch tail remaining on the underside of your fabric.**

8. **Reinsert your needle through the front of the fabric's hole, diagonally to the right (up or down) and across the first square.**

9. **Continue to make this slanted part of the stitch, working diagonally across the row and using the same color floss as the chart indicates, as shown in the illustration on the left in Figure 18-1.**

10. **After you complete a section of slanted left to right stitches, cross back through the fabric to make each stitch into an X, as shown in the illustration on the right in Figure 18-1.**

11. **Each time you run out of floss, weave the last bit of the remaining piece under a few stitches on the fabric's underside to secure your stitches. Rethread your needle and continue stitching.**

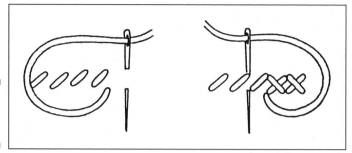

Figure 18-1:
Cross-
stitching.

Changing colors

When you begin a new design color, weave the floss under a few stitches on the underside of your fabric and then poke your needle up through the appropriate hole to begin the first stitch with the different color.

Don't carry one color across an area under the fabric where more than a few stitches exist. The floss's color shows through to the project's front side.

Correcting cross-stitch errors

Making errors, missing stitches, finding a letter inappropriately spaced, adding a row where one wasn't called for, leaving stitches unfinished — these are examples of some of the bothersome things that can happen when you cross-stitch. To avoid some or all of these problems, stop and check your stitch placements every now and then.

When you work on a border, for example, check your stitch position often to make sure that each corner meets where the graph indicates. Fill in the design details last, if possible. When you work on a quote, check to make sure that each letter starts and ends on the same row.

Before you start a new row, check to make sure that all the stitch slants lean in the same direction. Try to stitch your project's design as consistently as possible.

Remember that good lighting and a magnifying glass that hangs around your neck can add years to the health of your eyes.

Frame-Ups! A Trio of Fruit

A trio of cross-stitched fruit designs make perfect decorations for the kitchen. (See the photo in the color section.) You can also use these designs to make sachets or pin cushions. The following are the dimensions of the finished cross-stitch projects: The apple picture is 4½ x 4½ inches, the pear picture is 3½ x 5 inches, and the cherries picture is 3 x 3 inches.

The designs and color charts (with DMC color numbers and names) for the fruits are shown in Figures 18-2, 18-3, and 18-4.

Figure 18-2: The apple design and color chart.

Symbol	DMC	Color
⌂	817	Coral Red - vy dk
○	498	Christmas Red - dk
■	938	Coffee Brown -ultra dk
●	910	Emerald Green - dk
▽	3347	Yellow Green - med

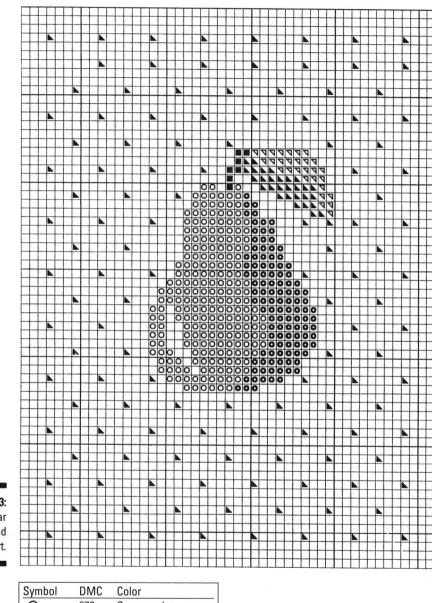

Symbol	DMC	Color
○	972	Canary - deep
●	921	Copper
■	898	Coffee Brown - vy dk
◣	910	Emerald Green - dk
◺	3347	Yellow Green - med

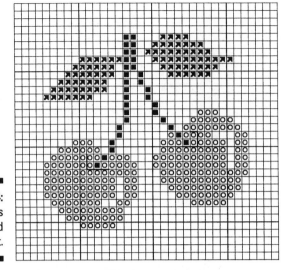

Figure 18-4: The cherries design and color chart.

Symbol	DMC	Color
■		Black
O	304	Christmas Red - med
↗	911	Emerald Green - med

Tools and Materials:

14-count yellow Aida cloth, 6 x 6 inches (for the apple)

14-count red Aida cloth, 6 x 8 inches (for the pear)

11-count white Aida cloth, 6 x 6 inches (for the cherries)

Masking tape (1 inch wide)

Embroidery floss (in the colors that the charts for each design indicate)

Tapestry needle

Embroidery hoop

Embroidery scissors

Steam iron

Fabric scissors

Mat and frame for each picture

Note: Use the following directions for all three fruit designs.

1. **Bind all the raw edges of the Aida cloth with masking tape.**

2. **Find the center square on the design charts (refer to Figures 18-2, 18-3, and 18-4).**

3. **Count the number of squares up and out from the center to the beginning of the first line of the design that you're working on.**

4. **Find the center of your fabric by folding the fabric in half vertically and then horizontally.**

Each square on the graph corresponds to a square on your fabric. Because the squares aren't always the same size, you count, but don't measure, the squares.

5. **Find the starting point for the first stitch of the fruit on the Aida cloth.**

   Although the pear and apple projects have a background pattern of stitches, stitch the fruit first and fill in the background stitches last.

6. **Cross-stitch the design pictured on the graph (see "Working Counted Cross-Stitch" earlier in this chapter).**

7. **After you finish cross-stitching, remove the masking tape from all the fabric's edges.**

8. **Place the project facedown on a padded ironing board and steam press (see Chapter 17).**

9. **Trim the excess Aida cloth around your design to fit the size of each frame.**

10 **Place the mat over the front of the project and frame it for hanging. (See Chapter 7 for framing directions.)**

Cross-Stitch Fruit Coasters

In most craft stores, you can purchase coasters that are made especially for crafting purposes. The coasters come with plastic rims and a plastic insert, under which you place your finished cross-stitch. You can purchase these craft coasters in sets of four and in different colors. The three coasters (shown in the color section of this book) feature summertime fruit slices of lime, watermelon, and orange to decorate the coasters, and they're quick and easy projects. Each coaster measures 3 inches in diameter. The designs and color charts are shown in Figures 18-5, 18-6, and 18-7.

Tools and Materials:

4 14-count pieces of white Aida cloth (a 5- to 6-inch square for each coaster)

Masking tape (1 inch wide)

Embroidery floss in the colors that the coasters' design charts indicate (see the figures for each coaster)

Tapestry needle

Embroidery hoop

Embroidery scissors

Steam iron

Fabric scissors

Craft coasters

Note: Use the following directions for all three coasters.

1. **Bind all the raw edges of the Aida cloth with masking tape.**

2. **Find the center square on the design charts (refer to Figures 18-5, 18-6, and 18-7).**

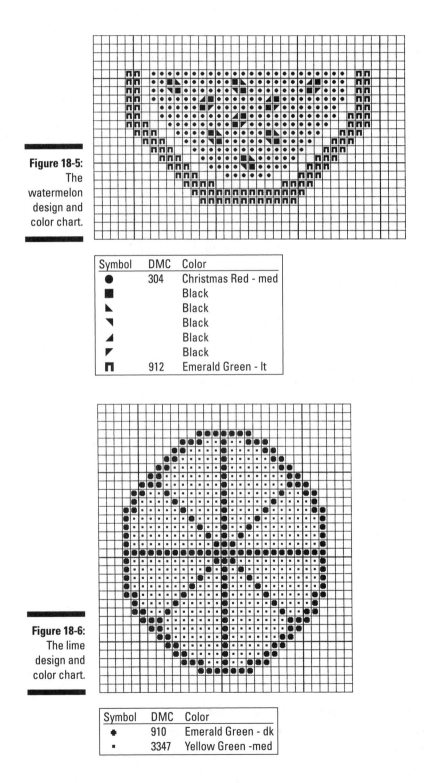

Figure 18-5:
The
watermelon
design and
color chart.

Symbol	DMC	Color
●	304	Christmas Red - med
■		Black
◣		Black
◥		Black
◢		Black
◤		Black
⊓	912	Emerald Green - lt

Figure 18-6:
The lime
design and
color chart.

Symbol	DMC	Color
✚	910	Emerald Green - dk
·	3347	Yellow Green -med

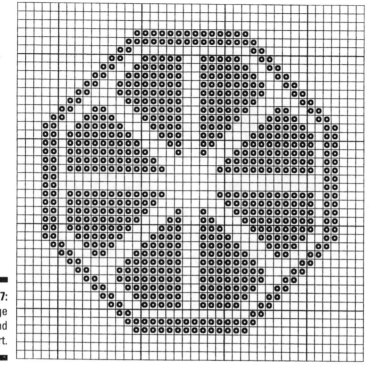

Figure 18-7:
The orange design and color chart.

Symbol	DMC	Color
⚪	608	Bright Orange

3. **Count the number of squares up and out from the center to the beginning of the first line of the design that you're working on.**

4. **Fold your project's fabric in half vertically and then horizontally to find the center.**

5. **Find the starting point for the first stitch of the fruit on the Aida cloth.**

   When making the coaster with the watermelon design, notice on the finished project (see the photo in the color section) that the fruit is placed at the bottom rather than in the middle of the fabric. Start the stitching with enough fabric above the design to fill the coaster. Leave approximately 20 rows above and 5 rows below the finished design.

6. **Cross-stitch the design on the graph (see "Working Counted Cross-Stitch" earlier in this chapter).**

7. **When you finish cross-stitching, remove the masking tape from all the fabric's edges.**

8. **Place your project facedown on a padded ironing board and steam press.**

9. **Center the plastic inset from the coaster over the cross-stitch design. Use a light pencil to draw the coaster's circle around each fruit design.**

10. **Cut out the fabric on the drawn pencil lines and place each cross-stitch picture into the coasters.**

Pictures for Baby's Room

Counted cross-stitch makes for fun and easy projects for a baby's room. You can turn the illustrations into pillows or frame them and hang them on the wall. The projects in this chapter (shown in the color section of this book) make lovely baby gifts.

Little Jack Horner cross-stitch picture

"Oh what a good boy am I" is the perfect wall plaque for a little boy's room. This is a classic children's storybook character. The finished picture measures 8 x 10 inches and fits in a standard size frame. The design and color chart are shown in Figure 18-8.

Tools and Materials:

10-x-12-inch piece of 11-count ecru Aida cloth

Embroidery floss in colors that the design chart indicates

Masking tape (1 inch wide)

Tapestry needle

Embroidery hoop

Embroidery scissors

Steam iron

Fabric scissors

Mat and frame

1. **Bind all the raw edges of the Aida cloth with masking tape.**

2. **Find the starting point for the first stitch.**

   The little boy's hair is the best place to begin.

3. **Thread your needle with three 18-inch strands of embroidery floss, separated and then rejoined.**

4. **Cross-stitch the Little Jack Horner design according to the chart. (See "Working Counted Cross-Stitch" earlier in this chapter.)**

   Follow the design graph to determine where you place each stitch of each color.

5. **Finish the boy design before you begin the letters.**

   All the solid straight lines that outline the boy design on the chart indicate a black outline, except along the legs, which you outline with brown floss.

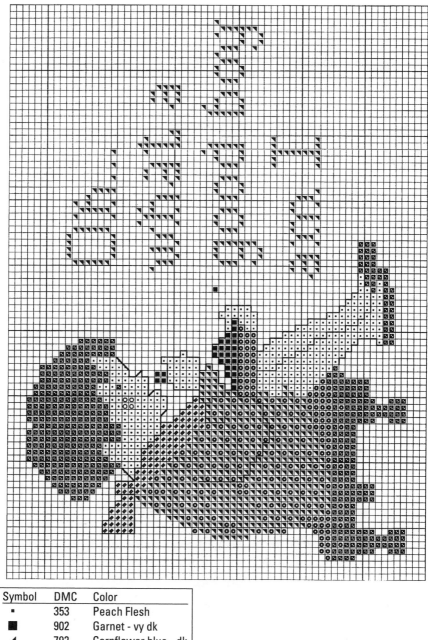

Figure 18-8:
The Little
Jack Horner
design and
color chart.

Symbol	DMC	Color
▪	353	Peach Flesh
■	902	Garnet - vy dk
◢	792	Cornflower blue - dk
◯	321	Christmas Red
⊡	801	Coffee Brown - dk
○	893	Carnation - lt
◇	970	Pumpkin - lt

6. **Use a backstitch in the outline areas.**

   The backstitch looks very much like machine stitching — the stitches are even and close together. To backstitch, bring the needle up from the underside of the fabric and reinsert it a half stitch behind where the thread came through, as shown in Figure 18-9. Bring the needle back up a half stitch in front of this point and then down again in the hole at the near end of the previous stitch.

   TIP

   As you stitch the letters, check your place often to make sure that it corresponds to the chart design. Make sure that you evenly space the letters.

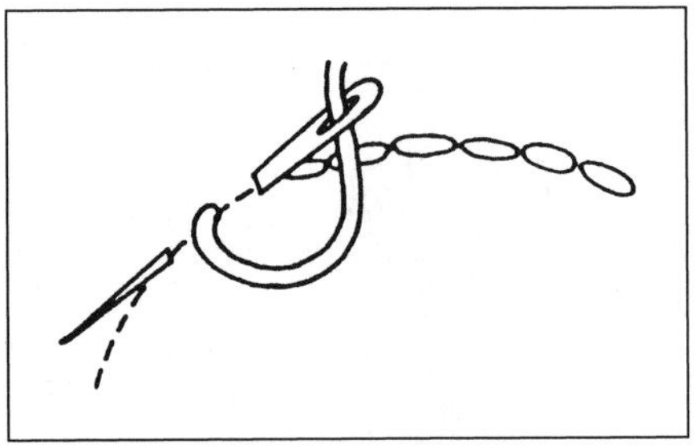

Figure 18-9:
Back-
stitching.

7. **When you finish the cross-stitch design, remove the masking tape from all the fabric's edges.**

8. **Place the cross-stitched work facedown on a padded ironing board and steam press.**

9. **Trim the excess Aida cloth around the design to the size of the frame with an extra inch all around.**

10. **With your cross-stitch project facedown, center the frame's backing on the back of the project.**

11. **Pull the extra inch of fabric to the back of the picture and tape it down with masking tape.**

    Check the front of your design as you tape the fabric to the back of the frame to make sure that you don't distort the picture or get it off-center.

12. **Place your finished work in the frame.**

Miniature hang-ups

Miniature pictures of teddy bears and sailboats (see the photo in the color section) are perfect for a small area in a baby's room. They also make terrific shower gifts or bazaar items because they take very little time to make and you can frame them inexpensively. For miniature hang-ups, you can use pop-together frames that come in various sizes and colors. These frames resemble embroidery hoops in the way they work, and you can buy them in any craft store. Each round frame for this project measures 2½ inches in diameter. You embroider the project right in the frame, cutting away the excess fabric when you finish. The designs and color charts are shown in Figures 18-10 and 18-11.

Tools and Materials:

4-x-4-inch piece of 14-count yellow Aida cloth for the teddy bear

4-x-4-inch piece of 14-count blue Aida cloth for the sailboat

Embroidery floss in colors that the design graphs indicate

Tapestry needle

Two 2½-inch frames in colors to match each design

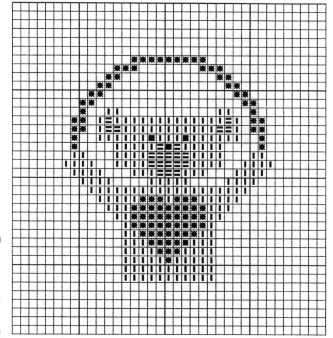

Figure 18-10: The teddy bear design and color chart.

Symbol	DMC	Color
❋	666	Christmas Red - bright
I	938	Coffee Brown - ultra dk
=	350	Coral - med
■		Black

1. **Put the fabric in the frame.**

2. **Find the starting point for the first stitch on the design chart and on the fabric. (See "Working Counted Cross-Stitch" and the steps for the projects earlier in this chapter.)**

3. **Cut an 18-inch length piece of embroidery floss and separate the embroidery strands. Rejoin two strands of floss for all the colors except white, for which you join three strands.**

   Because the sailboat background is blue, using three strands of white floss makes the background brighter in contrast.

4. **Cross-stitch each design according to its chart. (See "Working Counted Cross-Stitch" and the steps for the projects earlier in this chapter.)**

   Follow the design graph to determine where you place each stitch of each color.

5. **When you finish cross-stitching, cut away the excess fabric as close to the frame as possible and hang the miniature frame.**

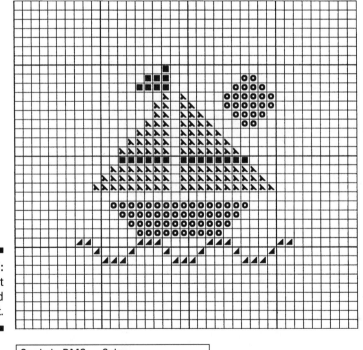

Figure 18-11:
The sailboat design and color chart.

Symbol	DMC	Color
◢	825	Blue - dk
■	666	Christmas Red - bright
O	972	Canary - deep
⋏	White	White

Part V

Nature Crafts

The 5th Wave   By Rich Tennant

@RICHTENNANT

"I decided to take up dried flower arranging. Most of the flowers in my house were halfway there anyway."

In this part . . .

Crafting with natural materials doesn't require any special training. And you don't have to live in the woods, by the beach, or have a garden to obtain the materials for nature crafts. You can go for a walk and pick a bouquet of flowers. You can gather pinecones in the woods. And practically everyone comes home from the seashore with some seashells. Almost everyone, at one time or another, has made something from nature. And if you can't get the materials yourself, garden centers provide it all.

In this part, you find out what you need to make simple seashell projects, fabulous flower arrangements, potpourri, decorative candles and soaps, a dried-flower wreath, and many small gifts. You also find out how to dry and press flowers, how to clean shells properly, and about the basic tools and materials you need to collect and craft naturally.

Chapter 19

Crafting with Materials from Nature

- -

In This Chapter

▶ Taking the right stuff with you when you gather materials

▶ Collecting seashells, flowers, grasses, leaves, and pinecones

▶ Gathering together the essential tools for nature crafting

▶ Using tips for techniques, tools, and crafting

- -

Collecting the materials for a craft is half the fun, and turning the collectibles into decorative projects and gifts is the other half. In this chapter you discover what bits of nature's bounty to collect for your craft projects. You also find out about different crafting techniques; the best way to dry and press flowers, leaves, and herbs; and how to clean shells before displaying them.

Gathering Nature's Supplies

No matter what time of year or wherever you go to collect material — the seashore, woods, fields, or the backyard — always take along a plastic bag for collecting material. A large shopping bag is good for collecting pinecones and branches that tend to be bulky. You need work gloves to protect your hands and, if you're going to be in the woods or fields, work boots. You also need a pair of clipping shears.

Regular scissors cut most materials. But clipping shears or small garden clippers are indispensable when you are out collecting material. You can use this handy tool to clip heavy stems and branches, remove pinecones from the tries, and cut dried stalks and vines easily. You can find clipping shears in most home centers.

Always wear long pants to avoid getting scratches or poison ivy.

Look around you carefully. Even if you don't know exactly what projects you want to make, collect a variety of things that interest you. You may find pieces of bark, interesting pieces of dried wood, feathers, shells, leaves, and fallen flower petals. Gather acorns, nuts, berries, twigs, and branches. Different pine trees have distinctly different kinds of cones — collect them in varying sizes. Balsam needles are especially fragrant, and you may want to fill a bag to make sachets. You can often find ferns in wooded areas. They are beautifully delicate, can be pressed and dried successfully, and are worth collecting.

Before going out on your hunting expedition, look through a book of plants. Get familiar with what you may want to look for and what you want to avoid. An inexpensive or free guidebook, available at most local area visitor's service centers, can tell you about the plants that grow in your area.

Finding seashells

You can find endless varieties of shells at the seashore, depending on the area or type of seashore you visit. The best time for beachcombing is at low tide. Because the shoreline is constantly changing, you can visit the same area over and over again, always finding something new.

Don't discard a pretty shell just because it's covered with tar — you find out later in this chapter how easy it is to clean shells.

You find the greatest variety of shells along tropical beaches, but every beach, even those lining freshwater lakes, can offer the crafter something of interest. If you crave exotic shells, they're easily obtained from shell shops and mail-order catalogs.

Cleaning shells

After you take a collection of shells home, you need to clean the shells before you use them for crafting. They may have seaweed, tar, or tiny little bugs on them. Rinse them in hot soapy water, with a capful of laundry bleach added to a pail or sink full of water. If you want to bleach the shells to pure white, soak them in equal parts of bleach and water, just enough to cover the shells, for several hours. Removing tar is easy with linseed oil, and the oil restores the shell to its original luster. For hard-to-remove stains, use a stiff copper brush dipped in bleach or laundry stain remover.

Look before you leap to pick flowers

Wildflowers grow almost everywhere. Many states maintain their roadside wildflowers. But hopping out of your car, scissors in hand, every time you see some beauties you'd like to take home is not a good idea. Many states now list the flowers that you are prohibited from picking. State and national parks usually prohibit any flower-gathering at all. Always check before wandering into an area with which you aren't familiar. And, where you are allowed to gather natural materials, please be sure to take only a limited number from one area so that you don't deplete a certain area of a particular flower, for example. You can get current information on whether you can pick wildflowers in a certain location at the Chamber of Commerce.

Everyone is attracted to different types of shells — some with specific shapes, some with a certain design, a pattern, or those with perfect symmetry. You can use whatever shells appeal to you to make a display or to use in a crafting project.

Collecting flowers and herbs

Even if you live in a city, you can find flowers for crafting in every season. Most wildflowers are considered weeds and usually grow in the poorest soil and under the worst conditions. However, you can use some of the loveliest wildflowers, such as blue chicory, Queen Anne's lace, buttercups, daisies, and dandelions, to make the prettiest craft projects. Enjoy garden flowers and herbs while they are blooming, and then pick them for drying and press them for crafting. Keep in mind that gardens are no longer limited to the backyard. Windowsill planters and gardening under lights in a city apartment yield a wealth of material for crafting.

Gathering grasses, leaves, and pinecones

Grasses, all sorts of leaves, and pinecones are great craft materials to gather from fields and forests. You can press blades of grass to use in a natural collage. Press leaves to decorate boxes or to make decorative cards and place mats. Honeysuckle vines and dune grasses from the beach are also good materials for crafting.

You can usually find pinecones and pine needles blanketing a woodland floor in the summertime; in the fall, pick up the dried needles from the trees in the backyard. Use pine needles to make elegant little sachet pillows to keep your drawers smelling sweet (see Chapter 16). You can also combine the fragrant pine needles with dried flower petals and herbs for a potpourri.

After picking or gathering dried pine needles, break them up into small pieces to release their fragrance.

Techniques, Tools, and How-To Tips for Nature Crafting

The tools you need for nature crafts aren't mysterious — many of them are tools you use for a variety of crafts — but they are versatile. You can choose from among several ways to dry flowers, leaves, and grasses — whichever method appeals to you the most. The tips in this section that describe how to work with these different tools and materials give you the freedom you need to concentrate on the creative aspect of nature crafting.

White craft glue works well for applying most materials to a background. For example, for a greeting card with dried flowers, put a tiny spot of glue on the area of the card where you want to apply a flower or petal. You use craft glue to make my flowering candle project (see Chapter 20) as well.

If you decide to make a wreath of dried flowers (see Chapter 20), using a glue gun (see Chapter 2) is more practical than craft glue. Hot glue is especially useful when working with shells (see Chapter 21).

A small pair of tweezers is a useful tool for working with dried flower petals. When creating a flower collage, for example, the dried petals are quite delicate and often brittle. Picking each one up with tweezers makes it easier to handle them and accurately place them in position.

Drying flowers

Drying flowers is so easy that it's hard to believe that you can achieve such great results. Most flowers retain their original color, if not fragrance, after they are preserved.

Begin by cutting flowers at the height of maturity. Light-colored flowers retain their color best. You can try two methods for drying flowers: air-drying and chemical drying.

Air-drying flowers

Air-drying flowers is probably the easiest approach because the air does all the work. Strawflowers, statice, and goldenrod are examples of some flowers that air-dry well. Just follow these simple steps:

1. **After picking the flowers, strip off all foliage from the stems.**

2. **Turn the flowers upside down and tie the stems together in small bunches.**

3. **Hang them in a cool, dark area.**

   Allow the flowers to dry for two or three weeks. Flowers with the most moisture take the longest to dry.

4. **Remove the flowers from their hanging position, throw away the string that holds them together, and they're ready for crafting.**

Drying flowers chemically

Silica gel is a powdery chemical you can use to dry flowers. It's available in craft and flower shops. This chemical is highly absorbent and lightweight.

To chemically dry flowers with silica, follow these steps:

1. **Fill a shoebox or plastic container with about 1 inch of silica gel.**

2. **Cut the stems of the flowers so that only short stubs remain.**

   Short stems let the flowers stand upright in the silica gel. Full-length stems bend, inhibiting the drying process.

3. **Stand the flower stems in the silica gel.**

   If you're drying fat, heavy flowers, such as roses, tulips, or lilies, place them head first on top of the gel. Otherwise, the heavy flowers bend before the drying process is complete. The silica gel has a powdery consistency and doesn't damage the flower in any way.

4. **Slowly sprinkle the silica gel all over the flowers until they are completely covered with the powdery substance.**

5. **Cover the container and seal it so that no moisture can get in.**

6. **After three days, check the flowers to see whether they are ready.**

   The flowers should feel crisp to the touch.

7. **If the flowers aren't completely dry, leave them undisturbed in the resealed container. Check for dryness every two days.**

8. **Remove the flowers from the container and blow away any silica that may be remaining on the blossoms.**

9. **Use wire florist's stems to replace the real stems that were cut off before drying.**

   These florist wires are available in florist and hobby shops.

Pressing flowers

Naturally flat flowers, such as the pansy, are the easiest to press. But that doesn't mean you have to limit yourself to flat flowers. Flowers that press well also include the black-eyed Susan, cosmos, daisy, heather, lavender, Queen Anne's lace, tansy, and zinnia, to name a few.

Pressing flowers is easy. Just follow these steps:

1. **Place a piece of paper toweling or blotting paper on a piece of corrugated cardboard or poster board of the same size.**

2. **Place several flowers on the paper so that they do not overlap.**

3. **Place another piece of paper toweling or blotting paper on top of the flowers and another piece of corrugated cardboard or poster board on top.**

4. **Repeat until you have a stack of two or three layers.**

5. **Pile several heavy books on top of the sandwiched flowers.**

   If you want to press one page of flowers only, lay the flowers between pieces of paper toweling and place them between two pages of a very heavy book, as shown in Figure 19-1. Stack a few more books on top to weigh it down.

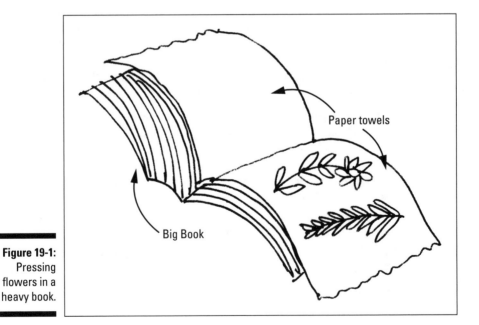

Paper towels

Big Book

Figure 19-1: Pressing flowers in a heavy book.

6. **Leave the flowers to press for a minimum of one week.**

The blotting paper or toweling absorbs the moisture in the flowers as they dry out. After the moisture is completely absorbed, the flowers are brittle to the touch; they need to be handled carefully. Lifting flowers with tweezers is a practical way to work with them.

Drying herbs to use in cooking and potpourri

If you want to dry parsley, dill, mint, and other leafy herbs, follow these steps:

1. **Remove the leaves from the stems.**

2. **Dip the leaves into boiling, slightly salty water.**

This step immediately wilts the leaves.

3. **Using a strainer, remove the leaves from the water.**

4. **Pat the leaves dry with a paper towel and lay them on a broiler pan.**

5. **Place the broiler pan in a medium-hot oven with the door open for about ten minutes.**

The leaves become dry and crisp, ready to be crumbled.

6. **Put the powdery leaves in a salt shaker for easy use while cooking.**

If you don't plan to use the herbs for cooking, place them in an airtight container to combine with other herbs for a potpourri.

Chapter 20

Fabulous Flower Crafts

● ●

In This Chapter

▶ Arranging dried flowers

▶ Making easy projects with dried flowers

▶ Making easy projects with pressed flowers

● ●

*F*lower arrangements made with dried flowers can last forever — or until you're tired of looking at them. You can use all sorts of creative containers for your arrangements. In this chapter, I show you how to choose flowers and containers that suggest a style of decorating. You also find out how to make arrangements for special occasions.

Making your own potpourri from dried flowers extends the pleasure of your garden long after the season. This chapter gives you a simple recipe for making your own scent. You can also use dried flowers to make a dried-flower wreath that looks as though it costs a fortune, when in fact, it hardly costs a dime.

After you create a nice group of pressed flowers, you can use them to make exquisitely decorated candles and soap. When you know how to dry and press flowers (see Chapter 19), this chapter shows you what to do with them.

Arranging Dried Flowers

Certain dried flowers look best in an arrangement. These arrangements may include globe amaranth, cockscomb, golden yarrow, tansy, and strawflowers. If you haven't dried your own flowers, look for dried flowers in a garden shop.

A flower-arranging project begins with a container. Look for unusual containers of different colors, sizes, and shapes, as well as styles. Choose a container and flowers that compliment the style of your home. For example, a ceramic pitcher, a basket, or a wooden box filled with strawflowers, chrysanthemums, or golden yarrow is perfect in an early-American or country-style home.

To make the perfect dried-flower arrangement, follow these steps:

1. **Place a large block of Styrofoam or florist's clay into a container.**

2. **Poke the stems of the flowers into the Styrofoam or clay.**

3. **If stems are weak or need lengthening, attach stiff green florist's wire to the real stem and then insert it into the Styrofoam or clay.**

   You can also use wooden toothpicks for this purpose instead of the wire.

   Attach these supports to the flower stems by wrapping the stem and support together with green florist's tape, which comes on a roll and is available in garden centers.

4. **To build the arrangement, place the larger, heavier flowers in the center of the container. Then fill in around these flowers with the lighter, more delicate sprigs, such as baby's breath.**

   Another option is to use statice, which comes in pink, yellow, white, blue, and purple. This flower dries nicely and can be used in almost any kind of arrangement. Purple larkspur and lavender add deep, vivid color and scent.

5. **Find the perfect place in your home for the arrangement and enjoy it!**

 An idea for an arrangement for a new baby is to use a ceramic baby shoe. Use pale colored flowers with baby's breath and tiny rose buds. Tuck a velvet ribbon in among the flowers.

Creating Easy Dried-Flower Projects

You can do many things with dried flowers. One of your options is to make potpourri, which is a mixture of dried flowers and herbs. *Potpourri* is a French word pronounced *po-po-ree* and meaning "rotten pot." Don't worry — potpourri doesn't smell rotten! Imagine creating a potpourri of lemon verbena, roses, geranium petals, and lavender, suggesting the freshness and fragrance of a summer garden — even in the middle of winter.

Making your own potpourri is fun, simple to do, and extremely satisfying. You can create your very own scent, depending on the flowers you've chosen to dry. Look for pretty containers that aren't too deep, such as a small bowl or saucer, at flea markets, yard sales, boutiques, and even in your own cupboards. Use the potpourri to create a pleasing scent and a pretty accent in your powder room.

Another option is to make a dried flower wreath. Find out in this chapter how to make one with a few simple tools, a wire wreath frame, and your own dried flowers.

Lavender potpourri

Lavender is a favorite scent for a potpourri. While dried rose buds have no scent, they do add color and texture and look quite pretty scattered over the lavender mixture. You can also add rose petals and dried herbs, such as rosemary.

In order to blend the various scents and to be sure that the fragrance lasts, you need to add a *fixative* (a chopped or powdered substance used to enhance the aroma) to the mixture. *Orris root* is the most popular fixative. Other fixatives include calamus root, benzoin powder, and oakmoss. Fixatives are usually available through florists, nurseries, some pharmacies, natural food stores, and places where herbs are sold.

Follow these directions to make a traditional lavender potpourri.

Tools and Materials:

1 large bowl

Wooden spoon

2 cups dried lavender flowers

½ cup dried rose petals

2 teaspoons of orris root

2 tablespoons dried lemon geranium leaves

2 tablespoons dried rosemary

3 drops lavender oil or
2 drops lavender oil and
1 drop rose oil

1. **Place all the dried leaves, petals, and buds in a large bowl and gently mix together with a wooden spoon.**

2. **Add the orris root and lavender oil drop by drop, mixing as you do so.**

3. **Place the mixture in an airtight container, filling it about three-fourths full. Store the potpourri in a dark, warm place for approximately four weeks. Shake it every few days.**

4. **To make sachets using the potpourri, place a tablespoonful of the mixture in the center of a lace handkerchief or a square of pretty fabric. Bring the corners together and tie tightly with a ribbon around the potpourri to make a little bundle.**

If you don't want to make a sachet, fill a small, low container with the potpourri and place it in a bathroom, on a night table in the bedroom, or on a coffee table in the living room. It looks pretty and adds a delicate scent to the room.

Dried flower wreath

Making a dried flower wreath like the one shown in the color section of this book begins with a *wreath form,* which can be a frame made of wire, a Styrofoam ring, or a natural grapevine wreath. They all come in different sizes, from 10 to 20 inches in diameter. A frame that is 10 or 12 inches is a good size to start with.

Thin florist's wire comes on a spool and is available in garden shops.

Tools and Materials:

Wreath form

Dried artemisia for the bulk of the wreath

A variety of dried herbs, spices (such as cinnamon sticks, bay leaves, and rosemary), and flowers of your choice for color (such as tansy, cardamom, wild iris pods, and strawflowers)

Thin florist's wire

Wooden toothpicks

Ribbon for a bow (3- or 4-inch-wide taffeta is pretty, but the choice is up to you)

1. **Lay two large bunches of artemisia around the front of the wreath frame so that their stem ends overlap each other and the flowers encircle the frame.**

   Check out the photo of a dried-flower wreath in the color insert of this book to get an idea of how to position the flowers.

2. **Using the thin wire, secure the artemisia to the frame. Start with the stems and wrap the wire in a progressive spiral up toward the blossoms. Use fresh sprigs of artemisia to insert here and there.**

   If you find that the material you are working with is too dry and therefore quite brittle, you can spray it with a little water while you work. This makes the dried flowers more pliable. If you find wiring the flowers to the frame too difficult, consider using a glue gun (see Chapter 2) to adhere the flowers where needed.

3. **Insert a variety of dried herbs and spices into the wreath in such a way to make it your own creation.**

4. **Use the florist's wire to attach wooden toothpicks onto pods and flowers that do not have strong stems. Hold the toothpick alongside the stem and wrap the wire around both the toothpick and the stem. Then poke the wrapped stems into the artemisia. The wired pods and flowers stay in place without glue. For more color, especially if you're creating a holiday wreath, consider adding dried peppers here and there.**

5. **Add more artemisia where needed to fill out the wreath.**

6. **Finish the wreath by adding a decorative ribbon bow. To make a nice, fat bow, secure the bow by wrapping a piece of wire around the center, leaving an inch or two of the wire ends. Insert the wire ends into the wreath. Glue a small flower bud to the center of the bow to cover the wire.**

Creating Easy Pressed-Flower Projects

The craft of pressing flowers (see Chapter 19) is just the beginning of crafting many creative projects with pressed flowers. You can use your pressed flowers to decorate and personalize greeting cards, stationary, candles, soap, and découpage boxes (see Chapter 9).

Flowering candles

Decorating candles with pressed flowers and leaves turns plain candles into lovely accessories and gifts. Although the flowers appear embedded in the candle, they are simply adhered to the outer surface with paraffin wax, a protective wax covering. You can see a photo of these candles in the color section of this book.

When making this project, consider assembling enough material to decorate several candles at one time. The brightest colored flowers work best for this project because the wax coating dulls their color slightly. Using large, fat, dripless candles is best because the flame burns down through the center of the candle and the wax does not drip down the sides. As the flame gets lower each time you burn the candle, it creates a glow from behind the flowers. The more the candle is used, the prettier it is.

If you use pulpy flower buds, you may want to iron them between pieces of brown paper after they are pressed to flatten them as much as possible.

Tools and Materials:

Fat, white or off-white, scented or unscented, cylindrical candle (3 inches or more in diameter looks best)

1 box of clear paraffin wax (available in supermarkets)

Baking pan (big enough hold the candle)

Pressed flowers

Tweezers

Paper towel (to wipe up any accidental spills)

Old paintbrush (optional)

1. **Begin by planning how you want to arrange the pressed flowers around the candle.**

2. **Place a cube of paraffin wax in the baking pan and melt it over low heat on the stovetop.**

   Melting wax can catch fire if it is overheated. Keep a lid nearby to smother flames, if needed. Don't use water on a wax fire!

3. **With your fingertips, hold the candle on each end and touch part of the candle to the surface of the hot wax.**

Dip only one section of the candle at a time, but work quickly because the paraffin begins to cool immediately after you remove it from the wax.

Be careful not to let your fingers touch the wax because it will burn.

4. **Lift a flower with the tweezers and place it onto the candle where the hot wax has made contact. Press it in place using the tweezers and tap it down carefully.**

5. **If the paraffin begins to cool before you can add all the flowers to the candle, dip the candle into the hot paraffin again. Keep dipping and adding flowers to the sides of the candle.**

6. **When all the flowers are on the candle, hold each end of the candle with your fingers again and roll the flower-covered candle over the surface of the hot wax so that the flowers are lightly coated. Do this step quickly to avoid a wax buildup. The more quickly you work, the smoother the candle surface will be.**

Don't submerge the candle. Let only the surface of the candle touch the wax.

An alternative method to rolling the candle in the paraffin is to dip an old paintbrush into the hot wax and brush it over the candle surface. Then lay the flowers on the wax and use the paintbrush to coat another layer of wax over the flowers.

7. **Place the pan of paraffin in the refrigerator to return it to a solid state so that you can easily remove it to use it again. Or you may want to pour the hot paraffin into a smaller can and put the can into the refrigerator to let the wax harden.**

Decorative soap

Decorating plain bars of soap with pressed flowers turns them into beautiful gift items or accessories for your guest bathroom. They make lovely stocking stuffers for Christmas, or you can gift-box a set of three for a bridal shower.

You can create this project with paper cutout flowers as well, which is similar to the craft of découpage (refer to Chapter 9).

You can use the soap as long as it isn't completely submerged in water. To display the soap in the bathroom, place a pretty, lace-edged handkerchief or linen napkin in a basket and put three pressed-flower soaps on top. Tie the handle of the basket with a velvet or satin ribbon in a color to match the flowers. Add a few dried rosebuds (see Chapter 19).

Tools and Materials:

Bar of soap (any color, shape, or size)

Pressed flowers (flat flowers, such as pansies, work best)

Cuticle scissors

White craft glue

Tweezers

Clear nail polish or clear paraffin wax (available in supermarkets or leftover from the pressed candle project described in the preceding section)

1. **Begin by arranging the pressed flowers on the top of the soap the way you want them to look. Cut away any stems with the cuticle scissors. If you're using flat petals, such as those from dried roses, arrange them to create a flower on the soap.**

2. **Using the tweezers, lift each flower one by one off the soap and apply a drop of white craft glue to the spot on the soap where you want the flower or petal to be. Spread the glue around with your fingertip. Then, still using the tweezers, carefully replace the flower and tap it down with the tip of the tweezers. The pressed flowers are quite delicate and handling them with your fingers could destroy them.**

3. **After you glue all the flowers in place on top of the soap, let the glue dry for a few minutes.**

4. **To protect the surface of the flowers, carefully apply a coat of clear nail polish. Let it dry and then apply a second coat. Repeat this process two or three more times.**

You can use hot paraffin wax instead of nail polish to create a protective coating for the pressed flowers. (Refer to the project, "Flowering candles" in this chapter.) Lightly touch the top of the soap onto the surface of the hot paraffin wax and then quickly remove it. Put the soap aside to dry. A wax film covers the flowers, but their color shows through.

Chapter 21

Using Nature's Bounty

This chapter is chock-full of good ideas for nature crafting. You discover how to use a few essential tools to make easy projects from pressed leaves and other natural materials gathered outdoors. Decorated miniature vines make great gifts as well as ornaments for your Christmas tree, and everything you need to make them is at your fingertips. Crafting with pressed leaves gives you a chance to personalize note cards. All the directions you need are in this chapter.

Everyone likes to take pictures at the seashore. In this chapter, you find out how to display shells or use the shells that you collect to decorate a frame for your favorite seaside photographs.

Easy Projects with Pressed Leaves

Pressing leaves is just like pressing flowers. As you gather leaves, avoid those that have fallen from the trees and have dried up crisp and curled. You don't want these leaves for your craft projects because they crumble when you handle them. Look for freshly fallen leaves in a variety of colors and sizes, or pick them from the trees. See Chapter 19 for how to press flowers and follow the same procedure for pressing leaves.

Pressed leaf box

After you collect a nice variety of pressed leaves in different colors and sizes, you can use them to decorate a painted box. The placement of the pressed leaves on the box isn't important. Any way you arrange them looks good. The result is a beautiful, collage-like jewelry-type box to give as a gift or to keep for yourself.

Tools and Materials:

Basic craft kit (see the Cheat Sheet at the front of this book)

Wooden box (any size)

Pressed leaves, varied in color and size

Paper towels

Sponge, damp

Rubber roller (optional)

1. **Spread craft glue over the back of each leaf and place them on the surface of the box.**

2. **Press down gently on the leaves with a paper towel and, with a damp sponge, remove any excess glue that oozes out from the edges.**

   (Optional) Use a rubber roller (which you can find in the wallpaper section of a home center) to gently apply pressure on the leaves, which ensures that the leaves press completely to the surface of the box.

3. **Let the leaves dry for two to three hours.**

4. **Coat the pressed leaves and box with clear, water-based varnish or polyurethane for protection.**

5. **Repeat the varnishing process five or six times, allowing each coat to dry thoroughly (read the label on the varnish container to find out how long to let it dry) before reapplying another coat.**

For another variation of this project, create a collage effect by overlapping the leaves as you glue them in place so that they cover the box completely. You may have to trim the leaves or cut them here and there to fit each side of the box, especially where the top and bottom come together. Use regular scissors to cut the leaves and apply each piece in position on the box.

Pressed leaf tray

A plain metal, wooden, or clear plastic tray is perfect for a pressed leaf project. You can find some great antique-type trays in flea markets or newer-looking ones in discount stores.

Tools and Materials:

Tray

*Pressed leaves, varied in color
and size*

*Spray paint, in an autumn or
other color*

Glass cover for tray

1. **(Optional) If the tray isn't in perfect condition, give it a coat of spray paint in an autumn color.**

2. **Measure the inside dimensions of the tray and have a piece of glass cut to size. (Most hardware stores provide this service.)**

3. **Next, arrange pressed leaves in a pleasing way all over the tray. Think about how the leaves would fall at random from the trees.**

4. **Set the glass over the leaves to hold them in position by placing one short end into the tray first and then lowering the rest of the glass down into the tray.**

   Although the edges of cut glass aren't rough, take care when lifting it.

When you want to change the design of the tray, remove the glass and the leaves. For variation, replace the leaves with pressed flowers, cutout paper flowers, photographs, pressed ferns, or pretty fabric cut to size.

Enjoying Easy Natural Gifts

If you've collected all sorts of natural materials, it's time to spread them out on your worktable and have some fun. For holiday gifts and decorations, make miniature wreaths. For example, natural grapevine wreaths work great for making wreaths of pinecones, small leaves, and dried flowers. Discover these other great projects in this section: framed picture note cards, leafy place mats, and decorative votive candleholders.

Leafy frame

Take a picture of your children playing in a pile of leaves and make a leaf frame to go with it. What a nice gift for a grandparent! And it really captures the feel of autumn.

Tools and Materials:

*Basic craft kit (see the Cheat
Sheet at the front of this book)*

Photograph

*Posterboard or foam board (in
the color of your choice)*

Small pressed leaves

Picture frame

1. Glue the photograph on a piece of poster board or foam board (available in art supply stores) with several inches of the board showing around each edge of the photograph.

2. Select small leaves and glue them around the photograph so that they cover the edges of the photo and create a frame of about 2 inches all around the edges.

   (Optional) Use small scissors or a craft knife to cut around the outside edges of the leaves surrounding the photograph to create a free-form frame following the outline of the leaves.

3. Draw a rectangle around the outside of the leaf frame area on the poster board or foam board background and, using a straightedge and craft knife or razor blade, cut along these lines.

4. Frame the photograph, surrounded by leaves, in a regular picture frame.

Leafy place mats

What can make you feel like you're outside having a picnic? Place mats made of natural materials, such as leaves, can. Try these leafy place mats to use for your next family meal.

Tools and Materials:

Basic craft kit (see the Cheat Sheet at the front of this book)

12-x-16-inch piece of foam board or poster board for each place mat

Clear self-adhesive paper (2 pieces for each place mat, each 13 x 17 inches)

Rolling pin, cylindrical water glass, or rubber roller

Pressed leaves

1. Cut a 12-x-16-inch piece of foam board for each place mat.

2. Cover the foam board with pressed leaves so that none of the background shows. The leaves should overlap one another, as well as the edges.

3. Peel the backing paper away from one piece of the self-adhesive paper and center it over the leaves so that an extra inch of adhesive paper extends beyond the poster or foam board all around. Press the self-adhesive paper down with the palm of your hand over the leaves and smooth it down firmly as you go.

4. Using a rolling pin, cylindrical water glass, or rubber wallpaper roller, go over the self-adhesive paper to smooth it down and remove any air bubbles.

5. Turn the place mat over with the leaf side down and apply the second piece of self-adhesive paper on the back of the foam board so the self-adhesive paper extends beyond the foam board an extra inch all around. Smooth in place as you did for the front of the place mat (refer to Steps 3 and 4).

6. Use regular scissors to trim the self-adhesive paper and any excess leaf ends as close to the edges of the foam board place mat as possible.

Pinecone wreath

Miniature grapevine wreaths (find them at a craft and hobby shop) are perfect to add your own decorations to. Make one wreath with pinecones; another with dried rosebuds, and another with leaves, bark, or shells. Select small items in proportion to the miniature wreath.

Tools and Materials:

Basic craft kit (see the Cheat Sheet at the front of this book)

Glue gun and glue sticks

Pinecones

Shells

Other decorative items for your wreath, your choice

Ribbon

1. Assemble the various elements that you plan to use to decorate the wreath so that you have plenty of material to work with. You can select the ones that look best together while you're planning your arrangement.

2. Arrange the pinecones or shells evenly spaced around the wreath. Or overlap the items so that they fill the entire front of the wreath. Either way looks pretty.

3. Allow the glue gun to become hot; insert a stick of glue in the glue gun and pull the trigger to release a drop of glue on the middle of one pinecone. Attach the pinecone to the wreath immediately, holding it there for a moment to make sure that it is secure.

4. Continue to attach each element in this way. You may want to combine items, such as a piece of bark, a small shell, a pinecone or two, or a cluster of pine needles and a leaf. The hot glue dries almost immediately, so your project is ready to hang as soon as you apply the last decorative item.

5. Tie a ribbon around the top and hang the wreath on your tree, front door, or give it as a gift.

Picture note cards

Use natural materials to make personalized note cards more personal and to give them a touch of the outdoors. These nature note cards are very popular in stores these days. Blank note cards and matching envelopes are sold in stationery stores.

Tools and Materials:

Basic craft kit (see the Cheat Sheet at the front of this book)

Blank note cards and matching envelopes

Tiny pinecone, leaf, or small shell

Tweezers

Blades of green grass

Hole punch

1. **Put a spot of glue on one corner of a card and attach a tiny pinecone, a small leaf, or a small shell.**

2. **To decorate the card with blades of grass, run a line of white craft glue around the card about ¼-inch in from the outside edges all around. Using a pair of tweezers, gently place a blade of grass on the glue, making a line of grass and overlapping each end to create a continuous green border.**

3. **For another design, use a hole punch to make evenly spaced holes all around the front of the card. Weave the blades of grass in and out of the punched holes. Secure the ends at the back of the card with a small dot of white glue.**

My own collection box

Take your children along with you on a nature walk and let them collect things that interest them. When you get home, let the children decorate the outside of a shoe box in which they can keep their collections. Whenever they find something new, they can add it to the box. Collecting things like rocks, leaves, nuts, and pinecones can provide hours of fun.

Using What You Collect at the Seashore

A walk on the beach inspires you to pick up shells, almost unconsciously. When you get home, you usually put the new shells in a jar or some other container with shells from previous trips to the seashore. The nice thing about shells is that it doesn't matter what you do with them — they always remind you of that great feeling at the beach. You can try many ways to display your shell collection — you find out about a couple of ways in this section.

Displaying seashells

One of the nicest ways to show off your shell collection is to display it in a glass container. Seashells are simply beautiful as they are. Sometimes the shells look prettiest when they're wet because they become dull when they dry out. You can fill the jar with water to get this wet look. You can also coat shells and stones with glossy varnish to create that underwater effect.

Seashell basket

If you have a variety of shells, you can display them in a small basket. The natural colors of the shells complement the texture of the basket.

If the shells are simply piled into the basket and not glued together, you can rearrange them at will. I find that visitors to my home enjoy feeling the shells and taking a few out of the basket to look at them more closely. Shells are appealing to touch.

Tools and Materials:

Seashells, varied in size and shape

Small basket

Florist's clay or Styrofoam

Glue gun and glue sticks

1. **Fill the basket almost to the top with florist's clay or a chunk of Styrofoam (both are available at any garden or flower shop).**

2. **Using a glue gun (see Chapter 2), glue the shells in place to form a nice rounded mound.**

   Start with the larger shells on the bottom. Glue each shell to the one under and next to it so that all the shells are glued to each other, making a nice pile of shells that looks natural. You can make any size arrangement, depending on the size of your basket and the number of shells you want to display.

You can also use a collection box — display boxes that are divided into small compartments — to display your seashells. Look for collection boxes in hobby and craft stores. Arrange the shells in each compartment. Then remove each shell, one at a time, to apply the hot glue, and then replace each shell.

Frame with shells

You can enhance your favorite picture from the seashore and create a nice keepsake by decorating a frame with seashells for it. See an example of a seashell frame in the color section of this book. If you don't have a collection of shells, you can purchase a variety of shells at a souvenir shop or craft store.

Tools and Materials:

Basic craft kit (see the Cheat Sheet at the front of this book)

Enough shells to fit around the photograph

Heavy cardboard or foam board, slightly larger than the photograph

1. **Glue the photograph to the center of the backing (cardboard or foam board).**

2. **Arrange the shells around the border in a pleasing way before gluing each one in place. The shells should cover the cardboard border area and the edges of the photograph all around.**

   You can fill the area heavily with shells or simply make a border of decorative, delicate shells. Starfish make an interesting decoration when you use one at each corner of the photograph.

4. **Remove one shell at a time and apply a small amount of glue to the underside of each shell. Reposition it around the photograph.**

5. **After all the shells are glued in place, let the glue dry overnight.**

6. **Attach a hanging tab (available in photo shops) to the back.**

Part VI
Holiday Crafts

The 5th Wave   By Rich Tennant

"Okay kids, today we'll be working on sock puppets, name plates, and glue gun safety."

In this part . . .

*E*ven if you've never done a single craft before, you've probably been tempted to make something for the holidays. You may want to make a tree ornament, a wreath for the front door, or a garland to wind up the staircase. The best thing about crafting for the holidays is the abundance of materials available at this time of year. In this part, you find out what those materials are and loads of quick and easy techniques for making gifts, ornaments, and stockings.

After you delve into this part, you can become an expert at wrapping creative packages, setting a holiday table with decorated hurricane lamps, creating interesting containers for baked goodies, and discovering great ideas for helping kids make gifts for their grandparents. Hostess gifts, stockings ready for stuffing, and a whimsical card-holder are just a few more fun things you can find out how to make in this part.

Chapter 22

Basic Crafting for the Holidays

• •

• •

*I*n this part, you find out what you need and where to find all the materials to make decorations, ornaments, a card holder, gift tags, gifts for giving and selling at fund-raisers, Christmas stockings and wreaths, and delightful food containers. You don't have to be a magician to know the tricks and techniques for quick and easy crafting. Making sensational hostess gifts is rewarding for you, and your friends will greatly appreciate the results.

Make a few extra gift items so that you have something on hand to take with you for your hostess if you're invited to a last-minute party.

Getting What You Need

The materials that you need for holiday crafting are simple and inexpensive: felt, Styrofoam, glue, ribbons, paper, sequins, buttons, and a variety of trims that you can find in fabric and craft shops.

> ✔ **Felt:** Felt is a fabulous material for many reasons. Working with felt is extremely easy and a lot of fun. It comes in an array of colors and is inexpensive. You can cut it into different shapes, the edges won't ravel, it's easy to sew, and you can paint on it. Felt is sold in 9-x-12-inch pieces, as well as by the yard in fabric stores. Felt pieces are also sold with a fusible backing for making no-sew projects (see Chapter 14). In this part, you find out how to make a variety of ornaments and stockings from felt.
>
> ✔ **Different fabrics for different projects:** A well-stocked fabric store is the place to start planning a craft project. Printed fabric, some with holiday patterns, can be used for stitching stockings and ornaments with a country look. Canvas and muslin are excellent materials to use for backing stockings, as well as for a background on which to paint designs and

shapes. For an elegant look, use velvet, satin, and taffeta to make your projects. Even-weave fabric is perfect for counted cross-stitch ornaments (see Chapter 18). Gingham fabric is a checked pattern that comes in different colors, including green and red.

Gingham is the perfect material for covering and decorating the tops of canned jellies and jams that people often make for gifts at holiday time.

✔ **Styrofoam:** A solid but light, white porous material, Styrofoam is molded into many shapes. At holiday time, garden centers and craft shops carry Styrofoam balls in different sizes that you can decorate and turn into handcrafted ornaments. You can wrap the balls with fabric or ribbons or encrust them with sequins or beads. You can also find Styrofoam cones for embellishing with trimmings to make them look like small Christmas trees. Styrofoam also comes in wreath shapes so that crafters can add their own creative decorations. Painting on Styrofoam with a brush or spray paint is a snap.

✔ **Wreaths:** Wire wreath frames are ideal as a base for adding dried flowers and other decorations to create an original wreath. You can find these frames, as well as natural vine and foam wreath forms, in craft and garden shops.

✔ **Scissors:** No longer limited to a straight-edge cut, scissors now make all sorts of fancy edges like scallops, zigzags, waves, and a variety of squiggles. You always need a pair of regular household scissors for basic crafting techniques. However, you can use the new novelty scissors available in craft stores to have a lot of fun making decorative edges on fabric and paper. Experiment with different effects. Using decorative scissors for making ornaments, decorations, and gifts gives your projects a creative edge.

✔ **Glue:** Different kinds of glue are meant for different materials and craft projects. Regular white craft glue, such as Elmer's Glue-All, is perfect for most projects where you must attach paper to paper or fabric to fabric. But, for example, when you want to affix dried flowers to a wire wreath frame, you need a special glue gun and glue stick, which are available in craft stores (see Chapter 2). The heated glue is more effective than craft glue for holding heavy and three-dimensional objects. Tacky glue comes in a squeeze bottle and is often used to adhere something temporarily. Tacky glue isn't permanent; therefore, you can remove and reposition the item if you make a mistake.

Techniques for Quick and Easy Crafting

Making stockings, ornaments, and decorations doesn't require any difficult crafting techniques. Nobody has extra time during the holidays for stressful projects, no matter how much you enjoy the crafting process. Holiday crafting involves all the basic things you learned to do in elementary school — measure, cut, and paste — with a little simple sewing here and there.

Enlarging stocking patterns

To make a Christmas stocking, you need a pattern. The projects in this part provide patterns that you must enlarge to a specified size. Enlarging a pattern is easy to do at a copy center. If you don't have access to a copy machine, you can enlarge the pattern on a grid (see Chapter 3 for directions).

Dressing up with finishing touches

Adding the finishing touches like buttons, ribbons, sequins, and other fancy trims turns any plain item into a work of art. After you make a lush, red velvet Christmas stocking with a wide, white satin cuff, for example, you can then trim the cuff with bands of embroidered ribbon. Outlining the edge of the stocking with bells or colorful glass beads further adds to the elegance of the finished project. You can find all the fixings for decorating and personalizing your craft projects in craft and hobby or fabric stores. These *notions,* as they are called, are inexpensive, but they make a big difference in your projects. Best of all, you can attach them with a few tacking stitches or a drop of glue. Browsing through stores simply to find out what is available is as much fun as actually choosing the decorations that make your project look the best.

Making it personal

Christmas ornaments and stockings have more meaning when they are personalized. Embroidering or painting a name on a stocking gives it an extra quality that turns it into an heirloom. Cross-stitch ornaments (see Chapter 23) are easy to personalize with each family member's initials or name stitched on the project. Personalizing gifts makes them special, which is just what you discover how to do when you make the craft projects in this part.

Painting on different material

Whether you're painting on fabric, wood, glass, metal, ceramic, or fabric, one type of paint usually works best. Most crafting projects can be done with water-based paint. Acrylic paint, which is water-based, is the most popular kind of paint for all your crafting projects.

You can find a wide variety of colors of water-based paint made especially for working on fabric in most craft and art supply stores. When applied on the fabric, this type of paint dries soft rather than stiff, meaning that you can safely wash the fabric.

All-purpose craft paint is also water-based. You can use it to paint anything for which a specific paint isn't specified. All-purpose paint is available in small- to large-size containers, so that you can buy only the amount you need for the project you're working on.

For stenciling projects, you can use acrylic or oil-based paint, which is available in craft stores. I prefer water-based paint because it makes cleanup easier. The projects in this part all use water-based paints.

Chapter 23

Making Tree Ornaments

● ●

In This Chapter

▶ Bringing back Jurassic Park with dinosaur ornaments

▶ Welcoming a star and the little drummer boy to your tree

▶ Stitching up some festive cross-stitch tree ornaments

● ●

Decorating your tree with handmade ornaments makes your tree special — one-of-a-kind. Making lots of ornaments at the same time is easy and quite economical. Call in your friends, neighbors, and relatives and have a craft party. Your guests will have a good time making a variety of ornaments for their Christmas trees.

Dynamo Dinosaurs

These jaunty, colorful dinosaurs (see the photo in the color section of this book) are so much fun to make that my friends and I had a pre-Christmas party and spent the evening making a whole bunch of them. Everyone who came into the studio wanted to make a dinosaur. They're especially appropriate for a household that includes young children. One woman wanted to make them for her tree and then use them as a mobile over her baby's crib. I think that this idea is a great way to extend the use of the ornaments, which makes a nice Christmas gift for someone on your list.

Tools and Materials:

Basic craft kit (see the Cheat Sheet at the front of this book)

Tracing paper

Heavy paper, such as manila folder

Assortment of brightly colored felt pieces, each approximately 5 x 7 inches (one per ornament)

Black embroidery floss

Embroidery needle

Stuffing, such as Poly-Fil

1. **Trace the dinosaur patterns (see Figure 23-1) and transfer them to heavy paper for templates (see Chapter 3).**

   You need to enlarge these patterns by 250 percent. The easiest way is with a copy machine; if you like to do things the hard way, see Chapter 3 for how to enlarge a pattern by hand. Be sure to make separate templates for the spines of the three dinosaurs that have spines.

Figure 23-1:
Enlarge
these
dinosaur
patterns by
250 percent.

2. Make two outlines of each dinosaur template on a piece of felt. (One piece is for the back of the ornament, and one is for the front.)

3. For each dinosaur that has a spine, use a different color felt piece and draw around the spine templates. When cutting these pieces out, add ¼ inch outside the drawn line along the curved edge of the body.

4. Cut out all the shapes.

5. Referring to Figure 23-1, use black embroidery floss and a chain stitch (see Figure 23-2) to sew the mouths and eyes where indicated.

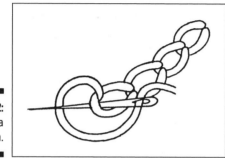

Figure 23-2:
Making a
chain stitch.

6. Using felt in a color that's different from the color of the body, cut out small circles (or use a paper punch to make circles) and glue them at random over the front pieces of the spotted dinosaur.

Use up the scraps of felt that are left after cutting out the bodies and spines to make the circles.

7. Pin the front and back piece of each dinosaur together, with the spine in between the two pieces, so that your dinosaurs look like the ones in Figure 23-1.

8. Stitch (by hand or machine) around the outside edge, leaving a small opening at the top of each ornament for the stuffing.

9. Fill your dinosaur(s) loosely with stuffing. Use the eraser end of a pencil or a crochet hook to push the stuffing into the points and narrow neck areas.

10. Cut a strand of embroidery floss 6 inches long. Fold it in half to make a hanging loop and insert the ends into the center of each opening.

11. Stitch or glue the opening closed.

Toyland Felt Ornaments

These Toyland felt ornaments match the Christmas stocking in Chapter 24 and the gift tags in Chapter 25. You might want to make them all for a coordinated theme. They are fun to make and fun to give. You can see a photo of the ensemble in the color section of this book.

Tools and Materials:

Basic craft kit (see the Cheat Sheet at the front of this book)

Tracing paper

Heavy paper, such as manila folder

½ yard white felt

Piece of fusible red felt, 4 x 6 inches (or use regular felt and glue)

Small pieces of felt in red, green, blue, and gold

1 skein black embroidery floss

Embroidery needle

1. **Trace the patterns of the Toyland ornaments, shown in Figure 23-3, enlarge them 165 percent, and transfer the designs to heavy paper to make templates (see Chapter 3).**

   Place the template for each design on a piece of felt in the color of your choice and draw around the outline of the template. Make two for each ornament (one for the back and one for the front). If you are making only one ornament, trace the pattern and pin the tracing to the piece of felt.

2. **Use three strands of embroidery floss and a running stitch (see Chapter 13) to embroider the details on the drum and for the eyes and mouth on the star.**

3. **Place the front and back of each ornament shape together with the fusible sides facing. Place a clean cloth over the front of one side and press with a warm iron for three seconds. If you are using regular felt, glue the matching front and back felt pieces of each ornament together with a thin coat of glue. Let dry.**

4. **Glue the felt cutouts to each ornament to complete them (like the bow to the wreath and the ribbon on the present; refer to the color photo). Let the glue dry about five minutes.**

5. **Cut a 4-inch length of embroidery floss and thread the needle. Poke the needle through one corner of the ornament, pull the thread through the felt, and remove the needle. Tie the ends of the thread to make a hanging loop.**

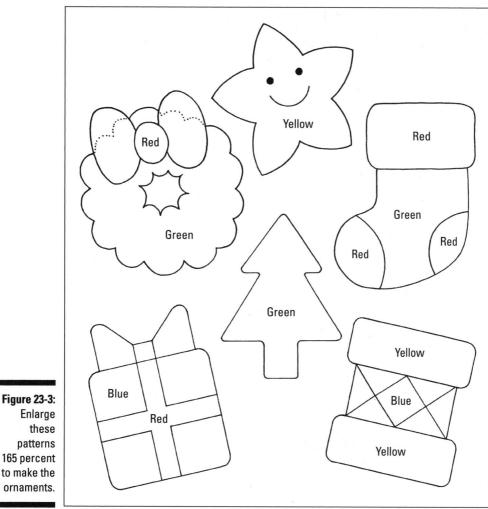

Figure 23-3:
Enlarge
these
patterns
165 percent
to make the
ornaments.

Cross-Stitch Cuties

Counted cross-stitch ornaments (see the photograph in the color section of this book) make wonderful gifts or trimmings for your tree. Because the designs are small, the projects are quite easy and quick to finish. All the ornaments are done on 14-count, even-weave Aida cloth and trimmed with lace or colorful piping. The cross-stitch materials are available in craft stores and yarn shops. The projects list the color numbers and names for DMC brand embroidery floss, but you can use similar colors of any brand of floss.

Always work with a piece of even-weave cloth that is twice the size of the finished ornament so that you have plenty of fabric around the design while doing your embroidery. This size is more comfortable to work with and makes it easy to center the design.

Here are the finished sizes of the ornaments in this section: tree ornament, 2 x 3 inches; reindeer ornament, 2½ inches in diameter; church ornament, 2½ x 3½ inches; and Santa ornament, 3¼ x 5¼ inches.

Tree ornament

The design pattern and color chart for the cross-stitch tree ornament are shown in Figure 23-4.

Tools and Materials:

Basic craft kit (see Cheat Sheet at the front of this book)

Masking tape

14-count red Aida cloth

1 skein embroidery floss in each of the following colors: white, green, and yellow

Embroidery needle

Backing fabric (can be Aida cloth, felt, or colorful fabric)

10½ inches lace trim

Stuffing, such as Poly-Fil

6 inches of ⅛-inch-wide white satin ribbon for hanging

Reindeer ornament

The design pattern and color chart for the cross-stitch reindeer ornament are shown in Figure 23-5.

Tools and Materials:

Basic craft kit (see Cheat Sheet at the front of this book)

Masking tape

14-count white Aida cloth

1 skein embroidery floss in each of the following colors: red, brown, and black

Embroidery needle

Backing fabric (can be Aida cloth, felt, or colorful fabric)

8 inches lace trim

Stuffing, such as Poly-Fil

8 inches of ⅛-inch-wide red satin ribbon for hanging

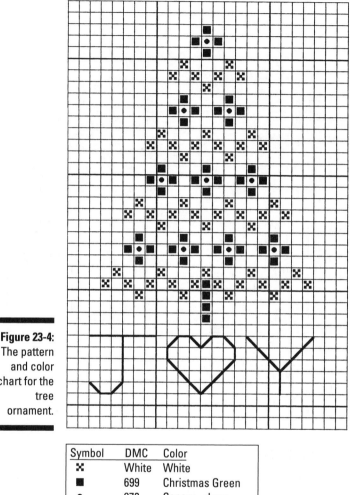

Figure 23-4:
The pattern
and color
chart for the
tree
ornament.

Symbol	DMC	Color
✖	White	White
■	699	Christmas Green
●	972	Canary - deep
–	White	White

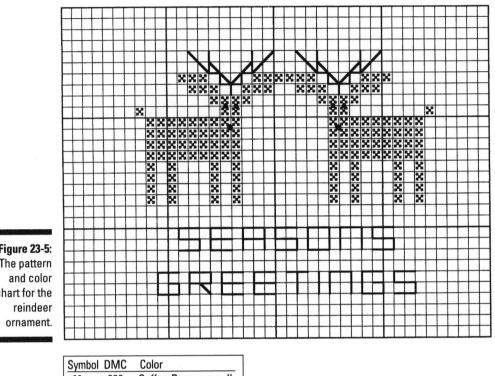

Figure 23-5:
The pattern
and color
chart for the
reindeer
ornament.

Symbol	DMC	Color
✖	898	Coffee Brown - vy dk
−	310	Black
●	304	Christmas Red

Church ornament

The design pattern and color chart for the cross-stitch church ornament are shown in Figure 23-6.

Tools and Materials:

Basic craft kit (see Cheat Sheet at the front of this book)

Masking tape

14-count white Aida cloth

1 skein embroidery floss in each of the following colors: gray, red, green, and blue

Embroidery needle

Backing fabric (can be Aida cloth, felt, or colorful fabric)

12½ inches lace trim

Stuffing, such as Poly-Fil

8 inches of ⅛-inch-wide red satin ribbon for hanging

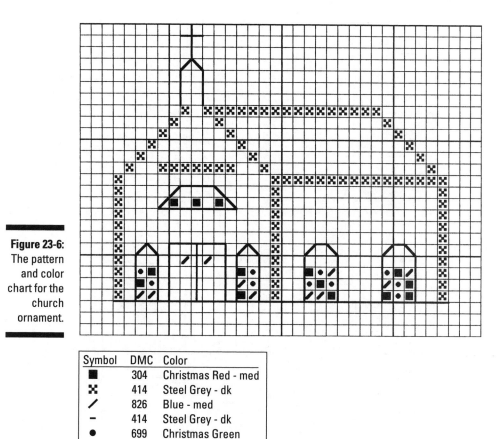

Figure 23-6:
The pattern
and color
chart for the
church
ornament.

Symbol	DMC	Color
■	304	Christmas Red - med
✕	414	Steel Grey - dk
╱	826	Blue - med
▬	414	Steel Grey - dk
●	699	Christmas Green

Santa ornament

The design pattern and color chart for the cross-stitch Santa ornament are
shown in Figure 23-7.

Tools and Materials:

*Basic craft kit (see Cheat Sheet
at the front of this book)*

Masking tape

14-count white Aida cloth

*1 skein embroidery floss in
each of the following colors:
red, black, white, navy blue,
peach, and green*

Embroidery needle

*Backing fabric (can be Aida
cloth, felt, or colorful fabric)*

1 package green or red piping

Stuffing, such as Poly-Fil

*6 inches of ¼-inch-wide red
satin ribbon*

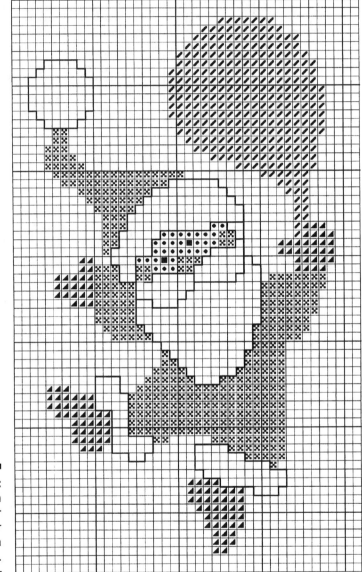

Figure 23-7:
The pattern
and color
chart for
the Santa
ornament.

Symbol	DMC	Color
✖	666	Christmas Red - bright
●	353	Peach Flesh
■	310	Black
◢	336	Navy Blue
╱	699	Christmas Green
–	310	Black
☐	White	White

Making the cross-stitch ornaments

The patterns and color charts provided for each ornament (refer to
Figures 23-4, 23-5, 23-6, and 23-7) indicate where to place the stitches needed
in each color to create a design on the even-weave fabric. Each square on the
chart represents a square on the cloth. (See Chapter 18 for complete counted
cross-stitch directions.)

1. **Tape the edges of the cloth so that they don't fray.**

2. **Using a pencil on the even-weave fabric, center and draw a rectangle
   or circle to the size given for the finished ornament you are making.**

3. **Cut a piece of embroidery floss approximately 18 inches long. Separate
   the six strands of the piece of floss and rejoin three of the strands.
   Thread the floss through the embroidery needle (see Chapter 18).**

4. **Follow the directions in Chapter 18 to find the placement of the first
   stitch. The charts in the figures indicate the color of this stitch.**

5. **Work the stitches as directed in Chapter 18, referring to the chart for
   the placement of each color in each square of the fabric.**

   Note: If you're working on an area that has few stitches in each row, you
   may prefer to cross each stitch as you work it. With this method, you
   have to make sure that each stitch is crossed in the same direction as
   the others so that the finished work looks neat. Holes are worked twice
   when the stitches are adjacent with no spaces between. When working
   on isolated stitches, always complete each stitch, end the thread, and
   move to the next area.

6. **Use a backstitch (see Chapter 18) for outlines and for the lettering of
   "JOY" and "Season's Greetings."**

7. **Use a French knot, shown in Figure 23-8, for the reindeer's eyes and
   nose.**

   Insert the needle from the underside, bringing the needle out on the
   right side of the fabric where the stitch is indicated on the chart. Wrap
   the thread two or three times around the point of the needle and insert
   the needle close to the spot where the thread came through. Hold the
   knot in place and pull the thread to the wrong side.

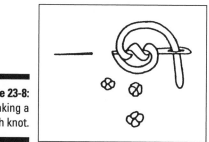

Figure 23-8:
Making a
French knot.

8. When you finish cross-stitching the ornaments, remove the tape from around the edges.

9. Cut out each ornament ¼ inch larger than the drawn lines all around. This ¼ inch is your seam allowance.

10. Cut a piece of fabric for backing that's the same size as the Aida cloth.

11. With raw edges aligned, pin the lace trim or piping around the front of the ornament. Stitch around the edges.

12. With right sides facing and raw edges aligned, pin the front and back pieces together, with the trim between, leaving the top edge open.

13. Stitch around the fabric, leaving an opening in the top for turning.

14. Clip the corners and curves and then turn right side out. Steam press from the wrong side of the fabric.

15. Fill the ornament with stuffing.

16. Fold the ribbon in half to make a loop and insert the raw ends into the center of the top opening. Slipstitch or machine-stitch the opening closed, across the raw ends of ribbon.

Chapter 24

Stockings for the Whole Family

. . . .

In This Chapter

▶ Enlarging and cutting out a stocking pattern

▶ Making a felt stocking

▶ Putting together an elegant patchwork Christmas stocking

. . . .

*I*f you're looking for Christmas stockings to add a festive touch to your mantle, you've come to the right place. In this chapter, you find out how to enlarge and cut out a basic stocking pattern to use on any fabric. You also discover how to turn scraps of colorful felt into delightful Christmas stockings covered with images of toys. (You can also use the toy patterns to make simple felt ornaments and gift tags that will personalize your tree and your packages with a theme — find out how in Chapters 23 and 25.) In addition, you have the directions for making a quilted patchwork Christmas stocking from scraps of fabric.

Cutting Out a Christmas Stocking

You can cut a basic stocking pattern from any material. However, felt is a good material for this type of project because it is heavier than many other types of fabric, such as lightweight cotton. When you cut felt, the edges have a clean finish because this fabric doesn't ravel when cut. For these reasons, a stocking made of felt does not require a lining.

Before you can cut a stocking pattern, you need to enlarge the pattern (see Chapter 3) shown in Figure 24-1 by 310 percent. Next, pin the pattern to two pieces of the fabric of your choice, with wrong sides of the fabric together. Making a stocking requires two pieces of fabric, one for the front and one for the back.

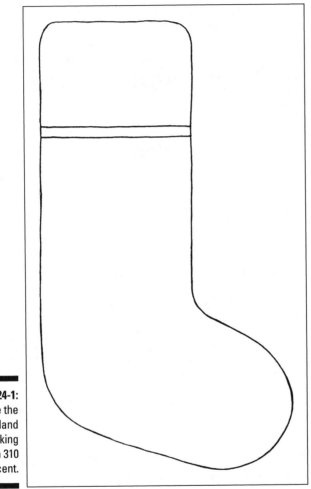

Figure 24-1:
Enlarge the
Toyland
stocking
pattern 310
percent.

If you're making the stocking with felt, you can cut it out to the exact size. However, if you're making the stocking from another fabric, such as velvet, satin, cotton, or taffeta, cut the pattern with an extra ¼ inch of fabric around the stocking outline for a seam allowance.

Toyland Felt Stocking

The Toyland felt stocking matches the Toyland felt ornaments in Chapter 23 and gift tags in Chapter 25. You can see a photo of all three items in the color section of this book.

The felt stocking and its appliqué can all be made with fusible (iron-on) felt or regular felt with fusible webbing (see Chapter 22). Or you can attach the felt pieces with regular craft glue. After you make the stocking and see how easy the project is, you're sure to want to make the gift tags and tree ornaments to complete the theme.

Tools and Materials:

Basic sewing craft kit (see the Cheat Sheet at the front of this book)

Tracing paper

½ yard white felt

Piece of fusible red felt, 4 x 6 inches (or regular felt and fusible webbing)

Small pieces of fusible or regular felt in red, green, blue, and gold

1 skein black embroidery floss and needle

Heavy paper, such as manila folder

1 package green or red piping (or other decorative trim)

1. **Trace the stocking pattern (including the cuff) shown in Figure 24-1 and enlarge it 310 percent (see Chapter 3).**

2. **Pin the enlarged stocking pattern to the white felt and cut out two pieces of fabric.**

3. **Trace the cuff section of the stocking and pin it to the 4-x-6-inch piece of red felt. Cut out the cuff. If you are using regular felt, cut a matching piece of fusible webbing.**

4. **Pin the cuff in position on the front of one stocking piece (with the fusible webbing, if used, between the cuff and the stocking).**

   Cover the cuff with a clean piece of fabric. Then press over the cloth with a medium-hot iron for five seconds to fuse the cuff piece in place on the stocking.

5. **Trace all the appliqué pattern pieces in Figure 23-2 (refer to Chapter 23). Pin each to the appropriate felt color (refer to the color photograph or use the colors of your choice) and cut out.**

6. **Refer to the photo of the Toyland stocking in the color section and arrange the appliqués on the front of the stocking piece with the cuff as shown.**

7. **Place a clean cloth over each appliqué and press with the iron as described in Step 4.**

8. **Cut a piece of piping, ribbon, or decorative trim slightly longer than the width of the bottom edge of the cuff. Pin it across the cuff, with the edges of the trim tucked under at each end. Hand- or machine-stitch the trim across the cuff.**

9. With the wrong sides facing each other and the trim between the two pieces, pin the front and back of the stocking together, leaving the top edge open.

10. Cut a 4-inch length of piping and fold it in half to make a hanging loop. Insert the raw ends of the loop between the stocking pieces at the back, top edge.

11. Starting at the loop, stitch around the stocking as close to the outer edge as possible, leaving the top edge open.

Country Patchwork Stocking

Red and white patchwork has always been a favorite color combination for any quilted project, but it's especially bright and cheerful for a Christmas stocking. Use this easy patchwork design (see Figure 24-2) to make a stocking for everyone in the family. You can make each stocking with different fabric combinations, such as solid colors or calico prints. The right triangle method (see Chapter 15) is used to make the squares, which you then arrange in a pinwheel pattern. The stocking is a generous 20 inches long — perfect for stuffing with plenty of goodies!

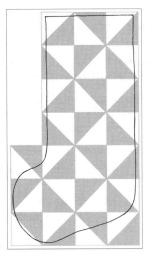

Figure 24-2:
Each square on this pattern equals 3 inches.

Tools and Materials:

Basic sewing craft kit (see the Cheat Sheet at the front of this book)

½ yard of 45-inch-wide white fabric

½ yard of 45-inch-wide red fabric

½ yard of 45-inch-wide thin quilt batting

8 inches of ⅛-inch red or white satin ribbon for hanging loop

Tracing paper

Note: All measurements for cutting include a ¼-inch seam allowance.

1. **Cut one piece of white fabric measuring 12 x 16 inches and one piece of red fabric measuring 12 x 16 inches.**

2. **On the wrong side of the white rectangle, measure and mark 12 squares, in a 3 x 4 grid, each 4 x 4 inches.**

3. **Use a ruler and a pencil to lightly draw lines diagonally through all squares in the same direction (refer to the right triangle method in Chapter 13).**

4. **With the right sides together and the raw edges aligned, pin the white fabric to the same-size piece of red fabric.**

5. **Make a row of stitches on either side of all the diagonal lines, ¼ inch away from the line. (The stitching can be done by hand if you don't have a sewing machine.)**

6. **Cut along the lines you used to draw your original 12 squares. Open the seams and press. You have 24 squares made up of white and red triangles.**

7. **Refer to Figure 24-2 for placement of the squares. The shaded triangles are red. With right sides facing together and the raw edges aligned, stitch two squares together along one side edge. Open the seams and press.**

8. **Continue to join another square, alternating colors so that you always stitch a white square to a red square. You now have a row of three squares. Make three more rows of three squares each.**

9. **Join four squares to make a row. Make two more rows.**

10. **Arrange the rows as shown in Figure 24-2. You have four rows of three squares followed by three rows of four squares.**

11. **With right sides facing together and the raw edges aligned, join row 1 to row 2 along one long edge, making sure that all the seams match. Open the seams and press. Continue to join rows in this way.**

12. Use the enlarged stocking pattern (see "Cutting Out a Christmas Stocking," earlier in this chapter) to cut one stocking shape from the remaining white fabric, one from the remaining red fabric, and one from the quilt batting.

13. Pin the pattern to the red and white patchwork fabric and cut it out (the seam allowance is included in the pattern).

14. Trim ¼ inch around the quilt batting stocking shape.

15. Pin the red and white patchwork piece, batting, and white stocking piece together.

16. Using a small running stitch (see Chapter 13), quilt ¼ inch on each side of all seam lines. Do not run the stitches into the outer ¼-inch seam allowance all around.

17. When all the quilting is complete, remove the pins.

18. With right sides facing together and raw edges aligned, stitch the red backing piece to the quilted top, leaving the top edge open. Clip around the curves into the seam allowance. Turn right side out and press.

19. Fold ¼ inch of the top unfinished edge of the stocking to the inside and press. Fold another ¼ inch of fabric to the inside and press. Pin the fabric in place temporarily.

20. Fold the ribbon in half to make a loop. Cross the raw ends of the ribbon and slip the ribbon ends inside the stocking at the top of the long side seam.

21. Stitch around the top of the stocking as close to the edge as possible.

Chapter 25

Giving Gifts from the Heart

In This Chapter

▶ Stenciling plain paper with pretty designs

▶ Painting containers for food gifts

▶ Spicing up your packages with felt gift tags

▶ Making gifts your hostess will love

*W*rapping presents is part of the joy of the holidays, and in this chapter, you use simple techniques to make sensational gift packaging. Use holiday stencil designs to create fabulous gift wraps. Painting freehand designs on plain jelly jars, plastic containers, aluminum-foil pans, and juice glasses turns them into delightful gift containers for homemade jams, jellies, breads, and cakes.

This chapter also shows you how to make adorable felt gift tags for kids of all ages. And if you've ever felt stumped by what to take to a party as a hostess gift, this chapter has more terrific ideas than you can use in one holiday season.

Here's a clever idea that I discovered by accident. Last year I sent most of my presents to relatives who live far away. The bows all got crushed in the mail. This year I'm drawing my bows with markers right on the packages. No ribbons, no crushed bows!

Sensational Stenciled Wraps

Designing your own wrapping paper makes all your packages special (see the photo in the color section). In fact, making your own wrapping paper is nicer and less expensive than buying it. You can personalize each gift with my easy method for making these pretty, colorful wraps — see the how-to in Chapter 11. Using simple stencils (shown in Figures 25-1 and 25-2) and colored markers, you can decorate plain paper (shiny paper looks festive) with different holiday symbols as well as initials, sayings, and names. Stencils of ribbons, bows, bells, artificial greens, candy canes, and so on, will make your packages look so pretty that no one will want to open them.

All the materials for cutting my stencil designs are available in art stores. An alternative to cutting stencil designs is to use Christmas cookie cutters for your patterns.

Figure 25-1:
Enlarge
these
stencil
designs 200
percent.

Trace this half of the bow pattern, then turn the tracing over and trace again for the other half.

Figure 25-2:
Enlarge these stencil designs 200 percent.

Tools and Materials:

Basic craft kit (see the Cheat Sheet at the front of this book)

Colorful markers (use a white marker on colored papers)

Stencil letters (from craft or art stores)

Solid color wrapping paper (or use plain shelf lining paper, available in rolls)

Ribbons, bows, bells, artificial greens, candy canes (optional finishing touches)

1. **Wrap your packages in solid color paper.**

2. **If you're using pre-cut stencils or cookie cutters, you're ready to go. If you use the designs provided in Figures 25-1 and 25-2, begin by tracing each one.**

3. **Tape the tracing to the stencil paper and place on a cutting surface.**

4. **Using a craft knife, follow each traced line and cut through the tracing paper and stencil paper beneath. Remove all cutout pieces.**

5. **Place a stencil design in position on the package and fill in with the desired color marker. To vary the look of your packages, apply the stencil design on all sides, top, and bottom of some of the packages.**

6. **Choose one of the smaller designs for small packages, such as a star or one bell. For small designs, place the stencil on one side of the package and, using a pencil, draw the design inside all cutout lines of the stencil. Then fill in with the marker color of your choice.**

Try the white marker on red, green, or blue papers. The white is good for creating snowmen or snowflake designs (see the blue package in the photograph).

7. **To personalize a package with words such as "Noel," trace stencil letters in position on paper to use as a guide for planning the spacing and placement of the letters exactly where you want them on the package before actually doing the stenciling. Use this tracing as a guide to refer to when actually stenciling the letters on the package.**

Stencil the name of each person on his or her present.

8. **Add ribbons, bows, bells, artificial greens, candy canes, and so on, to each package.**

Painted Food Containers

Save up all your empty coffee cans, mayonnaise and jelly jars, aluminum-foil loaf pans, plastic plant pots, and inexpensive juice glasses to use for this project. You don't need any painting talent to use acrylic paint and a paintbrush to create random patterns of dots, swirls, and scallops on the containers.

Tools and Materials:

A variety of containers in various sizes

Red and white acrylic paint

Paper plate

Artist's paint brush

Paper doilies

Scraps of red-and-white checked fabric

Christmas ribbons

1. **Wash the food containers thoroughly and let them dry.**

2. **Squirt a small amount of each paint color onto a paper plate.**

3. **Dip the brush into the white paint and draw small circles at random around the containers. Rinse the brush in water and then dip the brush into the red paint and put a dot inside each white circle.**

4. **Paint a scalloped edge around the top and bottom rims of a few jars or glasses. Write words like "Noel" or "Jam" in freehand with a brush and paint.**

5. **Cover the tops of the jars with doilies or red and white fabric. Using pinking shears (see Chapter 2), cut a square of red-and-white fabric so that it is large enough to cover the top and sides of a jar lid. Secure the doily and fabric covers with a rubber band around the neck of the jar. Cover the rubber band with red and white satin ribbon wrapped around the neck of the jar and tie the ends of the ribbon in a bow.**

6. **To give loaf cakes or bread that you have baked as a gift, decorate a loaf pan as per directions for the glass jars above. Wrap the baked goods with clear or colored plastic wrap and tie with red or white ribbons. Place the wrapped food in a decorated aluminum-foil loaf pan.**

Toyland Felt Gift Tags

Make colorful felt appliqués for decorating all your holiday packages. The appliqué shapes match the Christmas stocking in Chapter 24 and the ornaments in Chapter 23 to complete a coordinated holiday theme.

Making appliqué gift tags is a great way for kids to craft with you.

Tools and Materials:

Basic craft kit (see the Cheat Sheet at the front of this book)

Tracing paper

Heavy paper, such as manila folder

½ yard white felt

Piece of fusible red felt, 4 x 6 inches (or regular felt and fusible webbing)

Small pieces of fusible or regular felt in red, green, blue, and gold

l skein black embroidery floss

Embroidery needle

White card paper

Hole punch

¼ satin ribbon (any color) or embroidery floss for ties

1. **Trace the Toyland project patterns in Chapter 23 and cut one piece of felt for each gift tag. If you're making several tags in one design, trace all patterns and transfer the designs to heavy paper to make templates (see Chapter 3).**

2. **Using three strands of the black embroidery floss, add embroidery details to the drum and stars, as shown in the photo in the color section.**

3. **From the white card paper, measure and cut a 3-inch square for each gift tag needed.**

4. **You can glue the felt pieces to the card or fuse the felt to the card with a medium-hot iron. The fusible felt adheres in three seconds. Center a felt appliqué piece on each card, place a clean cloth over the felt, and press with the iron.**

5. **Punch a hole in one corner of the card, thread with embroidery floss or ribbon, and tie the tags to your packages.**

Wowing Your Hostess with Great Gifts

You can turn plain, everyday store-bought items into wonderful, handcrafted hostess gifts by adding a decorative trim. It takes only minutes, but the results are impressive. The following are a few quick and easy suggestions:

- ✔ Stitch a band of decorative ribbon across the edge of plain hand towels. Make up a box of four.

- ✔ Tie lavish organdy ribbon around a clear glass votive candleholder and insert a candle.

- ✔ Using a Styrofoam ball and a package of brass upholstery tacks (from a fabric shop), insert the tacks so that they completely cover the ball. Your gift will look like a medieval ornament.

✔ Cover an inexpensive fat candle with upholstery tacks, inserted in a random pattern, to take the candle from plain to exquisite.

✔ Personalize an everyday canvas apron by stenciling your hostess's name across the front (see Chapter 11 for stenciling tips).

✔ Spray a bunch of pinecones with silver or gold paint. When they are dry, pile them into a pretty basket and tie the handle with a fat bow.

✔ Decorate a few bars of plain soap with pretty stickers on top. Nestle the soap in a bed of pastel tissue for gift giving.

✔ Make a set of napkins from leftover fabric prints. Using pinking shears (see Chapter 2), cut 16-inch squares, each from a different color or print. Roll each one up, tie with yarn or ribbon, and you have a no-sew set of napkins! (See Chapter 14 for more no-sew crafts.)

Chapter 26

Holiday Decorations

● ●

In This Chapter

▶ Decorating hurricane lamps

▶ Adding a festive touch to your windows

▶ Making a snowman card holder

● ●

*T*his chapter shows you how easy it is to decorate ordinary items like glass hurricane lamps and windowpanes with holiday designs. You can use permanent markers if you want the design to last, but if you use water-soluble markers, you can wash away the designs after the holidays. I also show you how to use your scraps of felt to make a holiday card holder to hang on your door.

Glass Hurricane Lamps

Glass hurricane lamps with candles add a glow to a holiday table, especially when they're decorated with a holiday motif. You can find these lamps, which are quite inexpensive, in various sizes in home centers. The lamp that I made (see the photo in the color section of this book) sports a design of a red bow, holly leaves, and berries. You can use the design provided in Figure 26-1 or any design of your choice.

Tools and Materials:

Glass hurricane lamps	Tracing paper
Red, green, and black water-soluble markers	Tape

1. **Trace the complete design shown in Figure 26-1. Make a slit at the top and bottom of the tracing paper and tape the paper in position inside the hurricane lamp. The slits help the paper conform to the shape of the lamp.**

Figure 26-1:
Holly design
for
decorating
on glass.

2. **Place one hand inside the lamp and press the tracing paper against the glass. Use the other hand to fill in the color of each design element.**

   The bow and berries are red, and the leaves are green. The markers are easy to apply on the glass, and you can easily remove the ink with a damp cloth if you make an error.

3. **When the leaves are dry, use the black marker to draw a line down the center of each leaf as indicated on the tracing.**

Decorating a Windowpane

Kids and adults alike enjoy decorating windowpanes or glass doors with holiday designs. You can make up any designs that appeal to you, such as snowflakes or ornaments, or write holiday greetings like "Noel" or "Joy." Remove the markings (they wash off with a damp sponge) after the holidays. You can enlarge the design using a copier or manually (see Chapter 3). I suggest enlarging the design 200 percent.

Tools and Materials:

Basic craft kit (see the Cheat Sheet at the front of this book)

Tracing paper

Tape

Red, green, and black water-soluble markers

1. **Enlarge and trace onto the tracing paper each design element in Figure 26-1 as a separate piece of art. Cut out each piece.**

2. **Tape the designs in position on the windowpane and outline each with the appropriate color.**

3. **Remove the tracing pattern pieces and fill in each color. In places where the marker doesn't cover completely, let the ink dry and go over the area once more with the marker.**

Decorate champagne glasses with a gold marking pen. You can use this method to make dots, snowflakes, swirls, and all sorts of free-form designs, even initials and names. Or you can write a toast such as "Cheers!" on your glasses. Be sure to use water-soluble markers unless you want the designs to be permanent.

Holiday Cardholder

Making a decorative snowman cardholder, shown in the color section of this book, is the perfect solution for containing all the holiday cards that pile up. As each new card arrives, you can place it in the pocket of the holder, which you can hang on your door as a decoration. You can easily remove the cards whenever you want to look at them. After the holidays, pack away the cardholder with the cards intact. The finished size is 8½ x 14½ inches. The navy blue-and-white dotted fabric is the perfect background for the white snowman, and you can iron on or glue the felt appliqués in place.

Tools and Materials:

Basic craft kit (see the Cheat Sheet at the front of this book)

¼ yard of 45-inch-wide blue pin-dot fabric

8½-x-12-inch piece of fusible white felt

Tracing paper

Small pieces of fusible felt in red, green, black, brown, and pink (or use regular felt and white craft glue)

Hole punch (optional)

2½-x-9-inch piece of red gingham, calico, or ribbon for trim

Black embroidery floss

Embroidery needle

2 small plastic curtain rings for hanging

1. Cut a 9-x-15-inch piece (which includes the seam allowance) from the pin-dot fabric.

2. Turn under the raw edges of the fabric ¼ inch and press. Turn the edges under another ¼ inch and press. Machine or hand-stitch all around to finish the edges.

3. From the white felt, cut a 7-x-8½ inch piece.

4. Enlarge all the pattern pieces in Figure 26-2 200 percent and trace them on the appropriate colors of felt. The body and arms are one piece, and the head is another piece. The bow is made up of three pieces, and the broom is also three pieces.

5. Cut out all pattern pieces. A hole punch is handy for cutting out circles for the snowman's eyes and nose.

6. Refer to Figure 26-2. The numbers indicate the order in which you should place the pieces.

   Put the larger green tree on the pin-dot background approximately 1 inch down from the top edge and 1 inch in from the left side to the top branch. Cover the felt with a piece of fabric to protect it and fuse with a medium-hot iron for five seconds. If you're using regular felt, apply each piece with a small amount of white glue.

7. Position the smaller tree approximately 1½ inches down from the top and 1 inch in from the right edge. Press to fuse, or glue in place.

8. Position the eyes, nose, cheeks, bow tie, and buttons on the snowman as indicated in Figure 26-2. Fuse or glue as described in Step 6.

9. Center the snowman 2 inches down from the top edge of the pin-dot background and fuse or glue it to the background.

10. Add the top hat and shovel pieces to the snowman.

11. Place the 7-x-8½-inch piece of white felt across the trunk of the trees so that the felt abuts the bottom edge of the snowman and aligns with the side edges of the background. Fuse or glue in place.

12. Fold under the raw edges of the gingham, ribbon, or calico trim ¼ inch and press with a medium-hot iron for three seconds.

13. Pin this strip of fabric to the top 2 inches of the plain red felt and stitch (by hand or machine) across the top and bottom of the trim edges.

14. With the bottom and side edges aligned to the background, pin the pocket piece to the cardholder and stitch (by hand or machine) along the sides and across the bottom edge.

15. Using three strands of embroidery floss and a chain stitch (see Chapter 23), create a smiling mouth between the rosy cheeks on the snowman's face.

Figure 26-2:
Enlarge this
pattern 200
percent.

Part VII
The Part of Tens

The 5th Wave   By Rich Tennant

@RICHTENNANT

"Let's see, I've made an herb wreath, a fruit wreath, a flower wreath, a berry wreath, a shell wreath... Say- what are you planning to do with those egg shells?"

In this part . . .

Company's coming, and you want to spruce up your home. Don't fret. You can do many last-minute decorating projects that won't look like you threw them together. Best of all, most of the materials are leftover from other crafting projects or items that you may have around the house. This part gives you ten great holiday decorating ideas that are easy to do.

You can use throwaway containers for crafting, and they don't cost any money. Believe it or not, you can turn your trash into treasures that are good-looking enough to give as gifts. You find ten of these projects to make in this part.

Making small but elegant craft projects to sell at fund-raising events that churches, schools, and community groups hold can be very satisfying. You can use scraps of fabric, ribbons, trims, and paper to make items that everyone likes to buy at a bazaar. You find out how to do it all in this part.

Chapter 27

Ten Last-Minute Holiday Decorations

During the holidays, nobody has extra time for crafting, but almost everyone still likes to create homemade gifts or decorations. The projects in this chapter are your answer to this problem because you can complete them in very little time. Just imagine a beautifully decorated tree, an original centerpiece for your table, and boughs of greenery on the mantel — all made without any fuss!

This chapter tells you how to trim your tree with beautiful ornaments, fill baskets with sweet-smelling pomanders, set a table with easy-to-make candleholders, welcome guests with a felt banner, create a country theme, make miniature wreaths, add pine boughs to your mantle, and make an elegant gift bag. This is no time for stress, so these last-minute projects are easy and fun to do and definitely don't have that last-minute look.

Marbleized Ornaments

Marbleizing can turn a plain glass or plastic ball ornament into something extraordinary. Fill a pail with water and spray the surface of the water with gold paint. Hold the ball by the hanger, dip it into the water, and swirl it. Remove the ball and perch it on something like an egg carton to dry. No need to add more water or paint for the next one; you can use the same mixture for about a dozen ornaments. It's just like dyeing Easter eggs, but the effect is quite spectacular.

Use pale pink or blue ornaments for heavenly results.

Fruity Candleholders

Use fruit such as pears and apples (red or green) for candleholders. Polish the fruit and cut a hole in the top of each. Insert a small, tapered, red or white candle in each hole. Line up the candleholders on the windowsill or cluster them on a table.

If the candle doesn't stand up straight, remove the candle from the fruit and light the wick. Then hold the flame over the hole so that the wax melts and drips into the hole (5 or 6 drops). Insert the candle back into the hole while the wax is hot and hold the candle upright while the wax dries. It takes just a minute or two for the wax to harden, and then the candle holds in an upright position.

Welcome Banner

You may have discovered how easy it is to use glue and colored felt for crafting in Part VI. Now is the time to put those skills to work. Draw a design of holly leaves and berries on green and red felt (see the pattern in Chapter 26). Cut out each drawn piece with scissors. Arrange and glue the leaves and berries to the center of a rectangular piece of fabric that's the size you want for your banner. Using a piece of felt in a color that is different from the background of the banner, draw block letters (or use stencil letters) to spell out "CHEERS" or "NOEL." Cut out each letter. Evenly space and glue the letters to the felt background just above or below the leaf-and-berry design.

Sparkle Star Ornaments

For quick and easy ornaments, use a cookie cutter to cut stars from a sheet of Styrofoam approximately ¼ to ½ inch thick (available in craft stores). Coat the cut edges and one side of each star with glitter glue (also available in craft stores). Let the glitter glue dry and repeat the process on the reverse side.

Use an embroidery needle to weave thread or gold cord through the end of one point of each star to create a loop for hanging. Tie the thread or cord ends together and hang the ornament.

Golden Centerpiece

Save those empty throwaway containers like tin cans and glass jars. When decorated, they are perfect as candleholders for a holiday centerpiece. Each container should be large enough to hold a fat candle.

Spray the containers with gold paint and decorate each one with faux gems around the rim. Attach these gems, available in craft stores, to the containers with craft glue. Use a glue gun for the larger, heavier gems. Insert the candles and group the finished candleholders together on a pretty tray in the center of your table.

Spicy Basket

Pomander balls made from oranges, lemons, or limes studded with cloves are a sweet-smelling accessory. They look especially good in a wire basket on a coffee table.

Using a toothpick, puncture the skin of the fruit. Insert a clove into the punctured hole. Continue making holes and inserting the cloves in rows around the fruit so that the cloves are very close together. For an even quicker way to do this project, simply make a circle of cloves going around the fruit in a spiral, leaving sections of the skin showing.

Country-Style Tree Ornaments

Homespun plaid fabric, which has no wrong side, can be found in red and white or green and white. Most fabric shops carry this type of country fabric, especially during the holiday season. Use plaid homespun fabric to make stuffed ornaments in the shapes of hearts, tiny stockings, and pine trees. These shapes are easy to draw freehand, or you can use cookie cutters as patterns.

Draw the shapes on paper and cut out this pattern with an extra ¼-inch around the outside edges for seam allowance. Put two pieces of fabric together with the right sides facing, pin the pattern to the fabric, and cut out each ornament. Stitch the two pieces of fabric together, right sides facing, leaving an opening. Turn the ornament inside out and stuff it with cotton batting or cotton balls. Stitch the opening closed. Attach a loop made from ribbon, yarn, or embroidery floss to one corner of the ornament for hanging.

Miniature Wreaths

Small wreaths made from grapevines are available in craft stores and garden centers. These miniature wreaths are perfect for decorating with buttons, sequins, shells, dried rosebuds, bows, or small bells. Using a glue gun (see Chapter 2), attach each decoration to the front of the wreath until you have a pleasing arrangement. Tie a piece of ribbon around the top and form a bow to making a hanging loop.

Taffeta Gift Bags

Making an exquisite drawstring bag from luscious taffeta is an easy project. You can use these bags to bring a bottle of champagne or wine to a holiday party, or you can fill the bags with a bunch of fresh-picked evergreens to dress up a table and give your home a holiday scent.

Cut two rectangles approximately 8 x 16 inches. With the right sides of the fabric facing, hand- or machine-stitch across the bottom edge and along each side edge, leaving the top edge open. Turn the fabric bag right-side out. Turn ¼ inch of the top raw edge to the inside and press with a warm iron for three seconds. Turn another ¼ inch of the fabric edge to the inside and press. Stitch around the turned edge. Insert the bottle and tie a fat gold braid or wide wire-edged organdy ribbon around the neck of the bottle, on the outside of the fabric.

If you want to fill the bag with evergreens instead, first insert a glass that's filled partially with water. Insert the greens into the water glass so that they fan out over the top of the bag. Tie the cord or ribbon loosely around the middle of the bag for decoration.

Fill fabric gift bags with potpourri for a gift (see Chapter 20 for instructions on making your own potpourri mixture).

Pine Branch Decorations

Arrange pine branches across a shelf or on top of kitchen cabinets or a fireplace mantel so that they overlap and hang over the edge slightly. No matter how haphazardly you arrange them, they look great, and the room smells wonderful.

Next, add small silver and gold Christmas ornaments here and there among the boughs. Wrap small jewelry boxes with silver or gold paper and tie each one with a ribbon. Arrange these on the pine branches as well.

Add pinecones in various sizes to the arrangement. For sparkle, add a string of tiny, clear tree lights. For a country theme, weave a garland of cranberries through the pine branches.

Chapter 28

Ten Treasures to Make from Trash

· ·

In This Chapter

▶ Découpaging a jewelry box

▶ Disguising glass bottles and jars

▶ Converting paper paint pails into planters

▶ Beautifying berry baskets

▶ Turning a Band-Aid tin into a sewing kit

▶ Converting coffee cans into colorful containers

▶ Covering clay pots with fabric flowers

▶ Wrapping pencils in pretty paper

▶ Stringing buttons into a bracelet

· ·

Don't throw it away! There's treasure in that trash. Before throwing away the plastic food container from the take-out deli, take a second look. By the time you've finishing reading this chapter, you'll be looking at every container in a new light and asking yourself, "What can I turn this into?"

With your newfound knowledge of découpage (see Chapter 9), you can turn a plastic food container into a jewelry box, a glass pickle jar into a cosmetic holder, and a paper paint pail into a planter. With a little paper crafting, an ordinary cardboard berry container from the supermarket becomes a lovely desk accessory, and an empty Band-Aid tin becomes a sewing kit for all your mending supplies.

Pressed flowers convert the lowly coffee can into a pretty canister. And you'll never throw away scraps of fabric, tiny bits of paper, or unmatched buttons after you find out how to recycle those materials into quick gifts.

Découpage Jewelry Box

You can recycle those throwaway clear-plastic food containers from the deli for many uses. My favorite trick is turning it into an elegant jewelry box. You can see a photo of one in the color section of this book.

Tools and Materials:

Basic craft kit (see the Cheat Sheet at the front of this book)

Colorful wrapping paper with pretty flowers

Clear-plastic deli container with a hinged lid, thoroughly washed and dried

Sponge

Spray paint (I used white paint, but you can choose any color as a background for your cutouts).

4 inches of 1-inch-wide ribbon

Stapler

1. **Cut out the flowers from the wrapping paper and arrange them on top of the container lid. Trim the paper cutouts if necessary to make them fit.**

2. **Spread white craft glue on the *front* of each cutout. Working from the underside of the lid, apply each cutout to the lid. Press firmly in place with a damp sponge. Let the glued cutouts dry for an hour. Don't worry about the white film on top of the cutouts; the glue dries clear.**

3. **Using spray paint, coat the entire inside of the top and bottom of the container, right over the back of the cutouts.**

4. **Fold the ribbon in half lengthwise and position the overlapping raw ends in the center of the inside of the front of the lid. Staple in place.**

   This ribbon is a little handle so that you can open the lid easily. If the staple is visible, you can make it disappear with one quick squirt of the spray paint. Let the paint dry before using the box.

Bottles That Blossom

Disguising empty pickle, mayonnaise, and jelly jars with reverse découpage (see Chapter 9) is a cinch, and no one will be the wiser. These dressed-up throwaway items look sensational for holding makeup brushes, cotton balls, and dried flowers.

Tools and Materials:

Basic craft kit (see the Cheat Sheet at the front of this book)

Pretty wrapping paper

A variety of empty, clean jars and bottles, each with an opening wide enough for your hand

1-inch sponge paintbrush

Water-based acrylic paint (in colors of your choice)

1. **Cut out suitable paper designs from the wrapping paper for each jar or bottle. Small bottles need only one small flower, for example.**

2. **Spread white craft glue on the *front* of the cutout and insert it into the jar. Press the design against the glass from the inside.**

   If this is difficult to do with your hand, insert a damp sponge brush and press it against the back of the paper cutout. Let this dry for a few minutes.

3. **Using the sponge brush, paint the inside of each jar right over the back of the cutout.**

   You get the best results if you dab, rather than stroke, the paint on. Let the paint dry thoroughly. Add another coat of paint if needed.

Don't use the glass jars to hold liquid because prolonged moisture peels the paint away from the glass. To protect the painted finish, apply a coat of clear varnish over the paint.

Planters from Paper Paint Pails

You can find paper paint mixing pails in most paint and hardware stores. Made of sturdy white paper, these handleless pails come in two or three sizes and usually cost under a dollar. The largest pails can hold a full gallon of paint, so these pails are sturdy enough to hold any plant.

Spray or brush paint on the outside of the pail in a bright color. Then decorate the pail with a paper cutout (turn to Chapter 9 for découpage instructions), decal, or sticker. Stenciling is another crafting technique for decorating the pails (see Chapter 11). Place a saucer in the bottom of the pail before inserting a plant.

Decorate several paint pails to organize desk supplies, hold hats and mittens, or serve as a pretty container for wooden spoons on a kitchen counter. If you think about it, you'll probably come up with a dozen more uses for these versatile containers.

Beautiful Berry Baskets

You can convert paper berry baskets from the supermarket into handsome containers for more uses than you can think of. They are available in at least three or four sizes. After you transform them with a little paper crafting, you can use them to hold small pots of herbs on a kitchen windowsill, line them up on a shelf to hold odds and ends, or place one by the front door as a mail basket.

Tools and Materials:

Basic craft kit (see the Cheat Sheet at the front of this book)

Wrapping paper, wallpaper, or self-adhesive paper in a decorative pattern (a small overall pattern is best)

Berry basket

Sponge

Can of clear high-gloss spray varnish

1. **Place the basket on the paper. Trace around one side and the bottom, separately. Cut out these pieces.**

2. **Use the cut pieces to trace and cut a piece of paper for each side, inside and out, as well as the inside bottom.**

   This method for cutting pattern pieces is easier than measuring, because the shapes of the baskets are rather irregular.

3. **When cutting out the paper pieces, cut each piece slightly larger than the actual drawing to allow for overlap of paper at the edges.**

4. **Spread glue over the back of one side piece of paper. Center it on one side of the basket and press it down, smoothing the paper over the side, top, and bottom edges of the basket. (If using self-adhesive paper, peel off the backing to expose the sticky side rather than spreading glue.) Continue to apply the paper to all sides in the same way. Attach the paper pieces to the inside of the basket as well. Cover the inside and outside bottom of the box last.**

5. **Wipe away any excess glue with a sponge. Let the basket dry for at least a half hour.**

6. **Spray the finished basket with clear varnish inside and out to give the paper a high gloss. Let the basket dry for a few minutes and spray with varnish another three or four times. Coat the bottom of the basket as well.**

   The basket is sturdy and waterproof and looks like ceramic when finished. Suddenly a scrap material is glamorous!

Turn a Band-Aid Tin into a Sewing Kit

An empty Band-Aid tin can easily become a handy traveling container for sewing supplies. You can decorate the outside of the tin with paint crafts (see Part III) or paper crafting (see Part II). For an unusually delicate design, use a lacy paper doily to decorate the outside.

Tools and Materials:

Basic craft kit (see the Cheat
Sheet at the front of this book)

Small sponge brush

Acrylic paint (color of your
choice)

Band-Aid tin

Paper doily

Sponge

Clear nail polish or spray
varnish

Felt, fabric, or paper to line
the tin

Narrow decorative ribbon

Small piece of cardboard to fit
inside lid

Small piece of batting, polyester, or three cotton balls for
padding the inside of the lid

Small piece of felt or delicate
cotton slightly larger than the
inside lid

1. **Paint the entire outside of the tin. Prop the lid open while the paint is drying. After the paint is dry, apply another coat of paint for complete coverage.**

2. **Coat the back of the doily with white craft glue. Carefully lift the doily and place it on the front of the tin. Using a damp sponge, pat the doily down on the front and so that it wraps around the sides of the painted tin. Press the top and bottom edges of the doily to the inside and onto the bottom of the tin.**

3. **Let the doily dry thoroughly.**

4. **Coat the entire surface of the tin with clear nail polish or spray varnish. One or two applications of protective coating give the box a shiny finish.**

5. **Line the inside of the tin with felt, fabric, or paper, or paint it. If desired, trim the inside rim with a band of narrow decorative ribbon glued all around.**

6. **To make a pincushion on the inside lid, cut a piece of shirt cardboard to fit loosely inside the lid. Remove the cardboard piece and use glue to pad one side with batting, polyester fiberfill, or three cotton balls.**

7. **Cut a small piece of felt or delicate cotton print slightly larger than the cardboard. Cover the filler with the felt or fabric and overlap the edges to the underside of the cardboard.**

8. **Coat the inside of the lid with glue and set the pincushion in place. Don't let the pincushion touch the hinges at the back of the tin or the lid won't close. Press the pincushion down so that it is secure in the lid. With the lid open, let the tin dry for several hours before using.**

Uncanny Coffee Cans

Why keep coffee in unsightly coffee cans when a little paper crafting or pressed flowers can turn the containers into colorful containers?

Tools and Materials:

Basic craft kit (see the Cheat Sheet at the front of this book)

Coffee can

Pastel wrapping paper or wall-paper with a small overall pattern

Clear spray varnish

1. **Cover an ordinary coffee can with the pastel wrapping paper or wallpaper.**

2. **Cut out large paper flowers and glue the flowers around the can, over the wrapping paper. Protect the paper with two or three coats of clear spray varnish.**

Here's another way to dress up those coffee cans.

Tools and Materials:

Basic craft kit (see the Cheat Sheet at the front of this book)

Spray paint

Coffee can

Pressed flowers

Clear self-adhesive paper

1. **Spray paint the coffee can and let the paint dry thoroughly.**

2. **Arrange pressed flowers (see Chapter 20 for directions on pressing flowers) around the can and hold each flower in place with a dot of craft glue here and there.**

3. **Cut a strip of clear self-adhesive paper slightly longer than the circumference of the can. Peel away 1 inch of the backing paper from one short edge of the self-adhesive paper.**

4. **Position the sticky edge on the side of the coffee can and smooth it down. Slowly peel away the backing paper while, at the same time, smoothing the sticky paper around the can and over the pressed flowers. Using the palm of your hand, smooth the self-adhesive paper down all around the can. For better contact, use the edge of a credit card to smooth and remove air bubbles from under the self-adhesive paper.**

Stamp-Covered Pill Containers

Cough drop and candy tins are ideal pill or vitamin containers for your purse or pocket. Covering these little tins with unusual postage stamps makes them look as though they came from an expensive boutique. Using white craft glue on the back of each stamp, cover the top, sides, and bottom of the tin with a collage of stamps. Coat the entire tin with three or four layers of clear nail polish.

Fabric-Covered Clay Flower Pots

Use scraps of fabric to make appliqués for decorating your plain clay flower pots. The secret to this project's success is using fabric flowers cut from a large floral cotton print. Using sharp embroidery or cuticle scissors, cut out the fabric flower. Spread white craft glue over the back of the fabric cutout and press it onto the surface of the clay pot. Apply several coats of clear spray varnish to the entire surface of the pot, allowing each coat to dry before applying the next coat.

Pretty Pencils

Paper boutiques sell paper-covered pencils, but you can easily make your own with leftover scraps of paper. Gather up a batch of new pencils and scraps of wrapping paper or leftover wallpaper pieces. Cut strips of paper, the length of the pencil, wide enough to wrap around each pencil. Coat the back of each paper strip with glue and roll the paper around each pencil. Make a set by tying several together with pretty ribbon to give as a gift.

Button Bracelet

Everyone seems to have an odd assortment of buttons that they don't know what to do with. Use them to make an unusual bracelet. String as many as you can on a piece of thin elastic (sold in fabric shops) that you've cut to fit your wrist. This bracelet looks best when buttons of different sizes, shapes, and colors are bunched together.

Chapter 29

Ten Bazaar Best-Sellers

In This Chapter

▶ Knowing what it takes to make a bazaar best-seller

▶ Five ways to make your homemade foods sell like lightning

▶ Five best-seller projects to get you started

Some of the most familiar and popular fund-raising events are craft bazaars. Crafting for a bazaar is different from crafting gifts or decorations for your home. Items made to sell are usually made in multiples and should cost very little to make.

Bazaars are a lot of fun when your homemade crafts sell well, especially when the money is going to a good cause. In this chapter, you find the basic requirements for bazaar crafts, how to craft with scraps, and projects that have proven to be the best sellers. Get out your fabric scraps, your paper scraps, notions, and trims. You can put them all to use for creative crafting projects for your next craft bazaar.

Choosing Craft Projects for a Bazaar

If you've ever been to a craft fair, you know that one or two booths are always the most popular. They attract the most attention, maintain attendance throughout the day, and usually sell the most. To be successful, crafts for a bazaar must be

✔ Easily recognizable. Strange merchandise doesn't sell.

✔ Easy to make.

✔ Inexpensive to make and, therefore, reasonably priced.

✔ Made of readily available materials.

✔ Well designed.

✔ Well made.

✔ Made with a popular technique or one that people are interested in knowing about.

✔ Displayed nicely.

✔ Signed. This is an optional feature, but it's a nice touch to let people know that the items are handmade.

Making Creative Food Wraps

Food is always a big seller at craft bazaars. Make your goods look delectable with extra-special packaging.

✔ Wrap loaves of home-baked bread with red-and-white or blue-and-white checked linen dish towels. Tie with a red plaid ribbon and insert a sprig of rosemary under the bow.

Don't forget to add in the cost of the dish towel when pricing your baked goodies. If the cost of the towel makes the price too high, wrap the bread with checked fabric sold by the yard in fabric stores.

✔ Gather several empty baby food jars and lids. Paint the tops with colorful spray paint, let dry, and then glue red or white rickrack trim around the rim. Fill each jar with homemade relish or jam and screw on the decorated lid.

✔ Coffee cans are the perfect size to hold cookies. Spray paint the cans in a color of your choice and let the paint dry. Glue buttons all around the outside of a can (use white craft glue or a glue gun to attach buttons), line with colorful tissue, and add the cookies.

✔ Cover an oval wooden mushroom basket with pretty paper and glue a band of ribbon around the top edge. Use the basket to hold jars of relish, a loaf of bread, or cookies.

✔ Cover an oatmeal box with pieces of different colored wrapping papers so that the scraps of paper overlap and completely cover the box (use white craft glue to apply the paper to the box). Coat the outside with clear spray varnish for a sturdy, long-lasting container. Add a label with the name of your cookies to the outside of the box.

Adding a Special Touch to Familiar Items

Everyday plain items like ankle socks, combs, barrettes, T-shirts, guest towels, and bookmarks are easy to decorate with trimmings like buttons and bows to make them special.

✔ Decorating cotton ankle socks is fun and easy and opens up another way for you to creatively express yourself. Begin with plain white socks in sizes ranging from infants to adults. The first step is to dye the socks in fabric dye according to the directions on the package. (To obtain different shades of one color, leave the socks soaking in the hot water dye bath for different lengths of time. The longer they soak, the darker the shade. This technique enables you to economize by using fewer packages of dye.) Dry the socks. Then decorate the cuffs with buttons, sequins, rickrack, appliqués, and other trimmings, making each pair different.

✔ Assemble plastic hair combs, barrettes, bobby pins, and all the trimmings, such as ribbon, silk flowers, plastic fruit, buttons, beads, and bows, to make smashing hair ornaments. Glue different trims on each hairpiece, using white craft glue for the flat items like ribbons and buttons and a glue gun for three-dimensional items like silk flowers, bows, and beads.

✔ Plain white T-shirts are inexpensive and make good bazaar items after they have been decorated. Begin by dying them pastel colors. Next, use stencils and fabric paint to create all sorts of designs on each one. (See Chapter 11 for stenciling tips and directions on fabric painting.)

✔ An ordinary hand or guest towel can be trimmed with beautiful ribbon, embroidered tape, a satin applique, or lace, and suddenly it's no longer ordinary. Choose your trimming carefully and stitch a band of decorative trim across the bottom of each towel. Make sets of a wash cloth, hand towel, and bath towel — or three guest towels — and tie each set together with a pretty 1-inch grosgrain ribbon or a ribbon to match the ribbon that you use to decorate the towels.

✔ Use a variety of pressed flowers to make bookmarks. (See Chapter 20 for advice on pressing flowers.) Cut a 9-inch strip of 2-inch-wide satin ribbon. Cut one end on the diagonal. Cut the corners off the other end to form a point. Arrange pressed flowers on the ribbon. Cut a piece of clear self-adhesive paper so that it fits over the pressed-flower section only. Press the self-adhesive paper down to secure the flowers on the ribbon. That's all there is to it! Make as many as you think will sell — and then make an extra one that you can give as a gift with a new book.

Appendix

Where to Find What You Need

If you're interested in more information about crafts, plenty of additional sources are available, including books, magazines, cable television shows like the ones on the Home and Garden Television Network, and the Internet. The lists here are only a sampler of what's available.

Don't assume that craft resources that are several years old are necessarily outdated. Crafting techniques are as old as the hills, and sometimes the only things that get updated are the designs and the language. Materials sometimes improve, but new doesn't always mean improved. Judge for yourself.

Books about Crafts

You can find many books available on all the subjects in this book in bookstores, craft shops, or online bookstores.

Craft books fall into a wide range of categories or levels. For example, titles can be as broad as *Complete Book of Crafts* or as narrow as *Stenciling*. You can even find books that focus on a single style, such as *Country Patchwork Quilts,* or a single item, such as *Make a Wedding Ring Quilt.*

Dover Publications, Inc., publishes over 900 copyright-free books that contain designs, alphabets, symbols, découpage illustrations, and stencils. Because they're copyright free, you can "borrow" the designs for your own use in crafting. You can find Dover books in bookstores, craft and art materials stores, and online.

If you look through any British craft books, you'll probably notice that their specialty is embroidery, although many books on all craft subjects are also produced in England and distributed in the U.S. Although British craft books can be inspiring, too often the materials are not easily accessible, especially in the area of fabric crafting.

Craft Magazines

In addition to the craft magazines listed later in this section, you can find special issues of the following magazines on newsstands during the holiday season.

Sew News

Rubber Stamper

Memory Makers

Crafts 'n Things

Arts & Crafts

The Cross Stitcher

The Stitchery Magazine

Just Cross-Stitch

Kids' Crafts

Family Fun

Handcraft

Quilter's Newsletter Magazine

Quilt

McCall's Quilting

Decorative Woodcrafts

Weekend Crafts

These general magazines often include craft projects:

Family Circle

Woman's Day

Better Homes & Gardens

Martha Stewart Living

Mary Englebreit's Home Companion

Crafts Online

If you're connected to the World Wide Web, you can participate in discussions with others interested in crafts, obtain technical information about techniques and materials, and track down sources for buying supplies.

For a comprehensive book on computers and crafts, Judy Heim's *The Needlecrafter's Computer Companion* is an excellent resource. It includes information on computers, old and new, Windows and Mac, as well as online resources in great detail.

Usenet newsgroups

Usenet is a world-wide discussion system made up of newsgroups that are classified by subject. A message that is posted to a newsgroup over the Internet can be read and responded to by anyone who logs on to that newsgroup. If you access `rec.crafts.textiles.quilting`, you can find messages from people all over the country, and possibly the world, who are interested in some aspect of quilting. You can respond to their messages, ask questions, or write your own message. People interested in crafts are very active in newsgroups.

Check out `www.dejanews.com` for a comprehensive provider of newsgroup information. Here's a list of some craft newsgroups, arranged by type of craft:

Quilting, patchwork, and appliqué: `rec.crafts.textiles.quilting`

Needlepoint, cross-stitch, crewel embroidery, and so on: `rec.crafts.textiles.needlework`

Sewing: `rec.crafts.textiles.sewing`

Rubber stamping: `rec.crafts.rubberstamps`

Memory books: `deja.comm.scrapbooking`

Christmas projects and beading: `rec.crafts.beads`

Sources of supplies: `rec.crafts.marketplace`

Advanced craft issues: `rec.crafts.professional`

Other craft newsgroups: `rec.crafts.misc`

British craft enthusiasts: `uk.rec.crafts`

Craft projects on the Net

Visit the Web site of Clapper Communications, a publisher of craft magazines, at `www.clapper.com` to find out about the magazines and download free craft projects to try yourself. The Clapper site is just one example of many commercial Web sites that offer free projects to crafters.

Another craft magazine that offers free craft projects is *Crafts 'n Things,* at `www.craftsnthings.com`. This site provides many different crafts and activities and offers a message board where you can ask the editor questions about projects and techniques.

You can find a wealth of free craft projects and a well-organized message board for getting answers to questions about crafts at *craftnetvillage.com* (www.craftnetvillage.com), a shopping and learning site.

Family Fun Magazine, at www.familyfun.com, provides scads of fun crafts, activities, and creative ideas for kids to do with a parent or by themselves.

Arts-n-Crafts, at www.inmotion-pcs.com/amass/theboss/artsn.htm, offers over 40 craft ideas and activities that are perfect for a rainy day when the kids are restless. The projects are good for preschoolers and parents to do together. The directions are easy to understand, despite a lack of illustrations.

Craft information on the Net

The Quilt Channel, at www.quiltchannel.com, gives you access to the major quilting sites on the Web and features sites of individual quilters' pages, tips, techniques, and much more.

World Wide Quilting Page, at www.quilt.com, is a broad-based information center offering basic and advanced techniques and everything you ever wanted to know about quilt blocks. The site includes a bulletin board for questions and a trading post for finding quilters who want to trade fabric and patterns.

The Counted Cross-stitch, Needlework, and Stitchery Page at www.dnai.com/~kdyer/ provides links to designs, supplies, media information, organizations, and history of needlecrafts.

Index

• *Y* •

• *Z* •

Discover Dummies Online!

The Dummies Web Site is your fun and friendly online resource for the latest information about ...For Dummies® books and your favorite topics. The Web site is the place to communicate with us, exchange ideas with other ...For Dummies readers, chat with authors, and have fun!

Ten Fun and Useful Things You Can Do at www.dummies.com

1. Win free ...For Dummies books and more!
2. Register your book and be entered in a prize drawing.
3. Meet your favorite authors through the IDG Books Author Chat Series.
4. Exchange helpful information with other ...For Dummies readers.
5. Discover other great ...For Dummies books you must have!
6. Purchase Dummieswear™ exclusively from our Web site.
7. Buy ...For Dummies books online.
8. Talk to us. Make comments, ask questions, get answers!
9. Download free software.
10. Find additional useful resources from authors.

Link directly to these ten fun and useful things at
http://www.dummies.com/10useful

SURF THE NET

WWW.DUMMIES.COM

For other technology titles from IDG Books Worldwide, go to
www.idgbooks.com

Not on the Web yet? It's easy to get started with *Dummies 101*®: *The Internet For Windows*®*98* or *The Internet For Dummies*®, 6th Edition, at local retailers everywhere.

IDG BOOKS WORLDWIDE BOOK REGISTRATION

Register This Book and Win!

We want to hear from you!

Visit **http://my2cents.dummies.com** to register this book and tell us how you liked it!

✔ Get entered in our monthly prize giveaway.

✔ Give us feedback about this book — tell us what you like best, what you like least, or maybe what you'd like to ask the author and us to change!

✔ Let us know any other *...For Dummies*® topics that interest you.

Your feedback helps us determine what books to publish, tells us what coverage to add as we revise our books, and lets us know whether we're meeting your needs as a *...For Dummies* reader. You're our most valuable resource, and what you have to say is important to us!

Not on the Web yet? It's easy to get started with *Dummies 101*®*: The Internet For Windows*® *98* or *The Internet For Dummies*®, 6th Edition, at local retailers everywhere.

Or let us know what you think by sending us a letter at the following address:

...For Dummies Book Registration
Dummies Press
7260 Shadeland Station, Suite 100
Indianapolis, IN 46256-3945
Fax 317-596-5498

™

**BESTSELLING
BOOK SERIES
FROM IDG**